THE FILM AND AUDIOVISUAL INDUSTRY

*The truth about
writing, financing,
producing, distributing
and working in movies.*

Alan Smithee

THE FILM AND AUDIOVISUAL INDUSTRY
© Alan Smithee 2018

All rights reserved. No part of this publication may be reproduced, distributed, or transmitted in any form or by any means, including photocopying, recording, or other electronic or mechanical methods, without the prior written permission of the publisher.

ISBN: 978-17-08461-51-5

*To anyone who finds it useful,
and particularly to all those
who would have liked to know
this information from the very beginning.*

CONTENTS

INTRODUCTION	11
1. ART AND THE INDUSTRY	17
The Balance Between Art and Business	23
Small Independent Companies	29
2. DISTRIBUTION AND EXHIBITION	39
Festivals and Markets	44
Distribution Deals	50
The Real Business of Exhibition	56
Film Marketing	65
3. ECONOMY AND LAW	**73**
The Budget	77
Law and Taxation	82
Intellectual Property and Copyright	85
The False Protection of Ideas	96
Internet and New Technologies	100
4. THE STUDIO SYSTEM	109
The International Influence of Hollywood	115
5. GETTING INTO THE INDUSTRY	121
Agents and Managers	127
Entourage	136
Communication: The Meaning of Words	141
6. SCREENWRITERS' REALITY	153
The Script Format	155
Criticism and Self-criticism	158
Being a Professional Screenwriter	162

7. THE DIRECTOR'S JOB — 171
Directing a Film Shoot — 177
The Beginner Filmmaker — 183

8. MEETING THE PRODUCER — 203
Film Production Breakdown — 211
The Gods of Olympus — 215
Friend or Enemy? — 221

9. THE WORLD OF ACTING — 231
Talent and Skills — 238
Self-knowledge — 250
Physical Appearance — 254
The Star System — 259

10. CREATIVE INDUSTRIES WORKERS — 271
The Film Crew — 280
The Benefits of Being a Salaried Employee — 288
The Future of Entertainment — 296

*Dedicated with love, to
all the friends and family
who are always supportive and
willing to provide unconditional help.*

INTRODUCTION

Why is this book different from others? There are tons of publications dedicated to film and audiovisual matters that describe, in more or less detail, the many elements that make up this complex industry. Most of them effectively gather large amounts of theoretical information with which enthusiasts, students, and beginners can satisfy their respective interests. However, you cannot expect them to be interesting or especially revealing reads. Actually, they are not too different from the extensive curricula and educational training contents that you can find anywhere. Whether it is formal or non-formal training (authorized by an official educational system or not), there has never been as much training on subjects like: courses, workshops, specialized academies, universities, masters, etc. Not to mention the wealth of documentation available on the internet. The most appropriate option depends on each person's interests and needs. Some of them are barely more than simple lecture notes and others are almost encyclopedic glossaries.

There are monographs that could be interesting if it were not for, in the name of an excessive rigor, them becoming incredibly tedious. Some are too serious, others too informal; and many go too deep into physics, chemistry, mathematics, economics, politics, psychology, or philosophy. All that information may be true, accurate, and complete, but it is not content that most people consider useful or readable.

This book belongs rather to another kind of writing you can find on the market: the expository essay. Usually they focus on a mythical figure, published as a personal and/or professional biography, where you can learn some details about the business, if you know how to read between the lines.

Within this same division, we have anthologies too, where experts and film critics write about a broad variety of topics. That can be any specific period in cinema history, the author's favorite genre, or perhaps some kind of personal obsession with one single film. This usually requires exhaustive research or deep reflections on higher thoughts. Some authors prefer to focus on more casual and entertaining points of view. Then you can also find screenplays at stores, as well as the popular "novelized" scripts: An inverse process of adaptation where, apart from changing the narrative tense, the author can add nuances and story-arc stories that are impossible to include or develop in the original film or series. And finally, if there is required reading for aficionados, students, and amateurs, it is without a doubt, screenwriting books.

However, there is something that all these publications have in common: None of them tell you anything about how things really work from the inside. When it comes to moving from theory to practice, no one talks about the reality of the industry—about how it really functions. We would appreciate some honest information that is useful for the professional development of newbies or the satisfaction of suspicious curiosities.

Beyond overwhelming numbers, encyclopedic descriptions, peculiar anecdotes, and theoretical schematics on the cycles and phases of audiovisual production, no one is addressing the internal mechanics and rules of the business. The norms, principles, motivations, and reasonings behind everything.

THE FILM AND AUDIOVISUAL INDUSTRY

Nobody seems to be interested in sharing how things are related and how they affect the lives of the people who work or want to work in this industry. And the last one mentioned is especially relevant. Anyone interested in starting a career wants to learn as much about it as possible. It is the law of life; amateurs are always eager for knowledge. And the logic here is obvious: The more you know about it, the more you like it. In turn, you want to know more and more in an endless cycle. That is the reason for this particular vindication. Why is so much theoretical content available, yet no one explains the industry with honesty and objectivity? Is there anything to hide? (It is a rhetorical question, for the record.)

We all understand that doing is the best way of learning. But if it were that simple, all education and training would be questioned. It is true that through your own experience, little by little, you could learn every profession's secrets. But there is no way that we can accept the fallacy that everybody is trying to sell: That we are living in a healthy, successful meritocracy.

They say talent, effort, and tireless dedication are fairly rewarded in life. Anyone could tell you, according to their own experience, how much that is applicable to their own lives. Winners will always say that they worked very hard to get to where they are, with no one giving them anything for free. Losers will always hold a strong grudge against anyone who doubts how much they tried, without having received anything in return. Of course, eventually you may get some results with tenacity and sacrifice, but how fair the proportion is would be a different discussion. It is not a matter of personal perspective that is coming from conceited or resentful individuals. Something is wrong when we are all surrounded by people who are not rewarded proportionately to their talent, effort, or dedication.

The audiovisual industry is not so different from others. The artistic factor provides that fascinating aura we all know, but it quickly disappears once you go behind the scenes. Interestingly, it is very hard to get into the industry, but very easy to leave. Once inside, you do not know exactly where you are. You cannot know the distance you have moved, the direction, nor the destination. From your perspective, nothing is transparent. No matter what you call it: discretion, secrecy, confidentiality, or elitism; that will not make it more transparent. The film and audiovisual sector enjoys international recognition and popularity, so this lack of information can be shocking. But, it is easy to explain if we look at how some products are manufactured. Why do big corporations not want you to know much about the production process of the food we eat? Or the drinks we drink? Or the clothes we wear? Or the medicine we take?

Everyone is free to make their own conclusions and decisions after reading this. You can agree or disagree with the content. But you can be sure that the only intention of this essay is to provide a better understanding of the overall business of the film and audiovisual industry—the real one. We assume that that is exactly what you are looking for if you have this book in your hands. A global vision which, as you can imagine, tends to be highly manipulated by the press and insiders, for the simple reason that keeping up appearances is an essential need. Not only in this industry, but in any other business and professional context. We are talking about the adult world. Real life, in short.

We have compiled all kinds of conclusions and experiences, accumulated over the years, by a wide variety of international professionals. After categorizing the information, we tried to explain it in an understandable way. However, always focusing on those uncomfortable details that everyone conveniently avoids. And in case you are wondering, there is no need to mention specific names. What matters is the general overview, not the particular cases (simple truth does not need excuses).

Finally, a book that fills the gaps. You will know what is never mentioned in television interviews. You will start to understand things that do not mean what you thought they did and understand people you never thought you would understand. Although, there is also one important thing to keep in mind before you continue reading: it is possible that you will never watch movies the same way again.

THE FILM AND AUDIOVISUAL INDUSTRY

The way some people face their own reality, and the maturity they have to deal with the new things they learn, is a very personal matter and an important part of their lives. It is no coincidence that a love for movies starts at an early age, like childhood, because we still live in a world of dreams, fantasies, and illusions. Perhaps you aspire to become a professional. Or maybe your only intention is increasing your awareness and understanding as an aficionado. Taking a look behind the magic of film is a journey that not everyone will like. For many, this might not be new. Most movie lovers already know a lot about filmmaking and it affects the way they watch movies. Perhaps it is screenwriting, photography, editing, and digital effects? Whatever it is, this knowledge allows you to enjoy films but also changes your perceptions. You must be careful because the greed for knowledge is a beast that will demand to be fed.

We may mention personal and emotional highlights, not due to sentimentality, but because these are significant parts of such an intense profession. You cannot talk about such an industry without mentioning its most critical and relevant issues. There are a lot of artists and technicians with very good jobs around the world. However, it is time that someone explain what happens when these jobs are not as good as they seem, or why some people cannot get a job in the industry at all. The same happens in any other industry, some people succeed while others do not. You can find happy and unhappy people in any field.

We will talk about all of that in this book. Both the beautiful and the ugly parts. Not due to optimism or pessimism, but rather as an information analysis. You may already know a lot about pre-production, production, and post-production. Or maybe some things about distribution and exhibition. Perhaps you are one of those box-office geeks; you are obsessed with any cinephile stuff you can find online, and even have a cool Variety magazine subscription. But, if you still have this book in your hands, it is because you feel that the pieces of the puzzle do not fit and maybe you are missing a few.

THE FILM AND AUDIOVISUAL INDUSTRY

On behalf of all those who would have liked to have such information at the beginning of our careers, we sincerely hope that you enjoy it and can find something useful.

THE FILM AND AUDIOVISUAL INDUSTRY

ART AND THE INDUSTRY

The industry side is always the most difficult to understand for movie buffs and any visual arts lover. This is because their emotional ties to the stories, personal admiration for their idols, or the mere understanding of films as pieces of art, make any business matter boring and frivolous. Most audiences of films, theater, television, or music (not to mention video game players) do not have much interest in the industrial manufacturing process of their favorite consumer product. Nevertheless, due to the artistic nature of film, there is a lot of curiosity for creative processes. But again, not every process. People are usually attracted by the most seductive side of the profession (the most visible and obvious). It is hard to resist the temptation of doing work that you love. No one seems to care about the utopian goal of such reverie. Meaning, no one thinks about the things they don't know, which is almost everything. In these cases, possibilities' remoteness does not affect high ambition and expectation.

Career and professional decisions related to this industry always come from very strong personal motivations like passion for the arts, attraction to fame, or an eagerness for wealth. The problem is that such personal motivations are so vital in life that they usually turn against you. Said factors can easily make you lose your impartiality, in turn, affecting the way you feel when working in such a hard industry. In show business, the "show" side has its own complications, as well as the "business" side.

For ordinary people, the business world already represents a strange monster full of mysteries. And in this case, it is even worse; since everything related to the "show" side makes it even more complicated, considering its artistic and subjective nature. Every company is related to their consumer product by codependency. The products need the company to be sold, and the company needs the products to be created and distributed. (Additionally, it is important to avoid competitors that can create or distribute the same type of products.) On top of that, most relationships between art and industry are tense, irrational, and frustrating. (Exactly like codependency.) Indeed, art and the industry have completely opposed interests. We will examine how they are related to each other, where they clash, where they connect, and where they complement each other as well.

To begin on the art side, movies are composed of many traditional art resources. They merge to form the final piece of work. For example, literature can be found in scripts. The most basic story is divided into three parts: the setup, the confrontation, and the resolution. This is the basic three-act structure that every aspiring writer should know. In Chapter 6: "Screenwriters' Reality," we will see that there are a few formal differences between a script and a novel. However, the important thing that must be mentioned now, is that literary works are intended to be beautiful pieces of art in themselves, while scripts are just tools. Although it is a piece of literature, a film script does not seek to be beautiful. The pleasure is not focused on the reading, but rather, in the watching of the final product. A script is something designed to be transformed from paper to screen. This is the first example of the necessary symbiosis between art and business, and the sacrifices both sides must make.

THE FILM AND AUDIOVISUAL INDUSTRY

In regard to the final product, once finished, photography is the most relevant of the arts involved, mostly because of technical reasons. The mechanics of cinema are based on a very long strip of photographic film. When this film is projected at several pictures per second, our brain generates the optical illusion of motion, thanks to the retinal persistence. Like many other gadgets of the same period, the cinematograph captured pictures the same way, with the intent of being projected later onto a fabric screen or a white wall.

It was created by the Lumière brothers in France, around the late 19th century. The cinematograph improved various machines that other people were investigating in Europe during that time. Contrary to what many believe, the device patented in the United States by Thomas Edison, was also based on many of these investigations, but it was not cinematography's origin as we know it. (The kinetoscope was a big machine where only one individual could view the recorded pictures at a time.)

It is well known that the first films were silent and in black and white. They were a sequence of photographs projected at high speed, so cinema evolution has always been linked to the photographic emulsion. (And fortunately, the absence of color is not an obstacle for artistic expression and visual delight.)

In movies, we can see the volumetric strength of sculpture in every detail from the actors to the decorations; the grandiosity of architecture in sets and model construction; or the expressionism of painting in backgrounds, costumes and makeup. The iconic German Expressionism was the greatest exponent of film's artistic conception. It made its essential contribution to art history between the First and Second World War. Even the art of drawing had its own representation in films with the first animations. As a direct evolution of the zoetrope, which was already one century older, the first animated cartoons were done by painting directly on the film negative or by using photographs of handmade drawings.

THE FILM AND AUDIOVISUAL INDUSTRY

Regarding audio, considering that the cinematograph was mainly acknowledged as a frivolous invention, arousing slight curiosity rather than genuine interest, it was necessary to adapt the experience into something closer to what people considered an entertaining show at those times. The first screening rooms were variety/vaudeville theaters and concert saloons, which were considered to be low-end theaters. They had automated or regular pianos, so the musical accompaniment was present from the beginning, adding an entertainment value. At a certain point, musicians were hired to play live music and original scores were composed for better alignment with the content (eventually, the scores were even played by small orchestras). Being fully aware of the artistic and emotional impact that music added, the advent of sound in film came quickly. For many years, the industry replaced live music for simple gramophones, and synched the music with the screen. But the possibility of asynchrony was too high, making the option of including voices with dialogues impossible. (Although, from a technical point of view, it was not completely impossible, the synchrony was the real challenge.)

The final breakthrough came with a new approach: printing sound on the film strip, next to the picture negative, in a way where it could later be read by the projector. This new optical system was developed for military purposes, starting from a primitive, wireless telephone studied by Graham Bell. Sound films (also known as "talkies") began much earlier than people think. Several technical alternatives also thrived on the market for years, like different types of discs or projection rolls connected for synchronicity. But the advantage of using only one roll of film with image and sound together was undeniable.

So, the new 35mm film with an optical soundtrack soon became the standard. And just a couple of decades after the first silent films were created, filmmakers from all over the world could finally convey a much larger range of emotions, thanks to the power of music and spoken word. Since then, technical research has been focused on the optimization of the film strip, sound quality, noise reduction, and surround expansion.

Last but not least, we cannot talk about cinema as the confluence of several arts, without mentioning the one with the most important role, performing arts. Acting is the basis of any film. Actors playing fictional characters is a necessary condition in order to tell a story. Since the dawn of time, human beings have considered entertaining the concept of some people transforming themselves into others, in order to reenact a particular scene, due to some specific interest, be it pedagogical, humorous, philosophical, or political.

There are many factors involved in making the audience feel emotions. For instance, the situation is more favorable in a live show. Empathy is generated by human proximity to others, both on stage and in the audience. It conditions our minds and hearts, making it easy to be moved or entertained. In the movies, actors are just projected images, so the live empathy is lost. Fortunately, you still have it among the audience in the room, and that is why people audibly laugh and scream when watching comedy or horror films.

Similarly, on the one hand, the authenticity of the performance is weakened a little when it is recorded but, on the other hand, we have lots of new sensations reinforcing it, such as beautiful visuals, emotional music, or the psychology of the camera. For example, the type of shots, the camera angles, and the way they are connected, dramatically affect the emotions conveyed to the audience. Sensory perception and subconscious take part too. But it is not something that just happens magically. It is the director's job to control the actors' performances within one unified vision. We will see more of this in Chapter 7: "The Director's Job."

We will analyze who plays what, in the filmmaking process, but we should never forget that the end user (the audience) will judge the final result in a subjective way. Everyone is different. Some people can identify with characters, stories, or concrete actions, while others don't find that interesting. Hence the importance of being very clear about the target audience. Depending on how much they connect with certain stories, moments, and subjects, the whole industry will define (in "objective" terms) what is considered funny, moving, terrifying, entertaining, or boring, within a specific society and culture.

Our personal situations also affect our perceptions. One movie can make or break your day. Moreover, your mood is a two-way street: You can enjoy a lower quality product, simply because you are in a good mood; as much as you can hate a good product if you just had a terrible day. (Which you probably would have enjoyed more under different circumstances.)

Now we can see that filmmaking is both an industry and an art. So why is it often considered a controversial dilemma? Actually, this is not so much a real debate as much as it is an incessant tug-of-war between two opposing viewpoints, where each side wants the other to see that their view is more important. Business people and artists see their roles in radically opposing ways and according to their own interests. And that is the key: they both live from that place.

What is more, depending on the situation one can use the argument best fit, just to justify their particular opinion. You can always defend a more pragmatic stance and claim that the film and audiovisual industry is like any other. Its legal and economic issues are the same and money is always the most important thing. Some people invest significant amounts of their own money, so it makes sense that they will worry not only about recovering their investment, but also about getting a certain margin of profit. That would be the first and last aim of making movies, as in any other business.

But at the same time, if you prefer to go with a more cultural approach, you can always defend cinema's artistic essence. (For example, if that helps you make more money.) With this argument, you will have reason on your side, since there is an undeniable aesthetic along with conceptual and emotional value. (Well, not in all of them, but that is another story.) In fact, the best possible balance is not the argument of money's frivolity and other legal matters; in comparison to the argument of the value of creating pieces of art. It is defending the artistic quality that has a direct impact on the economic outcomes.

In short, depending on people's interests, no one can say which side of this argument is more important. However, separately analyzing the impact and influence of every single part of the filmmaking process could help to understand said impact, depending on the perspective.

THE BALANCE BETWEEN ART AND BUSINESS

The first thing any project has to do in order to succeed is present the idea. This can be an informal conversation, an email, or a more elaborate document like a first treatment, bible, dossier, or brochure. However, the official way to present a film project to decision makers and possible investors is called a "pitch." It does not matter whether it is a big producer, several studio executives, or a single private investor. They all belong on the listening side of the table, which is the side with money or the means to get it. Firstly, the most reasonable thing would be to understand their interests.

As in any conversation (not only in negotiations) first impressions are important. Once you have passed the initial value judgement during introductions, the sooner you start to mention the commercially-oriented highlights of your project, the better. That will draw the attention of the most demanding ears. Data shows that the suggestion of massive commercial success will peak more interest than artistic or culturally valuable motivations, which are less profitable by their very nature. This does not mean that such ideas are not valuable, it just means that most audiences are looking for light entertainment, rather than delighting themselves with a deep masterpiece of art. Like the majority of the public, most people who greenlight projects often lack artistic sensitivity. Moreover, the executives who could have an artistic inclination, must put their corporate responsibility above their personal preferences. In fact, when they bet on rare, personal, and risky projects, it usually ends poorly. Therefore, playing this card at the wrong moment and in the wrong way, could be catastrophic for your project; especially if it is presented as something that has never been done before. Every now and then you may achieve some interesting and artistic results because of originality and creative expression (rarely, we could say). But the project could be commercially disastrous due to the misalignment with the cannons accepted by society. The classic motivation to be special and different can be shared between artists and the audiences that connect with their artwork; but it is a philosophy diametrically opposed to mainstream reality. This industry is only interested in the likes and dislikes of the majority, because of the amount of money they represent. It cannot be compared, even remotely, to small niche markets. That is the simple truth.

Everyone wants to be, have, and crave the same as others. The different styles and trends that are sold to the general public are nothing other than that: commercial products cut from the same cloth. Fashion makes the philosophy of "being special" and "being different" mere superficiality. Perhaps most people are not prepared for something that is actually different or special, but perhaps they are not interested either.

Anything related to innovation is a dangerous double-edged sword. Surely you have heard producers and executives state that they are always looking for original, new ideas and innovative projects. But, if that is true then why do billboards seem to offer the same thing year after year? When someone tries to propose something unique, special, or experimental what they get in return is exactly the opposite philosophy, no one wants to run the risk. Nobody is going to bet on new ideas that have never been tried before. Decision-makers defend the idea that people will always want the same thing or that they do not know what they want. And when they say they want something different, it is just a lie. In the end, it comes down to the belief that success, measured by box office results, is dependent upon a simple

THE FILM AND AUDIOVISUAL INDUSTRY

standard formula: repeat the elements that we know audiences like and only modify the surface, so that the products are still the same but you can resell them as something different and special.

We can use soft drinks as an example. If success has been built on a particular formula, why change it? The only thing that you may want to change, and in fact is advisable, is to refresh the branding and packaging from time to time. You can assume that there is risk in releasing a new flavor or a "brand new formula," but are you willing to take responsibility for possible losses? That is the main reason why an executive will always be reluctant to abandon an established formula. They are held accountable for the final product's profitability.

With regard to a project's artistic value, the first thing we should mention is the script. Before you even start writing, you must make a decision about the overall direction you are going to go in and the appropriate ratios. Will the film be more commercial or more artistic? In the case of commissioned work, this intention must previously be agreed upon between the writer and whoever is funding the project, in order to avoid future misunderstandings. This is essential, because the direction of the film will determine the events and the characters' actions, and not to mention, their attitudes, motivations, and speech.

The future success of any work begins, to a large extent, at this stage. In the case that you choose to write a script on your own, without worrying about the direction, it is your responsibility to understand and accept the situation that you may find yourself in later, when you are trying to sell your film.

Writing is an art and a craft, so it has both objective and subjective parts. Writers with true artistic skills will be able to write lighter or more frivolous works with certain guarantees—even if it goes against their own principles. (Let us say that they are qualified to do this, if they so decide.) Writers' talents will accomplish any writing task with solvency. And in case a project's production stages meet their professional duties, any product supposedly designed to be a commercial and mainstream success will reach the goal correctly. Even if it does not have higher artistic pretensions. We say "supposedly" because even the most commercial script, when executed properly, can still fail as a product because of poor direction, photography, acting, publicity, or marketing. However, a bad script will always be a bad script. And it will be a heavy burden throughout production, unless someone decides to do something about it. In theory, that is what industry standards are for. Every business sector has a set of minimum quality parameters that separate professionals from amateurs. For instance, screenwriting standards, visual standards, or any other aspects of production. Even with acceptable skills, those with limited talent will be able to write an unambitious work, but will be unable to write a deeper, more artistic, or overall better, quality film (as hard as they may try). With just the basic theory of screenwriting, mediocre writers will not be able to obtain quality results in practice because they are coping with artistic challenges at a level that they cannot reach.

As previously mentioned, the film shoot is the next artistic element that can affect commercial outcomes. There are many artists working at the same time, each one responsible for a small part of what you see on the screen, like costume designers, set designers, make-up artists, and actors. In addition to this, a lot of technical workers, using the most diverse equipment, will also affect the visual look of the pictures captured by the cameras; therefore, they also have an impact on the artistic result, even if this part of the crew only has a technical profile.

The performance of each and every one will define the commercial success or failure of the entire thing. In fact, one of the most striking aspects of the relationship between commercial success and technical-artistic quality is that when all the work is done well, it tends to go unnoticed. In the case of big fantasy or period productions, these qualities are more evident, precisely because they have more money for better resources. But in traditional films, where such artistic elements are not the main focus, everything must remain of the highest professional quality anyway. No matter how natural it is meant to look, there are a lot of formal quality requirements that every single film must meet, both technical and artistic. Something that very few people understand, is that any movie that projects real life, no matter if they are realistic dramas or silly comedies, must use the same artistic audiovisual values and codes as any award-winning production. This is needed in order to have a decent, professional film. The crew may have to spend less time (which is to say less money) preparing, filming, and polishing these kinds of movies, since the requirements and expectations are not the same. But the most basic industry standards require some minimal artistic and technical challenges which are quite demanding by themselves. These challenges must be solved with advanced knowledge and resources, usually out of reach for both beginners and amateurs. That is why, even taking into account the massive amount of information and training we can find nowadays, and the low cost of audiovisual production equipment, there are so many independent works that are incapable of grabbing the industry's attention. It is technically possible, yes; but it is not that easy to get the best combination of time, dedication, knowledge, and talent needed to make something, with real potential to succeed, within the industry standards.

Something similar happens in regard to film music. Orchestral soundtracks are a well-accepted standard worldwide. Classical music, mainly with influences from 19th century Romanticism, is the most common tendency, happily embraced by composers and audiences. There are always exceptions, and surely modern music styles are considered more appropriate for contemporary movies but, in general, symphonic scores are practically the most immediate choice.

The fact is, the vast majority of the public do not notice or think about these details. Most viewers could enjoy a soundtrack, but it may not be something to remember. Music is a high-value artistic component and impacts the perception of film, but it is often underappreciated. Its presence and quality are taken for granted, which causes it to be underestimated. Only a small minority give it the attention it deserves; usually fans of that particular genre, who have personal tastes for music and art.

Not all soundtracks are classical music masterpieces, that is true. But actually, most of them present basic standards of incidental music that perfectly fulfill their audiovisual role, with a high level of sound aesthetics. Additionally, from an industry perspective, we also find an extra motivation: selling the OMPS (Original Motion Picture Soundtrack).

It is not a coincidence that each one of the major Hollywood studios have their own music division. For example, there is Disney music, Fox music, Universal music, Warner music, and Sony music. These all include their corresponding, specific labels for soundtracks and/or classical music, among the many subsidiary and associate companies that they own.

The business rivalry between studios results in a myriad of legal impediments. This is why occasionally, creators cannot use music for their movies from the artists that they want and are sometimes even forced to include music that they do not like. Again, the unavoidable clash between art and business.

There are more factors that affect the expectation and final performance of films, particularly within their first week in theaters, such as posters or promotional events. But the last essential part that affects the artistic quality of any audiovisual piece is without a doubt, the final editing. The rhythm, the understanding, and the meaning of images can all change substantially because of the final edit. This begs the question: is the editor an artist or a technician? Editors are at an interesting halfway point between both, but we will come back to that later. For the moment, the conclusion is that although the artistic content of a film is left up to the artists, it is always subject to more important business interests. Executives bring in the money and are responsible for the economic profitability; therefore, if the artistic finish affects the commercial success, they will have control of it.

THE FILM AND AUDIOVISUAL INDUSTRY

SMALL INDEPENDENT COMPANIES

As stated previously, the business world is usually an absolute mystery for regular people. Being an entrepreneur or businessperson of any kind is considered something too complex, compared to the traditional, easy choice of working for others. Theory says that good academic records will guarantee a fair salary according to your abilities. The problem begins when people find out the truth, sooner or later. In competitive capitalism there are always, by definition, much more demand than supply in the labor market. That is why unemployment is a serious economic and social concern, and not only in this industry.

Before we approach film and audiovisual companies, let us first have a generic look at the corporate world in general. People tend to think that companies make a lot of money and therefore, have plenty to pay for the annual expenses like hiring staff, providing good salaries, and complying with the applicable laws. In reality, that is a lot of money and it is far easier said than done.

The unknown truth is that most companies in the world are not profitable. Many of them can barely keep themselves in business after a few years. They underperform but are still operating thanks to lines of credit, subsequent loans, public or private funds, and similar solutions solely designed to perpetuate this precarious state. It may sound strange, but everyone running a company knows the brutal truth of our economic system.

The level of industry development is one of the most important indicators of a nation's prosperity. So, every single country in the world has a very specific interest to strengthen their business structure (which is based on our capitalist economy, which is based on mass consumerism). A greater welfare for the employees and higher product quality could be commendable and desired objectives, of course. But the questions that every company owner has to ask themselves are the following: If I did not have the means to do any of these things, would I shut down my company? Or keep it afloat, just operating under less favorable conditions?

If we apply this same logic over and over again, under worse conditions, we could easily understand the tricky situation facing most companies and workers around the world. Personal nuances also come into play, because business owners are humans too. Whether they are going through a difficult situation or not, they should consider, from the outset, the minimum quality standards for their products, as well as the working conditions for their employees. Now, and also in Chapter 3: "Economy and Law," we will review some business thoughts that will give you a better picture of the untold realities, beyond the Hollywood hills, about how production companies work around the world. Because, when it comes to small independent activity, the system is not exactly the same.

The main difference is the financial capacity to handle content production. And this means much more than having available capital, because in this market you cannot, or should not, operate without things like financial guarantees and insurances. To put it simply, imagine that you had a decent budget to create a film. Once finished, you distribute the work to theaters, TV, and other media outlets, and you start making money. When you earn more than what you invested, that is a profit, congratulations. Now, the higher the budget, the more comfortabilities you can afford for the crew or the higher complexity you can add to the film. However, a higher budget also has a negative side. The bigger the budget, the more time you need to gain a net profit once you make back the production costs.

In big, super productions everything is incredibly spectacular. They have the most advanced technical resources, a bunch of expensive stars, and constant mass-media advertising. Studios spend so much money because all of that guarantees a minimum certainty of expectations. But at the same time, that turns into a huge sum of revenues, only to recover the production cost. While most of these productions make hundreds of millions of dollars worldwide, imagine if you could have earned the same by spending 50 million less. And as a producer, you would want to avoid any unnecessary expenses. Needless to say, these large amounts of money are so hard for most of us to imagine. What is more, usually no one has a clear notion of how production money is spent even for regular movies.

It does not help that nowadays, anyone can record audio and video with decent professional quality (which has been called "the democratization of filmmaking"). Many amateurs, semi-professionals, and young, newbie producers/directors fail to understand the complexity of how big companies within the industry work. According to their own experience, with extra effort, passion, commitment (and even a bit of suffering), you can do decent things with little to no money. Most amateurs think that you can apply this same scenario even when you have a multi-million dollar budget. So, apart from being able to afford a star (as if stars could make your precarious production shine using their fairy dust) and substantially raise the salaries of your inexperienced crew, one may never know what to do with a large budget.

What is important, is that a low-cost production might look decent to some average viewers, but probably would not be meeting the high visual and technical standards of the industry. This quality is required in order to be marketed, distributed, and screened. Unfortunately, money does not magically make the transition from 'decent' to 'masterpiece' by itself. The vast majority of independent films or productions from small industries in other countries, do not get into the big game because they do not meet the minimum standards of Hollywood's distribution giants. In the best cases, an interesting movie can attract attention from the industry, as a way of talking about future collaborations. But the possibility of receiving a global distribution offer for that particular work is highly unlikely.

It is not that easy to produce something outside the studio system and expect it to compete at the same level of quality as Hollywood productions. The question is not about competition or fairness, but rather about what happens to small companies

THE FILM AND AUDIOVISUAL INDUSTRY

that cannot recover their investment? Things like bankruptcy, suspension of payments, and company shutdowns can take place. And after big failures, they may be unable to cope with debts, credits, interest, and taxes. But this is not always the case. Many small company owners also have different assets and big companies in other sectors, so their reasons for running a film production company may come from different business, fiscal, political, or personal interests.

The business world is a jungle and only the strongest survive. There are certain circles of influence that ordinary people are unaware of. In such a small guild, everyone must stand together and cover each other's backs, if they want to stay. Additionally, that circle must remain as closed and as tight as possible to be functional, or you will lose the advantages of being inside. For business people, it is convenient to keep their production companies in business, even in hard times of low profit margins or loss. This is better than closing their business, since they would lose the possibility of doing certain operations with other companies that are more profitable. (Apart from the fact that absolute losses are very rare.)

Most of these independent producers (the smart ones, at least) know exactly how much money they can spend, in order to not depend on box office success. Even by making movies that are not profitable, independent companies' survival is guaranteed with only a few fixed incomes. Such as, public funding and subsidies, some broadcast rights, national TV and international networks, and/or a fistful of favors that have been negotiated with third parties. More examples would be office use, promotional exchange, sponsorships, taxes discounts, programs for employment creation, cultural support, and R&D. The secret is not rocket science, never spend more money than you can raise, even if your production has to be done precariously. Of course this does not sound very good to your cast and crew, but we will talk more about that later.

THE FILM AND AUDIOVISUAL INDUSTRY

If these producers wanted to do what big studios do, they should spend the real cost of a decent production and rely on recovering that money, leaving it in the hands of fate. And that is the biggest controversy in the film industry, in many countries around the world. Apart from the already discussed dual conception of art and business, smaller film industries are also adding one new concept: culture. And they are not doing it without contention.

Every government has an obligation to regulate and promote film and audiovisual productions within its nation's territory. There is a lot of talk about national identity and cultural diffusion. But as with many other types of aid that exists in various sectors, this is just about an economic sustenance for an unprofitable industry. In the 21st century, any modern society cannot accept the shame of not having a proper film industry. (Exactly like many of the constitutional declarations of these countries explicitly mention.) Some industries consist of a small group of exclusive business people, who maintain film production activities in order to keep the industry alive. There is no other option than to support them through different ministries such as culture, tourism, employment, and defense. They also receive interesting benefits in return. After all, governments also use these industries to advertise their own national brand. (Hollywood, for example, does this all the time.)

In some countries, once producers recover the amount granted by the public fund, the law states that the money must be reinvested into producing new films or refunded to the government. But in most countries, these public funds are non-repayable grants, which is clearly an unsustainable model. It will only continue working as long as no one turns off the money tap. It can be considered as a sort of subsidy; like a misplaced civil service, that has somehow turned into an organized lobby. Let us analyze this system in more detail.

Earlier, we stated that economic profit is not a necessity. Because Hollywood blockbusters saturate the market, it is normal that few foreign countries' national productions may not be interesting enough for the majority of people. And do not forget that making a movie, no matter how simple it is, still costs a lot of money, no matter the currency. Which means that, according to statistics, in foreign countries, most national productions are destined to have a loss by default. But then, how do production companies survive in such a system? The key is their ability to cover all of their expenses with other people's money, either public or private. For example, government grants and loans usually do not cover 100% of the production budget, but are instead limited to a certain percentage. Depending on the legislation of each country, this could be a maximum of 50% of production costs. Likewise, you must also have money in cash to be able to spend it, since the bulk of these payments are usually received after proper justification of expenditure. (It is not rare to draw on loans for this purpose.)

But it is clear that you do not go into this game unless you know you can afford it. There are some different ways of increasing the budget percentage, in order to get as much money as possible. Like co-producing between several companies (if they belong to the same group of companies, even better) or submitting an application for more public funding with other projects, or using an oversized budget for something that actually needs much less money, like documentaries for example. Anything goes when it comes to reaching the only goal that really matters in business: making money. We can also highlight that considering these are usually sole trader companies or companies with a very small employee workforce, this is not about the real cost of your production, but much more about how much money you can save. Every amount is automatically dedicated to survival in the jungle. Whatever the production is, the goal is to spend as little as possible. Always. No exception. On the one hand, the most typical choice is to inflate budgets and on the other hand, to manipulate the expenditure accounts. It is not as easy as one might think, but not that difficult for those who know how. In fact, some people like to pretend this never happens, even in other industries. But there is no point in denying such an obvious truth, especially nowadays in this new world of information overexposure. The financial community even has a name for it: creative accounting.

THE FILM AND AUDIOVISUAL INDUSTRY

When you apply for any of these film grants, you first have to submit an estimated budget, along with many other documents. And as stated previously, even if your project receives some funding, as a producer, you have to spend your own money and account for every expenditure or you will never receive any help. Some funds are received in staggered payments, while others are always received in a single payment once production has finished. You must also be willing to expect the worst from government and institutional entities, like certain risks of delay or default. Let us not forget that this type of help will never cover the whole budget, but only a percentage of the overall cost. It can be a fixed amount (award-type) or any variable percentage defined through the subjective rating given by a committee of experts, appointed by each government. This causes two major lines of controversy. The first one is the possible favoritism within the committee (whose members are not publicly known) and the second is the insufficient fiscal control of submitted expenditures. These issues have always caused a tense social debate in the countries where it happens. Initially, only those who were left out of the exclusive elite who obtained the grants would complain against the system (a classic cake-cutting problem). Nevertheless, when taxpayers' pockets started to notice the crisis, and political scandals uncovered illicit activities as well, the public image of these small film industries was negatively impacted.

As time has passed, some improvements have been proposed, approved, and/or implemented in different countries. One such suggestion is that the commercial success of a film must directly affect the chances of producers' and directors' eligibility for further grants. The problem is that there are convenient interests behind this and a general lack of transparency. At this moment, what these grants and tax incentives do is guarantee their recipients an "automatic" return on investment, regardless of the quality or success of their products. In fact, an alarming number of funded films do not even get to be released, which proves that they have already fulfilled their purpose. And although many others do, it is usually in a limited way, mainly due to its quality.

THE FILM AND AUDIOVISUAL INDUSTRY

Some producers also own movie theaters, which allows them to schedule their own films, as long as they consider them appropriate. But although this is legitimate, it is an open door to fraudulent activities such as "selling tickets" even if there is no screening session. Selling to whom? Well, some producers who do not have their own screens may need to get a film premiere certification, for example, or have a minimum amount of success to meet the requirements for different types of grants, distribution programs, industrial subsidies, or to be eligible for awards, as some require theatrically released films and others do not. Perhaps they may just want to have a stronger position to negotiate international sales. Because, every movie screened in theaters will be of higher value than any failed product that no one wanted to distribute (or even worse, it could be considered a lower-category product, like direct-to-video).

From the opposite point of view, these actions are justified because of the impossible pressure these independent producers are under. Screens and dates available for their movies are minimal. In such a saturated market, only the flashiest products will attract mainstream audiences. And we all know that any low-budget production in Hollywood has more millions of dollars than any high-budget movie from a smaller industry.

You can always perceive money on screen (it is always a bad sign if you cannot) and Hollywood knows how to exploit that. In order to display an international success, movie theaters are forced to acquire an indivisible package including other smaller productions. If they want to screen the latest blockbuster, the exhibitors will have to find a way to fit those other movies on the billboards too. Most likely, reducing the sessions of even smaller, national productions. Everyone prefers movies that have better visuals and international actors. These are more preferred than unknown films, which can be deemed as less visually interesting and most likely, less entertaining. (Because the fact that one film has been proudly made in your country is probably not reason enough to get audiences interested.)

THE FILM AND AUDIOVISUAL INDUSTRY

These industries had to learn the hard way. No matter how government and industry-released associations in each country try to clean up their public image, it is the films' quality that fills the movie theaters. Every country has its own movie stars. Film and television celebrities, singers, elite athletes, and many other types of well-known faces. But that is not enough to compete. After all, it is a local level of celebrity. These industries are not fully mature yet, they have not found the balance between art and business.

Concluding the topic of public grants, we can assume that the artistic value must have some relevance for the committees in charge. However, instead of being a hopeful opportunity for a talent search, it is just another expression of formal vagueness. Another open door to the convenient subjectivity of the anonymous committee of experts. Some countries offer specific support to the development and the production of experimental works; as well as funding and promotion for festivals or alternative, arthouse cinemas. These distribution spaces do not have too much relevance, but let us say that they cover the need more or less proportionally to the size of the interested audience.

We can see that this economic and legal framework is not the most appropriate for industry growth. Therefore, (and this is hard to say) their professionals will not be sufficiently prepared either. Because there are no good references around them, you cannot establish proper comparative benchmarks. Aside from this, one of the most important strategies of the American economy is the recruitment of international talent (called "brain drain" as opposed to "brain gain"). This recruitment allows many artists and technicians from different industries to take the leap and go to Hollywood.

Talent is a natural ability to reach excellence in your field, whichever it is. In order to create an audiovisual product of the highest quality, everyone involved must demonstrate their talent first. That is why directors should surround themselves with the best possible artists and producers should look for the best means and technical staff that their budget can afford.

THE FILM AND AUDIOVISUAL INDUSTRY

Unfortunately, that whole situation contributes to a certain abandonment of responsibilities and a lack of motivation. When professionals do not feel properly remunerated, they do not think it is worth striving for, especially if they think that it is an average or poor project. Their only interest then becomes paying the bills at the end of the month, hoping the next job can be better. And now imagine that it never gets better.

That is how these workers end up becoming like the kind of classic cases of apathetic public employees, with no passion for their work or interest in improving or learning more.

Although these systems are clearly unprofitable and easily corruptible, some of these industries have managed to grow over the years, like the strongest countries in Western Europe for example. They are well known and criticized, yes, but the public image of their industries is much healthier now than it was twenty or thirty years ago, and the social debate is much more relaxed. This was possible due to the progressive increase of private investments, like TV networks, venture capital investors, and bank and insurance entities. And you can be sure that all of them will look for profitability. World economies continue to change (always in cycles, do not forget that) and it is no coincidence that a few years ago, Hollywood studios created several subsidiary production companies around the world. They are not producing many homegrown films from scratch in these countries, but it is certain that they will at the right moment. Now that private investors are more and more involved and commercial success is increasingly required, these small industries seem to have a future.

DISTRIBUTION AND EXHIBITION

Distribution is a necessity, but it is often overrated. While it may be true that the only complication should be to transport the manufactured product from factory to consumer or point of sale; at the same time, we also obtain comfort and benefit by having others do it for us, which ends up giving the distributor certain privileges. From a strictly trading standpoint, audiovisual products work just like any other industry merchandise. It has manufacturers and consumers therefore, it must have distributors. A distributor is someone who provides the manpower, infrastructure, and selling knowledge. Even the big Hollywood studio system considers distribution a totally separate area of business, despite the companies involved belonging to the same group or holding.

There must be an intermediary figure so that the different parts remain separate from each other. (We will see later that this distance is necessary at business level.) Distribution is also a way to facilitate regulation and study the market. Once the product is finished, its commercial life cycle does not have any relation to the previous process therefore, all the mechanisms and results should be analyzed in isolation.

THE FILM AND AUDIOVISUAL INDUSTRY

From the very beginning, the Hollywood system was aware of the necessity of having distribution and production companies separate, provided that they could continue maintaining control over the whole process. In a free-market economy like ours, it is not impossible to compete, but given the circumstances, it is quite difficult. Due to the international nature of this industry, some independent companies have managed to carve out their own niche. In fact, the roadmap is always the same. Every country in the world has a small group of distribution companies thanks to the introduction of cinema in their respective territories, and the development of telecommunications in general. And over the years, these companies have acquired extensive experience in film and/or the television business.

In such a small and closed circle, (and it is very important that it stays this way) global film distribution is 100% profitable and safe, even in the least developed country. Therefore, there is no need to take a chance on novel, risky, experimental, or unknown content. Your business can be stable, quiet, and comfortable, operating under safe conditions. So why would anyone want to complicate matters?

Due to this relative comfort, (at the end of the day, if you have a distribution company, you are still running a business) the only possible interest in occasionally taking a controlled risk, could be precisely when you find something special and exclusive that also has a promising commercial value. Perhaps a limited value to big studios but relevant enough to a certain (guaranteed) minority audience, which could be profitable for an independent distributor. After all, the economic risks of distribution are much lower. Since earnings are obtained in percentages, distributors will always get a proportionally higher profitability than any other link of the chain. In relation to the expense incurred, the difference can be overwhelming. This should encourage the search for new talent or different contents. It is like trying to be the first ones to find a new gold mine. But that is just the idealistic, theoretical part.

THE FILM AND AUDIOVISUAL INDUSTRY

Beginners and small business owners see the distribution sector as one more closed door. Just another select group with power, deciding what enters the market and what does not. However in this case, the door is not completely locked. Why would a distributor refuse to make money off a good product? With this open attitude, the problem from the production side will always be the same. Gathering enough money to make a quality product.

The industry logic itself (to make money above all else) outweighs simple elitism. Distributors are always looking for new job titles. Discovering a huge success can drastically change the prestige of a company and its business status in the industry, not to mention its financial situation.

With the critics' approval, for example in a film festival, the next goal would be to convince the audience. Massive success could depend on the right marketing strategy. Coincidentally, if anyone knows how to market a film well, it is the Hollywood system. Big studios' famous "indie" divisions are just subsidiary distribution companies (not so independent, right?) which may offer a seductive deal in advance. They could also give a second, international life to a previously successful product. (Usually a modest film that performed well in its own country with limited distribution.) Those previous box office results can be useful as market research. One can analyze the demographic of interest and detect the product's strengths and weaknesses.

The marketing strategy for independent films must focus on the artistic value and the awards obtained. These can either be the awards won in festivals prior to its first release or in its possible existing commercial life. But how can these serious, artistic products compete with the frivolous mainstream? The most immediate answer would be that these films are only capable of having some success, but never as big as blockbusters. There is usually only one reason for exceptional cases that garner millionaire success, and that is if everyone is talking about that film.

THE FILM AND AUDIOVISUAL INDUSTRY

Independent films with such a high level of hype, are so few that you can count them on one hand. Real moviegoers eagerly hope that some of these films come to their cities, while others could just be curious. Particularly, when the film stars well-known actors who have lowered their salaries because of artistic interest. But when everyone is talking about how good a movie is, no one wants to be the only weirdo who did not watch it. Suddenly, it becomes a social status of sophistication, and due to social pressure, everybody ends up going to the theater. Though the most common reaction to these titles is indifference. Nothing will change the taste of global audiences and their individual opinions about what makes a good or a bad movie.

The lack of competition that independent films have is, in fact, an interesting advantage. The market demand naturally maintains an adequate number of distributors (as well as exhibitors) who pay attention to this type of alternative product. It is a minor, niche market with its own audience after all. Without the commercial pressure of having to please the mainstream, some creators decide not to make concessions to the popular trends of the moment and voluntarily move away from the industry commonplace.

It is no coincidence that there are so few creators and distributors of this kind. Unable to stay in the business, a lot of them just disappeared over the years, and there are few opportunities for newcomers. However, even the major studios have understood the advantage of having an eye on these possible bargains. New talents and trends are considered strategic elements now. Every Hollywood studio has its own "indie" distribution division. These branches are dedicated to the acquisition of films that are more artistic or mature than usual, but also have good potential to be profitable with the right promotion.

Anecdotally, films can be considered "independent" when none of the major studios have been involved in their production. But the use of the term has become confusing, like some sort of quality seal. As if they are trying to sell more adult, serious films with a higher profile of artistic elaboration and intellectual maturity. Nowadays, many movies are labeled "indie" and categorized as "independent" despite the production company.

This turns us to the matter at hand: Depending on the quality of the product, one distribution company can receive substantial profits just by acquiring the distribution rights of a film. Essentially, any studio that shows interest in distributing a film, can put their offer on the table. Offers made by larger studios are more likely to be advantageous than those of smaller distributors, plus any attempt to outbid would be useless. But there are also cases in which studios detect an interesting movie, perhaps not good enough for them, but appropriate for a small, 100% independent distributor. As a strategic move, these large studios could put both parties in contact. It is not altruism, as they see an interesting opportunity but would prefer that others run the risk, just in case.

In these scenarios, everyone wins. Especially the creators. Besides getting a distribution deal with a specialized company (no matter how small it is), they also have the advantage of getting a Hollywood studio's attention. For independent production companies and distributors, there is no extra effort given to keep an eye out for promising talent and productions. Considering how few these companies are, they usually catch up to each other regarding the status of their projects. The calendar is checked for free dates in order to arrange passes for screenings, business meetings, and anything else needed to open or close deals.

A lot of people do not know this, but film festivals are perfect places to do all of the above. Apart from presenting movies to the press and selected audiences, festivals have the clear purpose of industry marketing for insiders. They are the most useful and efficient promotion tool for both national and international distribution.

THE FILM AND AUDIOVISUAL INDUSTRY

FESTIVALS AND MARKETS

The origin of film festivals is interesting. The first one was Venice Biennale (also known as The Venice Film Festival). It was conceived in 1932 by a wealthy Italian aristocrat and dictator, Benito Mussolini. Given the international and massive success of cinema in those years, Mussolini saw the opportunity to create an important touristic and cultural claim for Italy. It called the media's attention with the presence of some of the greatest celebrities of that time: Greta Garbo, Joan Crawford, James Cagney, Clark Gable, Vittorio de Sica, Howard Hawks, and stand-out artists like Frank Capra, James Whale, and Ernst Lubitsch.

Due to its fantastic turnout and its reach around the world, each new edition of the festival increased its fame; as well as the fascist political influence and pressure on the festival organizers. And not only the Italian fascism. In 1938, the award for Best Film (the Mussolini Cup) went to the famous documentary *Olympia*, about the Olympic Games in Berlin. Several members of the jury (coincidentally French and Jewish) publicly denounced that the film won without consensus, but was imposed by force. As a consequence, those same members created their own film festival the following year, in the French city of Cannes. They were supported by several celebrities of a high cultural profile, including one of the Lumière brothers. Sadly, this new festival was inaugurated on September 1st of 1939, coinciding with the fateful invasion of Poland. So, it was canceled and forgotten until the end of World War II.

Plenty of other festivals were created hereafter. Most of them were focused on luxury and glamour (ensuring that an elitist feeling was always present), but little by little they also gained prestige as audiovisual art exhibitions. It was not until 1960, in Cannes, that the first film market (in French, Marché du Film) was created. Since the world's main producers and distributors attended annually (or sent representatives), it was inevitable that they made a number of public relations, exchanged relevant information, and even sealed important deals.

THE FILM AND AUDIOVISUAL INDUSTRY

Therefore, it made sense to create a parallel area, exclusively dedicated to business affairs, apart from the media circus. In this environment, the main objective for companies was promotion, in order to get better sales abroad. However, at the same time, there was a growing interest in what was being done in other countries. In other words, they found the opportunity to make more money distributing foreign films, with the added value of being innovative or different, some would even say exotic.

Attending festivals with parallel markets became an important way to keep yourself up-to-date in the market, even without the specific intention of buying or selling. You could review catalogs, discover what was new and trendy, or simply get a forecast of what was to come. Markets were created on necessity and pleasure. An incomparable luxury setting, uniquely designed for meeting other industry members and doing business. Or more accurately, talking about the possibility of doing business in the future.

Attending international markets opens up new sales possibilities for your product. Companies that are established in their respective industries, will always have higher-quality products; but it is also a unique opportunity for smaller companies. They are able to stand out in an unknown environment. They can do this even if they are systematically excluded from the small elite of their own domestic market. The world is quite big, so there are a lot of markets and opportunities to explore. Although, this may also cause a negative effect on small producers and filmmakers because they often have too high an expectation (a kind of unrealistic hope). As we saw in Chapter 1: "Art and the Industry," many of these companies survive in their countries on certain conditions and, for the most part, do not depend on film production. Rather, they belong to a bigger holding or credit-worthy owner with other priorities. The more money you make with international sales, the better. But, in case your small company cannot sell anything and you come back empty-handed, just the travel and attendance expenses alone could be a disappointing loss.

The situation is different when you have a desirable product that everyone wants. If you have a poor catalog, at best, you can try to sell to a few markets that are weaker than yours, which means lower revenues.

Although it may be hard to accept, if no one wants to buy your products, either domestically or internationally, something is not working. Attending one of these markets is not particularly difficult or expensive for any professional production company. Accreditation fees and associated costs, like promotion materials, exhibit spaces, desks, booths, conferences, workshops, etc. should be affordable, especially if the company is not too small. But everything depends on how many festivals per year you want to attend, and with which purpose. Each owner/executive must decide whether it is worth attending these events or not. This will depend on the company's strategy and situation. At film markets, only a few attendees are real buyers or investors. You will hardly find producers and executives with capital in these places. If you do, they are looking to fund or buy projects that are in development or in early production stages.

There are basically two types of attendees. The first are the representatives of large trading companies. For example, film, television, new media agents, and networks and distributors. The second type is an infinity of small, independent companies that are in search of funding, pre-sales, and distribution agreements for their projects. But in general, no one is looking for ideas to produce or finished low-cost products to buy, unless they are really good. It is difficult to succeed at markets, but that does not mean that it is impossible. If you can afford the attempt, trying is worthwhile.

But definitely, being present in the most relevant festivals is a must for large production companies. It is important for the company and brand to stay up-to-date. They can check out how their competitors are doing, scout for emerging talent, and detect the latest trends. Lots of different festivals and markets take place throughout the year, all across the globe. And nowadays with the internet, it is really easy to research and make arrangements.

THE FILM AND AUDIOVISUAL INDUSTRY

Buyers have an elite and comfortable advantage. At markets, they can find more products on sale than they are actually looking to purchase. This is not by chance. This strategic superiority reinforces the competitiveness of the sector. Any company, big or small, should pay attention to what their industry rivals do. They should always aim to do more and get better products and deals. If you want to produce and distribute with a higher profitability than your competitors, you should strive to acquire independent products that are already finished. If there is anything interesting out there, you will find it at festivals and markets.

Distributors want new content to be released in their country (in theaters, on television, or any other window) and depending on their profile, interests, and needs, they could be as demanding as they want, in terms of quality, conditions, and budget. Countries that have a weaker audiovisual industry will not be able to afford expensive films, which might not even fit within their culture. The same goes for technological issues. Most modern countries broadcast high-definition television, but not all of them. There are old films whose image quality might lack technology and feel inappropriate. For instance, they may have low image definition, poor color, old audio, and/or video noise. This kind of catalogue is no longer available in modern countries. Even after digital restoration processes, some products still look old-fashioned or have too low a quality for western industries. However, they may obtain some profitability in the market of some developing countries.

The cost may depend on how new or old the content is, but there are many other factors that influence negotiations. Such as, demonstrable success over time and in different territories. That is why the main attraction in markets is the product catalogues. Apart from the most successful films and television and internet series, the bestselling products are usually recent projects that also have a solid, demonstrable track record in a few markets; at least in their own country of origin.

THE FILM AND AUDIOVISUAL INDUSTRY

As indicated previously, only a few attendees are open to investing their money in projects that are looking for funding or are considering a distribution agreement. With luck, independent producers can get a small amount of pre-sales from a few festivals, which can add to their budget; although it is necessary to emphasize that they are just business agreements, legally bound to the project termination. Namely, a lump sum negotiated and agreed upon before the film even existed. It is up to each buyer to trust the seller and require that they provide demonstrable references.

It may also happen, very occasionally, that a production company is open to the possibility of co-producing with another company in a similar situation and profile. Depending on the type of organization, project, and development status, these synergies can be useful. With similar size, financial solvency, and objectives, working together would double resources and efforts, so both companies could expect better quality in the final result. It is also an opportunity to produce something that would be impossible if done separately. There are many reasons in favor and against this practice, since collaboration with strangers is never easy, although common. Co-producing can also increase your chances for funding and distribution, as well as increase your chances of signing further production deals with third parties. Besides a relatively bigger financial strength, this projects a more business and professional appearance to others in the industry. Either way, no one will make easy deals with unknown newcomers.

Even in the best possible scenario, distributors or potential investors that show interest, will usually follow up with projects, companies, or talent at further events. Keeping in contact every once in a while, just to effectively check the solidness of your company and your project. (If you give up in under a year, there is not much more to add.) In short, think of it this way: "I am not going to help you now, but if I see you convince someone serious to go onboard and you demonstrate that you are getting things on your own, I might consider this again."

THE FILM AND AUDIOVISUAL INDUSTRY

That is the crux of the matter. Who will be the first to help newcomers? The misfortune of small, indie producers and filmmakers is always the same. A dog chasing its own tail and never catching it. "I never get funds because I do not have a distribution deal, which I will not get because I have no funding." This brings us to the basic, universal truth that everyone knows: You need a lot of money to get into the film industry. Many other things are needed, of course, but in order to try and produce something minimally serious within the industry, the first thing you need is always money—lots and lots of money. In business meetings you can meet people, yes. It is true that you talk a lot and may have very productive discussions. Perhaps, you even negotiate very promising remote possibilities, but a few months or years later, the vast majority of these conversations will fall into the most absolute oblivion. As if they never happened.

Any professional in this industry knows that slowness is one of its main features. For those who have started or have few resources to compete, the extreme slowness causes a sort of relentless natural selection, preventing many companies from surviving through the years. After trying again and again, with all kinds of projects, without reaching the next level (where the real money is), the most obvious consequence is that the producer or company ends up leaving. That might mean going out of business or perhaps just resigning themselves to operate at a reachable production level. This could mean adjusting to advertising, internet, services to other companies, or whatever the case may be. In the end, it is a personal decision which can be made after many years for wear, boredom, poor economic situations, or by realizing that you have been investing beyond your means.

Small producers usually attend international markets in one of three seasons. The first season is at the beginning of their business' activity. (If they have the required means. It is a particularly brave way of starting, but an excellent way to learn.) The second season might be at a relevant moment of economic growth. (This implies a certain overconfidence and probably an excess of investment.) And finally, the third season is before abandoning bigger aspirations, when they need a desperate attempt. Of course, the results you get will determine how willing you are to repeat the experience.

When these adventures go well, especially with the first, small distribution agreement alone, you can consider the executive expenses covered. Even if you are hiring a sales agency, with the percentage they will receive, they can consider their expenses covered too. However, sometimes there is no way of making money in these intrepid journeys and all you have are losses. A classic roadmap could be: You might believe you will triumph in your first attempt. For example, looking for funding or selling a finished product. Then, you might feel disappointed by the null impact of these efforts and the slow evolution of any actual opportunities. After that, you may have doubts about the usefulness of festivals and markets. And finally, the accumulated frustration, over the years, makes you realize that the situation is never going to change. This is how hopes of getting into the international industry are gradually replaced by frustration, until it completely disappears.

DISTRIBUTION DEALS

All independent newcomers must negotiate their first distribution agreement at some point. By default, it usually includes unfavorable conditions. And there is not much they can do about it. But knowing about the subject makes a difference. Rookies should be aware that they have a vulnerable position during negotiations. (For example, they may think: "I do not have a better offer so I will take the $20,000, which is better than nothing.") They can also be naive out of ignorance. (They may think: "I am not being paid with this contract, but all these promises are very impressive.") Or even worse, they can feel like victims of deception and be paranoid. ("How dare you offer me $20,000 when I heard that this other person was offered

$200,000 for their last movie.") The market price will always depend on the industry's global situation, the specific territory, and the fame of the product or its creators. Your work will be worth what others value it.

Ideally, a distribution deal is one of the first things that should be closed during the initial funding stage. No one wants to spend money on making a production, without the guarantee that it will be shown somewhere, so they can earn profits in return. That makes sense, but how do you convince someone to invest in something that does not exist yet? You could assume that your previous productions make others confident.

But how can beginners do this? Well, that is the thing, they cannot. Debutant producers and directors are always confident in their work's potential, of course. But they are the only ones seeing their films in their minds, so it is only natural that they attempt to sell it as a masterpiece. No matter how reluctant people are to buy it. When you do not have money to produce something within the industry's quality standards, you are forced to seek external funding. As long as you do not have a recognized and professional name, there is money that you will not get. And in order to obtain that status, you have to have at least one production that matches the industry's quality standards. Exactly, it is a never-ending story.

Even if they manage to finish their first production, most newcomers do not know what really happens next. The business part that comes after is usually a mystery to independent filmmakers. Precisely because there are things involved that have nothing to do with the creation process or with filmmaking itself. Most newbies visualize the moment when they can proudly show their finished product and an executive in a fancy suit makes them a million-dollar offer for their wonderful masterpiece, transforming them into a celebrity. This is, more or less, the mental scheme that beginners have in their heads. But when they are on the phone or in front of one of these executives trying to negotiate something, they have no clue. It is not easy to know if the deal they are negotiating is good or bad. In fact, many of them will have no choice but to just accept anything out of necessity or personal strategy. They have thoughts like: "I have to pay my bills to survive," "I will receive better offers over time," "My next project will go better," and "The important thing is that I am starting to make a name for myself."

For those who do not know, the first thing you need to understand about signing contracts (in this industry and elsewhere) is that they are negotiable by their very nature. If you do not like some parts of it, just change it. If you have a counteroffer to make, just make it. And, if you want to make an addition, just ask or demand for it. That is why it is called a negotiation. Something to keep in mind is that, given your inferior position, it is unlikely that you can make demands. So everything comes down to "take it or leave it," especially when it is accompanied by: "This offer expires on Monday, so sign it or else you get nothing." It is all part of the game. Each experience makes you learn something new. It is a quiet journey for some, full of cordiality and good deals, while others have to face a constant struggle of tensions, bad vibes, and litigations.

As you can see, everything in this industry starts and ends with the business world. It is an arena that creative people do not know much about, but the only true meaning of business is "to put deals in writing." Activities or partnerships that take place under certain terms and conditions in which both parties agree: "You do this and I do that, we both get this or that in return." In addition to this, the when and how this will happen and all the possible eventualities that may alter the agreed conditions. It may look simple on paper (well, not even) but the first time you face a contract of several pages, you will begin to understand that it is not a game. Large-scale audiovisual distribution (therefore, owned by Hollywood studios) is based on the so-called windows or distribution channels: movie theaters, DVD/Blu-ray, TV broadcast, Vision On Demand (VOD), or Pay-Per-View (PPV) services. There are also many other alternative or parallel channels, such as hotels, airplanes, trains, cruises, libraries, and schools.

THE FILM AND AUDIOVISUAL INDUSTRY

Traditionally, there is always a limited period of time that must pass before any product goes to the next window. However, this period is becoming shorter and shorter, due to the simultaneous pressure of two factors. Firstly, the increasingly fast consumption in movie theaters (partly because of the market saturation itself) and secondly, the unstoppable immediacy of the internet (including piracy, but also because of legal choices). Reality tells us that, in the not too distant future, the multi-window option will be the standard. Audiences will voluntarily choose what to see, when and where. This is already being tested and experienced around the world and, as usual, the big industry must delay the change as much as possible in order to give the traditional distribution model time to adapt. New technologies are not totally under their control (yet), which explains the huge impact it has made on the industry in the last couple of decades.

As for the formal content included in a distribution agreement, the first thing to clarify is that every distributor, as an intermediary, always negotiates two kinds of agreements. One with producers and the other with exhibitors (like movie theaters for example). Basically, everything is focused on defining the proportional amounts in which the benefits will be shared; apart from the most obvious: territory and duration of the contract. For film, it is usually 4 weeks in theaters with a minimum mandatory of 2 or 3. In some cases, it may be advisable to opt for the fixed amount payment, especially for small territories or films that are not guaranteed to be successful. But the most logical and common is a variable percentage, negotiated according to the context of film and country.

Using this example between distributor and theaters, the following calculation must be applied each week to box office results: After taxes are deducted, the revenue percentage that is usually negotiated is between 40% and 60%. But a minimum payment is also agreed upon, as a guarantee in case the results are far worse than expected. (Higher or lower, depending on the theater's territory and the film's fame.)

So, once you have the weekly data, the higher amount is applied in favor of the distributor. (The agreed percentage, or the minimum payment if the percentage is lower.) Although, it is also standard to modify these percentages as time passes, progressively favoring the exhibitor with each new week. If a movie is still on the billboard after one month, that means it has very good results. And do not forget that the success or failure of a film can be foreseen in their opening weekend (even more clearly during the first two weeks); so the additional compensation to the exhibitor will not be a significant loss. The number of tickets sold after several weeks may be enough to have it remain on the billboard, but not particularly significant in the end, from the perspective of the global results. So, exhibitors are allowed to receive higher incomes, once distributors have obtained the most relevant portion of their success (or failure, in which case it does not make a difference anyway).

Before we go any further, let us clarify a small detail here. Maybe you have heard of the famous 90/10 standard in these types of negotiations. 90% of the profit for the distributor and 10% for the exhibitor. Deals like this used to happen many, many years ago when the situation of the national and international industry was quite different. As stated before, the average is a theoretical 50/50, with a tendency to favor the distributor. But there is no doubt that professional secrecy surrounding these lucrative operations contribute to the convenient perpetuation of such rumors.

Distributors will have to distribute the money, according to the percentage that was previously negotiated with producers. The average is also 50/50 of net incomes, but open to more variants (such as making the calculations from gross income or reaching 70/30 for example). Without forgetting that independent producers could be using a sales agent to find distributors, who usually takes between 20% and 25% for their part. We must also mention that distributors have marketing and advertising expenses, as well as the theatrical copies that are released to the market. Unlike foreign distributors from small industries, since they do not have enough resources for that. The copies are ten times less now, in the digital era, and are expected to be nonexistent once movies can be played directly from the cloud. By the way, in regards to payment, we must mention that benefits are paid many months after the release or even one year later.

Studio executives meet every week to check the box office results and, using statistics, predict the revenues for the following weeks. This facilitates, among other things, the option to change the marketing strategy, if needed. From the beginning, they have to have several action plans, according to all possible scenarios of failure or success. As the weeks go by, these results are more predictable. Although, there are not too many things you can do to surmount a failure or empower a success that has already exhausted all its possibilities (so it is not worth spending more money in promotion).

Finally, the last link in the chain is exhibition. We already know that there is an executive side, focused on business negotiations from a slightly inferior position to distributors. But as business people, it is also part of their job to find alternative incomes which does not involve distributors. For example, it is typical for theaters to rent their facilities for galas, congresses, corporate presentations, and other kinds of events. They could also give discounts to schools or birthday parties with private screenings for children and even bachelor parties.

Something less alternative, but still aside from the traditional distribution is the streaming of concerts, operas, theater plays, and sports competitions. None of these activities are the greatest revenue sources for movie theaters, but all together contribute to the overall profit of the business. And do not forget that above all, exhibitors must ensure that the audience does not lose interest in the ritual of physically going to the movies and must help them fight against the dangerous comfort offered by the "home cinema."

Some of these broadcast services (operas, concerts, and such) began to be projected in 3D with this very objective in mind. Combining the broadcast of music or sports events with stereoscopic-3D live production, in general terms, offers a more enjoyable experience than being crammed among a mass of strangers. But considering that at home you can also sit on your couch in front of a big TV with surround sound speakers and even have 3D glasses, with a similar technology to movie theaters, the most immediate incentive to go to the movies, for now, will always remain on the giant screen.

There are many other personal comforts that exhibitors offer to make a difference. For example, a wide variety of food, multiple and spacious toilets, and private cleaning services. A series of details that make you wonder if it is not more practical to bring your friends together in a movie theater than your own home. In short, throughout the years, television manufacturers have been obsessed with bringing the spectacularity of movie theaters to the home, so exhibitors have decided to respond by trying to bring the comfort of home to the theaters.

THE REAL BUSINESS OF EXHIBITION

In the same way TV's transmission evolved (i.e. radio waves, television antenna, cable, fiber, satellite, etc.), cinema has been refining the screening format. But the intrinsic value of the big dark room remains unchanged. The concept of "magic vision" as a live show is just a projection of previously recorded images. Interestingly, the first cinemas were old, unused theaters. Theater enjoyed its last golden age of entertainment in the 19th century and with the advent of modern times, it began a progressive decline after it could no longer compete with the new popular sports sensations like baseball or football. Many other cinemas were old hangars that film industry pioneers possessed or bought from owners in troubling times, like in an abandoned state or were rented as warehouses for other companies.

THE FILM AND AUDIOVISUAL INDUSTRY

In those early days, besides being light entertainment, the technological novelty of the invention (bringing pictures to life with motion) together with the huge size of the screen, created a magical experience that was not easy to get used to (hence its continued and growing success). Although years later, because of television, video, computers, and the internet, that magic has become less new and shocking. Perhaps during childhood, we experiment with certain senses of wonder until we get used to it with age. But the group experience of going to the movies with friends or family is still intact today. Leaving your home and spending the day at the mall, going shopping, eating out, and going to the movies, are all perfectly complementary activities. We evaluate the pros and cons of going out, compared to the comfort of our home; but there are also many people who prefer to spend the day outside, doing activities that seem more special than being at home.

Additionally, we have many cultural traditions that are still alive. Modern society, not only the United States, would have to change drastically in order to erase the act of going to the movies from being an essential part of youngsters' courtship. Even in adulthood, it is still a very recurrent habit in any relationship. The good thing about it being a tradition is that it does not need to be an original thing. Quite the contrary, it is as socially accepted and stipulated as a nice restaurant for a candlelit dinner. Not to mention, the obligation of taking the kids to the cinema in this new "golden age" of 3D animation for children.

Exhibitors are supposed to be the customers of the distributors, yes, but taking into account the relation of strength and necessity, it seems that the first ones are those working for the second ones. Actually, although every part in this business is integral in order for the whole thing to be functional, we can all see the irony of having giant distributors enjoy such an obvious, strategic superiority in a time when the tendency is to eliminate intermediaries. The friction between both sides is apparent and there are many cases where exhibitors refuse to screen certain blockbusters because of the abusive conditions demanded by the few distribution companies from Hollywood; inflexible in the negotiation. They even prefer not to release copies in a number of theaters before making concessions to an exhibitor.

This relationship is much less problematic when the distributor and the exhibitor are the same. In both the US and the rest of the world, one company can own the land where the theaters are built directly or through its many subsidiary and associate companies. So, as an owner, you can rent the land to other people who want to run the business, or just run it directly as you prefer.

For half a century, many of the existing theater chains were owned or rented by the studios themselves, guaranteeing the possibility of scheduling your own films at your earliest convenience. This was also the easiest marketing strategy for them. Unfortunately, in the 50s it was declared illegal by an anti-monopoly law, which we will speak more about later. Eventually, in the 80s they began to find legal loopholes though.

Interestingly, a lot of countries imitated this practice. Nowadays, the larger distributors of each country also own a good number of theaters, multiplex chains, and production companies. This way, similar to Hollywood in the beginning, they can guarantee the best promotion and schedules for their films, at their own theaters. In addition to this, there are also interesting business maneuvers with different tax advantages, some more legal than others.

Movie theaters are, by definition, establishing direct contact with the consumer. As we said before, they are the last link in the industrial chain; or what is to say, the first ones touching the audience's money. When a customer pays to enter one of their buildings, the whole complexity of this business begins to make sense. The die is cast and the gods of Olympus are playing for millions in profits or losses, leaving their fate in the hands of simple mortals: the audience.

THE FILM AND AUDIOVISUAL INDUSTRY

Coming back to the percentage that exhibitors obtain from the box office, it is understood that it must cover the rent, supplies, employees, and everything else. But fortunately for all of them, cash registers are also filled with other sources of parallel income, much more lucrative than you think. And everyone knows the most famous one. Who does not know that the real business of movie theaters is popcorn?

Popcorn was undoubtedly the best idea that film exhibitors have ever had, or more accurately, stolen. The stalls and peddlers of this product have existed since the late 19th century when patenting all kinds of rare gadgets, like the popcorn maker, was the order of the day. The popcorn was already related to leisure and entertainment, being very common in fairs, festivals, carnivals, circuses, and the like. The key factors to their success are obvious: Surprisingly cheap ingredients, fast and equally cheap, preparation, and that salty, addictive taste that makes you thirsty. Considering the rapid fame of movie theaters in popular entertainment, popcorn booths (together with other snacks) made a fortune at the doors of the first cinemas. This disgusted exhibitors, who even prohibited the entry of outside food due to the noise, smell, and dirtiness. In Europe, the fascination and scientific curiosity caused by cinematograph, was transformed into elitist enjoyment to contemplate works of art in motion. The screenings were granted a cultural status of respectability, which therefore had to correspond with particular behavior from the audience. Instead in America, the possibilities of entertainment were immediately perceived with a much more entrepreneurial approach to profitability, without worrying too much about outside issues. There was no special reason for it to be considered a sectarian cult that only a few people should enjoy, regardless of their cultural or economic level. By setting a cheap entry price, people of the lowest and wealthiest conditions could enjoy the amazing magic of cinema. Just being in the dark screening rooms was attractive in those times. Even in our days, we are still attracted to that special, catchy feeling of the dark rooms in the theater, so full of psychological and sociological nuances.

THE FILM AND AUDIOVISUAL INDUSTRY

Not even the economic debacle of the early 20th century could end the flourishing film industry. During the Great Depression, the box office was not decreasing, but rather the opposite. It was one of the few whims that people wanted and could afford. It made them feel better, they could escape reality, even if for a few minutes. The same happened to popcorn consumption, which experienced an increase of more than 300% in the United States. The owners of the theaters opened their eyes to the perfect-selling product. So they decided to include popcorn makers at their entrances and in their lobbies overnight. They first had to prohibit street vendors from approaching the doors of their establishments (they did not have friendly methods of doing this, by the way).

As if this were not enough, during World War II film production significantly diminished (it was not a good moment for entertainment). However, people did not stop going to the movies. There were two great reasons for this. First, very few people had a television in their home, so the cinema was the only place where they could see the news with real images of war conflict as well as fictional stories to evade themselves later. The second reason was because of the popcorn. The perfect, tasty, cheap food that fulfilled its mission: to entertain the stomachs while the films entertained the minds. Both things were really needed in such turbulent times. Massive popcorn consumption was also possible because while sugar had to be rationed by the government, since most of it was destined for the army, salt and corn were more abundant and did not have to be rationed.

After this particular win against sweet snacks, in later years, during the Golden Age of Hollywood, popcorn started the ultimate stratospheric takeoff. With the progressive expansion of television into the American home, the amazing invention of the microwave appeared. Two isolated facts that were connected to each other, in the most unexpected and natural way, brought the habit of eating popcorn in front of a screen in theaters to the couch at home. And that is how exhibitors discovered their real business area.

THE FILM AND AUDIOVISUAL INDUSTRY

Unexpectedly, they became food and drink establishments, where films were exhibited as a claim. This successful system led, unavoidably, to increased ticket prices over the years, as well as product diversity. Theaters were turning halls, corridors, and roomy areas into the ultimate candy store, or even fast food chains. Looking at the prices, it is clear that such profits cover the costs of any business, including employee wages. With salaries as low as any other food establishment, cinemas only need to hire a minimal staff to be functional. Which is quite reasonable considering that there are no longer specialized tasks. Only box office, management, and cleaning and maintenance. Specialized projectionists do not exist anymore and any youngster with basic digital knowledge can operate the screening files. We are talking about temporary jobs that only interest young people. (Perks like discounted prices or free tickets are not enough to consider these jobs fantastic.)

With regard to the payment of supplies and the rent, that is also far from being a problem. The mount cannot be too high since there are barely two types of situations. You are the owner of the building and only supplies need to be paid, without any rent; or you are paying rent because you own a multiplex, where the chances for survival should be guaranteed. We say this because the very opening of a multiplex cinema should include its corresponding market study. And if this study had obtained a negative result, you would have never started the business in the first place. There might be sporadic cases in other situations, where losses may occur and end up leading to closure. This has been happening to old, small theaters for many years. They were unable to modernize their facilities, projection systems, or business relations with other players in this competitive industry.

Apart from all this, someone could think that the only decisive factor in determining if they can live off of the box office results is the ticket price. It is a controversial issue. People like movies but at the same time, there is a personal standard to which people determine if it is worth paying for or not. And the industry forces that limit too often.

THE FILM AND AUDIOVISUAL INDUSTRY

Being a mass entertainment, movies actually cost less than shows, like musicals or sports. But obviously, it is designed to be consumed more frequently and comfortably. (In fact, that is another reason to consider it a small luxury.) A majority of the world's population claim that they would go to the movies more often if the prices were lower. Just check the internet to find out what people think about the subject. There are continuous surveys and experiments that have been done, which proves it.

However, the market trends do not seem to be affected by such opinions. Neither is it affected by other factors like the last global economic crisis or computer piracy. Think about it, if box office results are so good, even in such adverse economic situations, the price will not only remain as is, but also continue to grow; and probably faster than the living cost, as it has happened thus far. It is not a coincidence, but a strategic process that has been thoroughly studied and planned.

The fat cats of this industry are always making sure that the price remains at an amount the public is willing to pay, to enjoy one of their favorite sources of entertainment. The best example is the success of new subscription-based television networks. Hypothetically, let us say that movie theaters suffer from an alarming decrease in revenues (note that the results are showing the exact opposite). You can be sure that the industry leaders would take the appropriate measures to balance expenditure and revenue. (They are not stupid, just greedy.)

Do not forget that Hollywood studios are the ones making the big decisions, for better and worse. However, at the same time, they are victims of that crazy race to make the most expensive film ever or the highest-grossing movie ever or perform well during its first weekend, and so on. If major Hollywood studios keep this excessive tendency, distributors maintain their usual inflexibility, adding even more pressure from their privileged position. Exhibitors are the only ones who might have the possibility of regulating ticket prices. But no one in their right mind would do such a thing selflessly, at the expense of their own benefit. Moreover, once the requirements of the studios have been filled, the local industry of each country regulates the ticket prices according to their own criteria. Supposedly this is based on the health of their local economy, taxes, and the cost of living. It is hard to say if increases are generated to compensate bad results in the box office. Their thought is: "We have to compensate the price because fewer and fewer people are going to the movies." But, that is precisely the excuse that justifies the opposite argument: "We would go to the movies more often, if it were cheaper," audiences would say. Opinions are divided depending on who you ask. It has also been considered that ticket prices may vary according to the potential interest in the film. In any market, prices are regulated in terms of supply and demand therefore, it makes sense. There is an open debate on this, and all the research done so far has demonstrated a clear, positive reception from the public.

Finally, we cannot conclude this chapter without mentioning the other big source of income for exhibitors. There is another bargain that, as usual, no one talks about and that is advertising. Cinemas typically charge high prices per ad, exactly like television networks do. The geographical scope may not be so global (nothing can compare to reaching every home in the world, at any time of the day); but the objective result is that movie theaters are still an established leisure place. Any city in the world with more than 10,000 inhabitants has at least one screen, if not several, depending on the economic conditions of the area.

Theaters offer unique environmental conditions. The giant screen maximizes the visual impact, the booming surround sound, the acoustic impact; and certainly the dark ambiance together with comfort and expectation, favor the concentration on the screen. Besides, there are many less tangible, but equally interesting, indirect advantages; like the fact that, being so selective, in such a short advertising space, means that products from direct competitors are less likely to be included. It is also true that all of these advantages for the advertiser can be perceived by the audience in a negative way. They can grow tired of seeing so many ads on the internet and on television that they might consider ads in the theater just as annoying.

In conclusion, even with having several problems here and there, the film industry seems to have the exhibition issue under control. There must be a reason for increasing the number of screens worldwide every year. In general, multiplexes in certain areas are directly integrated into large commercial complexes. This has proven to be the perfect model for modern life. In the case of smaller towns and villages, it is likely not profitable to maintain one single screen. In these cases, only the cinemas with a smaller number of sessions, fewer days, and reduced schedules will survive.

Additionally, it is very difficult to predict in an industry that depends on people's tastes and habits. Remember the famous drive-in cinemas? They began to decline little by little in the 40s. Nowadays for nostalgia, only a few of them are open.

Perhaps the format of the screening-room theaters will be obsolete in a few years. (We will have to see what virtual reality really offers.) But, this will not happen in the near future. Exhibitors still have a lot of time to adapt or die. Producers, distributors, and exhibitors can all take a sigh of relief. Unlike many other people in the world, they can all live off of their jobs. To change with the times is part of business people's responsibilities. (It is very easy to rest on your laurels and then complain about the changes happening around you.)

It is peculiar that everyone in Hollywood is always announcing how fantastic the billionaire box office profits are, the positive balances, and how production and distribution keep growing and expanding around the world. However, at the same time they are sending worrying and discouraging warnings about decreasing ticket sales and theater and production companies in bankruptcy. Never forget this, as we have said from the beginning, the most important thing to remember in this crazy land of Oz is that everything is part of the show.

FILM MARKETING

Competing with Hollywood's gigantic productions is usually considered impossible, for the simple reason that certain production levels can only be reached when you have a budget of several million. And do not forget that it is not limited to the production stage only, for it is also decisively applied to marketing and advertising arenas. We will not discuss how meaningful or ethical some marketing practices can be, so we will simply discuss the current situation. Hollywood generates hundreds of films a year (700-800 and growing) saturating the market intentionally with an agreed number of products that, in theory, cover the entire possible spectrum of mass audience tastes. This is decided in proportion to the type of genres and trends that are developing, according to people's reactions.

By looking back, anyone can easily perceive boom and bust cycles of movies with zombies, vampires, pirates, cowboys, dinosaurs, and natural disasters. There are also topics for minority groups, with sporadic representation, corresponding with specific interest from people like sports, addictions, psychiatry, religion, and existentialism. But the challenge here is how to anticipate said ups and downs in the trend. In other words, how can you tell if the next vampire or dinosaur movie will be the new billion-dollar success or a resounding failure? It is always erroneously assumed that the quality of films plays an essential role in their economic revenues. But, apart from the inherent subjectivity of the term "quality," there have been many cases where, even repeating similar and successful production operations, total incomes were less than half. This could have been caused by incorrect calendar decisions (some release dates in the year are more focused on consumption than others) or just the competitive nature. Having so many options on the billboard is difficult but usually, the script is the main culprit for this.

Even without any technical or artistic knowledge, all audience types can somehow perceive when stories are "more of the same" and get bored stiff with something they've already seen hundreds of times. Now imagine that happening with a simple trailer, even the least demanding of audiences would lose interest.

Subtle differentiation should suffice. Every film should find its own personality, beyond the anecdote. That is one of the alleged tasks of directors (at least the good ones). Besides official promotion, word-of-mouth marketing is one of the highest influences in the evolution of the first week box office results. The opinions shared by the first watchers will affect the rest of the potential audience, just like the effect of the specialized critique in the past (which hardly has any relevance now, at a time when social networks give the same value to everyone's opinions).

Nevertheless, if there is something that contributes to the first weekend, it is all the previous marketing work done in advance, before the release date (that anxious expectation caused by the hype effect). Additionally, standing out in such a saturated environment can only be achieved in one way, with having more money than others. Look at the billboard at any theater in your city. Whatever you find, every week you will have several Hollywood films, some national productions (much fewer, that is for sure), and a few other award-winning films from a foreign country. All those movies that are not produced or distributed by Hollywood majors, will have to be released on "irrelevant" dates, so that they do not have to compete directly against American productions. Because that is the harsh reality. Each person has a list of personal preferences and not everyone can spend the money they want to go to the movies, no matter how much they like a particular film. So you will have to distribute your time and money among the first few options on your list.

Coming back to the business point of view: Apart from production cost, films have to spend several millions in promotion for visibility. You want to reach as many people as possible and advertising is not exactly cheap. The common saying "money calls money" would lead us to deduce that the most expensive and spectacular films should always be in the first ranking positions of the box office, and yes, of course they are. Statistics are overwhelmingly clear on that.

THE FILM AND AUDIOVISUAL INDUSTRY

Let us say that the available ads in your city are 100 for television, 100 for metro and bus stops, 100 for road billboards, and 100 for magazines and newspapers. Well, the only thing you have to do is pay the price to occupy as many of those spaces as you can for as long as you possibly can. Besides, do not forget that if you can afford to pay most of them (and especially the most visible ones), apart from advertising your product, you will be preventing your competitors from advertising theirs, in the same spaces. So, if you add to the economic cost that no one can predict the promotional and release dates as early as Hollywood studios do, it is now clear how hard it is to compete in distribution terms.

It also costs a lot of money to create so much promotional content, in so many different formats: posters, brochures, live events, licensed promotions, TV commercials, and trailers. And the most important factor is how exponential said expenses are.

The more present your film is, in the everyday lives of people, the more curiosity it will raise. By pushing said exposure to the limit in each country's major cities, and maintaining it for several weeks before the premiere, we could easily be talking about an international investment in publicity between 50 and 100 million dollars.

Obviously, no one gets into anything like this unless they have a billionaire blockbuster on their hands. So you can be sure that even with handling such figures, the smallest unexpected slip can actually lead to a serious profitability failure. With gains around 100 million dollars (or more), there are productions that do not recover the publicity expenses, nor the amount invested in production. Revenues are never high or low in absolute terms, they are always relative to the money that was previously spent.

Within this industry, the people responsible for a film demonstrate their worth and credibility as executives, depending on the statistical profitability obtained, never on the number of zeros in the gross income. It is also important to highlight that all this advertising machinery for any Hollywood project, actually begins from the very moment the studio gives approval with the famous green light.

THE FILM AND AUDIOVISUAL INDUSTRY

Those who know something about marketing already understand the importance of thorough market research and its evolution. The investment in promotion is more intense and focused around the release date, no doubt, but the typical mountain starts to ascend as soon as the project enters the production stage. From there, it decreases after its first weeks (with the premiere being the highest peak) finishing during the last days of its commercial life.

While reading the script, you can identify a number of useful business synergies and product placements which can contribute interesting additions to the budget with minimal effort, as well as many other useful things for the film. For example, top-brand cell phones, computers, watches, food, vehicles, and clothing. Such things that, if necessary, could be included in the script expressly after making a good deal. This may sound very prosaic for more sensitive artists, but it might actually gather a decent sum of money, from a business profitability perspective. In the case of closing these deals, when a film is in the midst of production (or even wrapping up) it could be necessary to make script revisions and/or reshoot some scenes (regardless of whether it is live action or animation). These atrocities depend on how much money you are making with the deal to determine if it would be worth it.

Speaking now about the advertising format, everyone knows the most basic elements of promotion are posters and trailers. The goals are that the title of the film is remembered, the main actors/characters must serve as an attractive bait for audiences, and everything must clearly portray the genre and tone of the film. If all this is successfully achieved, the power of suggestion does the rest. The audience confides, in a subliminal way, to what the conjunction of these elements are promising; according to previous experiences with similar products. Let us say that the public is already predisposed to liking it. Of course, this is not an automatic mechanism that magically generates success. Any campaign can make a big difference by going in the right or wrong direction.

THE FILM AND AUDIOVISUAL INDUSTRY

In creative terms, the first challenge we find is that some concepts are harder to sell than others. The individual pictures that can be used in promotion (whether they are still photos or video clips) reflect the most "technical" quality of the film. The visual aspect can be more or less represented by the selected images, like the general tone of the film (the overall feeling it transmits).

The game starts there. Even a boring film can look entertaining with a good trailer, thanks to good editing. It is very easy to edit with disjointed, out-of-context-looking clips, creating an effective mini story. In two hours of filmed material, there will be enough footage that looks good enough to be used. Something of minimal visual or conceptual interest. In such a short time you can easily dodge any script failure or weakness, as well as disregard lousy pacing, directing, or acting. These small clips are made by distribution companies, using editors and directors that specialize in the field (there are cases of good faith where the director of the movie can give an opinion or even collaborate, but this is not considered necessary, or even relevant).

Bearing in mind that the first and last intention is to capture the audience's attention, we must try to get it at any price. This is not an exaggeration, some trailers cost one million dollars. If you need to manipulate the entire sense of a movie to make it look better, go ahead.

This does not only happen with trailers, the posters should also convey the film's genre. By association and previous design references, people can quickly deduce, for example, that a white background with characters in funny gestures and poses is mostly likely a comedy. Weapons, cars, explosions, and speed lines are usually used to promote action films and a spectacular composition of characters and scenarios means that we are about to see an exciting, epic, adventure blockbuster. (It would be stupid to have several stars in your movie and not include them in the poster.)

THE FILM AND AUDIOVISUAL INDUSTRY

Once in the movie theater, the audience will be the jury and they can be merciless, but the goal of promotion is to get you to the theater. Nothing else. That is the tricky purpose of marketing itself, to sell a product, no matter if the quality is good or bad; or whether you need it or not. The point is just to sell it. This is something that many people have experienced on their own when they find out that the film they watched did not fit the advertisement. It is not always a disappointment, but rather confusing, to say the least.

For example, it is very common that small dramatic films include small, trending elements, for example, ghosts, vampires, disasters, etc. to generate more attraction. But they are usually just minimal contributions, they are not even enough for the film to be considered a blend of genres; simply small, intimate dramas. This happens all the time in so called "romantic comedies." Comedy is a cheap and easy type of film to do (the hard part is to be funny, but not to be filmed). These films typically target females and are evidently focused on sentimental relationships, but they seem to forget the comical factor and often no one bothers to add one single scene that justifies the use of the term "comedy." Or even worse, in so many cases we are directly watching an undercover drama.

It may seem strange, but it has a fair explanation which comes, unsurprisingly, from the marketing world. Statistics indicate that when choosing a film option, more than looking for something specific, the female audience seeks to be guided by emotions; hence the classic indecision, when none of the options make them feel anything special. Additionally, this is against the cliché that says that women prefer tearful dramas. Results show that the most standard choice is to get rid of worry and have a good time. So, on the contrary, the most chosen option for this target audience is usually a pleasant romantic comedy, not a drama. All of them will contain the same common elements: love, heartbreak, sex, friendship, and family, but minimal drama?

THE FILM AND AUDIOVISUAL INDUSTRY

The point is that it does not matter. When leaving the room, this target will feel happier when they start and finish the movie with a smile, no matter how much drama there was in the middle. Audiences like that emotional rollercoaster. As long as the story is good, sensitive, and of course, contains a happy ending (in classical Greek literature, comedy is defined by "happy endings" as much as tragedy is defined by the opposite); no matter how many lies were used to sell the tickets (like saying that it is a "funny comedy"). The only thing the target audience cares about is their own happy ending and that they liked the movie they paid for. This does not only refer to this particular example, but any type of audience.

The amount of mass advertising around us is huge and constant, to the point that we do not even realize it anymore. Beyond the theaters themselves, publicity and media coverage for relevant movies have an enormous presence in the streets and on the televisions of any modern country. Relentless promotion tries to impart, within the depths of your subconscious, not only the need to go to the movies, but to go to specific films above any other option. With such saturation, the industry counts on everyone seeing it at some point in their day to day, at least one of the hundreds of ads spread throughout the city. Even the most "disconnected" person will end up seeing some of them and that might be enough to meet their goal. Even in the extreme case of people who do not go to the movies that often, on the rare occasion that they do go, they will most likely go to the most famous blockbuster, once more, according to the statistical data.

Indeed, there are countries that are very different from ours, and every culture has its own customs. But broadly speaking, from their conception, ambitious films aimed toward the international market are always concerned about the plot and premise being universal. If they want to have world-wide success, they will have to be understandable for any culture. For a few years now, smart producers have been using other cultures' exoticism to penetrate certain markets, while captivating our western eyes.

THE FILM AND AUDIOVISUAL INDUSTRY

It is not that simple, but it is definitely worth it. For a start, many parts of the story (if not the whole script) must take place in a foreign country. (Asian nations have gradually been in high demand over the last twenty years—and not by coincidence.) And by all means, you must offer the co-starring or secondary roles to that country's most famous actors. This type of synergy works in both directions, with numerous industrial and political agreements. Several co-productions have been underway in recent years. And some have even been fully produced with foreign capital, but globally distributed by Hollywood studios.

It is true that because of cultural differences, some film genres work better in certain countries. It will take a few generations to change that, since social issues are too complex for the relative influence of films. For example, in China there is a strong government censorship that allows editing, under their own criteria, of the visual content and dialogues before being released.

And do not forget that in every society, the impact on children and young people, plays an essential role (you know, manipulate children and it will be easier to control them when they are adults). So, the more all societies look like each other, the easier exchanging in the future will be. And we are not only referring to the famous social "westernization," but also to economies. The business class is always the main beneficiary of this progressive capitalism. While entertainment always plays a subtle role in social and cultural changes, bigger political challenges depends on factors far beyond its possibilities. That is the truth.

THE FILM AND AUDIOVISUAL INDUSTRY

ECONOMY AND LAW

Having a job is one of the fundamental pillars of our lives, it gives you the money you need to buy goods and cover your most basic essential needs. This may sound like a truism, but there are lots of people that apparently forget this. Especially young people who have the risk of growing up with a distorted view of the world. Until they are economically independent, in their adolescence they tend to take many things for granted; all the things their parents have been doing for them. Because of this, they do not have a clear notion on how money works, or even more important, how to administer it. We have all been told that money does not grow on trees. But the truth is, a large part of the population (and not only youngsters) do not know much about where it comes from or exactly where it goes. As explained in Chapter 1: "Art and the Industry," the business world is completely unknown for regular employees, but also for those self-employed, at least at the beginning of their careers.

Audiovisual businesspeople are forced to make important legal and economic decisions all the time. They do this from the very moment they register their business. No matter if it is for one small subcontract or the largest of the super-productions.

THE FILM AND AUDIOVISUAL INDUSTRY

Each detail will carry an economic expense. Personal and legal decisions must be made all the time. We have also seen that the final result of every production is not only conditioned by the actual capacity of the company or the workers, but also by executive decisions. Remember, businesspeople prepare the path to success or failure, by choosing certain options over others, among what their real capacities allow.

In less abstract terms, Hollywood studios have funding and budgeting systems that have been used and perfected since the birth of the industry itself. And this industrial sector has many unions that group and defend audiovisual workers, according to their professional branch. So, after one hundred years of experience making movies, the industry tends to operate within decent margins, in terms of working conditions and good practices.

Now, every penny counts and there are not many super productions that can get a "blank check" from the studio every year in order to get the best results possible. In fact, this morbid competition to spend more and more would not even make sense if it were not because they are also earning more and more money. It is true that no matter how strong an industry is, any global crisis can end up affecting all sectors in any economy. Despite having good health with bullish trends, it is natural that such external factors force us to never lower the guard, keeping production costs under control.

No matter the country, this industry generates a relatively small number of jobs compared to other sectors. As a general rule, they are temporary jobs for specific projects or occasional overloads. Meaning, as soon as that project (or the stage of the project your position belongs to) is finished, you will be unemployed again, waiting for the next job. And, as we will see later in Chapter 10: "Creative Industry Workers," new opportunities will only arise because of personal contacts or the outstanding quality of your work.

THE FILM AND AUDIOVISUAL INDUSTRY

On the other side, there are few options for permanent jobs with real stability, considering the obvious unpredictability of this business. Employees are barely reduced to being hired by some of those companies offering audiovisual services to third parties. Film, television, or advertising industries are the only way to have a permanent contract granted with your own desktop in an office, and an annual salary. If you are really really talented, you could also be one of the few permanent employees in some of the biggest production companies in the world (high shot, but not impossible). But now that the economy is beginning to recover a little, there is a new opportunity opening for the average audiovisual professional.

In the corporate world, large companies have traditionally been the only ones capable of affording strong public images, with the high-class that the audiovisual presence provides. However, in this new digital, multimedia era where everything is instant, the audiovisual presence is more than essential. Even more than basic, it is mandatory.

At the beginning, this meant more work for small production and service companies; but due to the constant need for new content, and the lower prices in production costs (everything is more and more affordable), nowadays almost every company is opening new positions for specialized jobs, in order to meet their audiovisual needs with a permanent staff.

The high financial risk that audiovisual companies run does not help employment stability. If we ask people for their perceptions of corporations, we will always get feedback like this: "They are owners and executives with lots of money, who earn a lot but do not do much." Or "Their gain is thanks to exploiting the working class." Or "Humble workers are sacrificed and they work more hours than stipulated; they earn less than they deserve, and are seriously struggling to make ends meet." Not for nothing, employment is often called the slavery of our time.

THE FILM AND AUDIOVISUAL INDUSTRY

It is easy to identify with that kind of pessimistic and victimized vision (and probably it would not be so widespread, if it did not have a grain of truth). But let us do something unusual, let us look at it from the employer's viewpoint. We always see it from the side of those working in exchange of money but never think of the opposite side, when we are the ones spending the money.

Every calendar day that passes takes money from the employer. The existence of any company is a painful race against the influx of revenues. You may have calculated your expenses well in advance and predicted your earnings, but it always depends on past results, since no one can predict the future. Therefore, any unplanned expense and below-expected income could have catastrophic consequences.

The film industry is no exception. When people talk about "X" millions in the budget, everyone assumes that with that amount of money you can do anything. No one stops to think that, even being that high, it is not a decidedly random number. As unattainable as it may sound, it is the sum of very specific amounts dedicated to external services, rentals, purchases, transportation, lodging, meals, and many other overheads. And this is only for shooting which means it does not include the specific needs of each project yet.

Putting promotion aside, production expenses are divided into two parts: "above the line" (creative expenses, like the salaries for stars, the director, screenwriter, and rights acquisition) and "below the line" (overheads and technical needs for filming). The first ones are variable, depending on the type of film and the dimension you want to give the production). They are the ones that provide a higher value when compared to the second ones; which are more predictable in relation to the schedule. These are also those that no one can avoid. The simplest thing in the world can be shot with actors or a voluntary technical crew, but even with the lowest budget it is very unlikely that you can film something without spending any money at all.

THE FILM AND AUDIOVISUAL INDUSTRY

THE BUDGET

The first thing any producer must do is make sure that the content of the film is feasible with the available budget. This is when frictions can first arise with the director, for his artistic vision will always have direct consequences on the film cost and vice versa. In the long finance stage (usually taking several years), this balance may be adjusted several times on both sides. And, in case there is not enough money, the parties involved can decide to adjust the content to the budget they have or keep waiting for the budget to be raised. The latter is always a risk, since it may cause the investors on board to lose interest.

It may also happen that the content of the project becomes obsolete for some reason or its viability becomes more complicated (or even impossible, in the worst case). To mention a few real examples, perhaps a similar production goes ahead of you; or maybe one of your confirmed stars is no longer available, due to physical reasons, health issues, or even death. (Now last minute cast changes do not seem so trivial.) Perhaps the producers/executives in charge decide to delay or cancel the project, without further explanation; do not forget that they can do that at any moment.

Making a film is nothing more than assembling the pieces so that the final quality depends on the success of those individual pieces. The human factor also affects the result, within the entire creation process as well as in every screening session. We can say that the result is doubly unpredictable. Any production may look like a winning horse in theory but fail in the box office; just like any lower-class project could be a success, contrary to expectations. There are no reliable guarantees.

It is normal for the general public and regular aficionados to ignore this side of the business, but the truth is, there are many beginners and semi-professionals who do not know much about it. Those at the amateur level have no real perception of how much things cost, since they are used to doing their best with the little money they have in their pockets. If someone is interested or curious, a valid solution is to interpolate public data, already known, and establish comparisons. If a super production would publicly announce to having spent 300 million dollars on a film, at least 100 would have been dedicated to a worldwide promotion (which does not strictly belong to the "production" budget, but to the total cost; which is not the same). That would leave 200 million, where surely about 90 would have been above the line and another 50 below the line, plus about 60 more in digital effects. The Visual Effects (VFX) have always been considered below the line, though nowadays separating them is recommended because they are a technical expense, but also take a more artistic relevance every day. They have a highly variable cost and add a great differential value in the film (meaning the old criteria for said two block separation is totally outdated now).

The more knowledge of the environment you have, the more you will learn to recognize the production value of what you see on screen. When you have enough experience on the business side, with eyes as the one who spends the money, you will understand the painful amounts that are lost every day in filming. Not to mention taxes, for example. Each country has its own rules and every company has its own way of coping with them. But it is always a headache. This proves that every production in the world (including Hollywood productions) are continually in search of the most advantageous tax incentives, public or private aid, and the cheapest, local labor force possible.

Back to the relationship between content and budget, in the studio system there are three generic divisions: High budget (more than 60 million), medium budget (between 20 and 60 million), and low budget (less than 20 million). And for those who never realized it, we will say that there is also an approximate correspondence between the film genre and the assigned budget. It is not an imposition, that must be taken as a rule, but rather it is a consequence of common sense. After many decades of analyzing the cost and profitability of similar products, it is not difficult to find significant patterns.

THE FILM AND AUDIOVISUAL INDUSTRY

For example, imagine a sci-fi movie full of digital effects, these movies are proof that you should not do it with a low budget, because you would not be able to pay for the demanding quality that such a production requires to succeed. On the other hand, if the initial approach was to offer an intimate drama with the simple premise of science fiction, (Perhaps in the future but not very different from ours or with a few technological advances that are introduced sporadically.) we would be talking about a simple drama. Drama is a genre that can be produced with a low budget, for sure. Science fiction would be an anecdotal nuance, not an accurate definition of the film genre. The same applies to period movies, which might involve the expensive creation of specific decorations and realistic clothing. But on the contrary, you could rent a few decent or average fake costumes and shoot in real, well-preserved historical places. (And most probably, a smart mixture of both options). We can say that the farther from present day the story happens, or the larger the scale of events is, the bigger the expense will be.

After the script, the next factor affecting the cost, and the main reason that the range is so wide, is the hiring of stars. In smaller industries, they can hardly consider hiring a Hollywood star, given that the cache of even a B-class star is usually the average cost of a full production in any other country in the world. Considering that these films are rarely blockbusters (usually they do not even recover the production investment), the sums do not add up.

In very few cases, the stars themselves decide to support these projects on a personal basis, lowering their cache or investing their own capital; but that would be a different story. Acting as an intermediary, a star can sponsor a modest film inside the studio system, assuming the role of producer or executive producer (or both). If the film is good, with some skills you could get high profitability. From the perspective of a studio or production company, working in a smaller industry implies much lower costs, so it could be a smart move.

The fact is that spending a big part of the budget on stars is considered valuable; something that considerably increases the possibilities of amortization. The reputation of the cast can bring economic results to the next level but, like other production assets, it is not risk free. Here is a simple example, in a standard romantic comedy, the difference between casting one pair of protagonists over another might mean many many millions of dollars in the box office. Two A-class actors or one A-class with one B-class, in theory would have a higher chance of success. But usually when one of them is a new "rising star" it is more than enough. The most economical formula would be counting on unknown actors for both characters (which studios are not willing to do, of course). They would spend way less money but at the same time, it would be much harder to obtain the same type of results in the box office. Even having a great script of unusual quality in this genre, without stars' support and/or a strong marketing campaign, the film would not have a strong media impact.

The budget scale ranges in each country, albeit in an equivalent proportion. There are no standards in low budget areas, but the range would be between one million dollars and anything below $10,000 (the so-called "micro-budget"). At the other end, we have projects designed to cost more than 100 million, we call these super productions.

Studios agree on a limited number of them per year, as they are a fundamental part of the market self-regulation. This regulation seeks to balance the supply and demand for content; which has to do with the economic performance of the industry and the real capacity of the consumers' pockets. But also the content, in order to control possible overexposure to certain social, political, or ideological trends.

If you do not pay attention to it, the contents may become abusive or repetitive. Therefore, before green lighting any new projects it is important to take all existing developments and considerations into account, even at the competitors' offices.

THE FILM AND AUDIOVISUAL INDUSTRY

From a business point of view, film industry tycoons must also play their cards well. They must be careful not to kill any goose, laying possible golden eggs too fast. These coveted creatures must always be exploited at their will, taking care that they never fall into other people's hands. Ideas, plots, and franchises which must be managed and diversified in the most appropriate way.

Studios plan and negotiate their own forecast, action, and reaction strategies, as well as those from their competitors. They do this to maintain an annual balance of diversity between the number of dramas, comedies, horrors, sci-fi's, and everything else. Plus they need to be proportionate to statistical results. The same goes for themes and their popularity: vampires, pirates, zombies, and natural disasters. As well as for ideological positions like republican, democrat, liberal, anarchist, or whatever else there is. (It can be explicit or implicit, but it is not a small thing in Hollywood.) Actually, this is not about having a global corporate position (although Fox and Paramount tend to be more conservative), as much as it is about the personal support from each producer. It is a peculiar situation because entertainment has always been traditionally attached to the political left, but the corporate caste always tends to lean to the right. That is why maintaining an appropriate balance between conservative and progressive ideologies in film, is recommended. For example, warmonger and pacifist, religious and agnostic, and similar antagonists. Considering the possible impact on the public, this regulatory responsibility is supposed to protect us from radical manipulations.

Changing the subject, in small industries outside of Hollywood (as well as in the American independent system), the consistency between budget and content is not so relevant. This is mainly because the amounts to be handled are already adjusted to the minimum needed to shoot anything, meeting the industrial standards. Starting from there, the budget may vary depending on the level of comfort or precariousness that each producer can and decides to allow.

THE FILM AND AUDIOVISUAL INDUSTRY

This means that if some people plan to produce a film with needs above what they normally could afford, it would imply that they have a higher budget than usual. But not necessarily. They might be the brave few, willing to accept the challenge. It may seem admirable, but more than anything it would be foolish. This excess of confidence in real life is often caused by naive ignorance, which is more than brave ambition. In these cases, the final results are never good enough. But sometimes, albeit very rarely, luck ends up being on your side and the impossible become possible. Imagine a small European production company. Let us say that this small company has been producing a modest film every two years for a decade, with budgets around one or two million dollars. This is the average that a company of this size and reputation would be capable of getting from government funds, bank loans, TV networks deals, and a few pre-sales. This status only allows them to produce dramas, comedies, and documentaries. But imagine if, due to a series of coincidences, they had the opportunity to shoot in a medieval castle for free for a few months in the summer. For whatever reason the decision is automatically made. The next project will be a period film, despite the precarious conditions that they would have to work in or how quickly they would have to improvise a script on the go, to ask for new subsidies in a hurry (which compromises the quality, of course). But none of that matters, you never miss an opportunity like that.

LAW AND TAXATION

The mass media is the most basic tool for dissemination and communication in every modern society. And as one of its main engines, the entertainment industry is used by everyone with very different socio-political purposes. This is why governments around the world participate in order to encourage and actively support the production, distribution, and exhibition of their own audiovisual industries.

Hollywood itself, even having immense private fortunes to operate, seeks government support in fiscal, bureaucratic, and diplomatic matters (to have support worldwide when it comes to filming, collaborating, or investing in other countries).

All these activities also enrich different industries in these countries, although many of them maintain tough protectionist policies to counteract the overwhelming machinery of Hollywood. Apart from hoarding the billboard every week, without leaving dates available for local productions, (many countries have a maximum number of foreign films allowed by law) American movies are perceived as highly invasive, both culturally and sociologically. On one hand, the imperialist policy of the United States is what it is and will not change after many decades of continuous expansion. But on the other, audiences will continue to reclaim Hollywood content as long as it stays as the head of production and development worldwide.

Getting to the point, government support for producers mainly comes from economic financing, i.e. direct cash contributions, concession of advantageous loans, amortization plans, tax deductions, or deferred taxes. But as we previously mentioned, whoever is publicly financed must have their own capital to incur the production costs in the first place.

Let us think about how the situation looks from the producer's perspective. The first justifiable expense must be the producer's salary itself. Laws in each country set a maximum allowed for this role within limits. The exact amount is voluntary. So, after covering your office overheads and the cost of your possible employees, the rest depends on how much you want to spend on making the film. If it is a cheap movie, wonderful; and, if it is an expensive one, well, you will have to do it anyway. Something must be done because any loan or public aid will be demanded back if the film is not finished.

The most obvious business mindset is to try and reduce all possible expenses. There will always be an inescapable minimum to cover the basic needs of any film shoot. Things like maintenance, accommodation, transportation, and social costs.

THE FILM AND AUDIOVISUAL INDUSTRY

And depending on each budget, the possibility of savings will be higher or lower. For example, you could use your own film material, either ceded, loaned, or co-produced (which all come in very handy for certain advanced tricks). You could also shoot in places where getting permission is cheap or even free in exchange for promotion (in extreme cases, it is very common to film on friends' or relatives' properties so you do not have to pay for a permit or insurance). Another option is to hire as few paid professionals as possible (you could use fellows, trainee students and/or beginners); or offer the crew capitalized salaries (payment is exchanged for a percentage of benefits however, the problem is that these types of productions are seldom profitable). A final choice is to extend working hours beyond the legal limit, as a sacrifice and personal commitment to the production.

These working conditions are not allowed in the United States, thanks to the work that unions and syndicates have been doing over the years. But unfortunately, it is very typical in low-budget productions. Not only amateurs or micro-budgets either, sometimes a producer wants to boast, and takes the production above its real possibilities; usually resulting in arrears, non-payments, and bankruptcy statements.

Producers have the maximum legal, fiscal, and financial responsibility for every production. You can use all the excuses in the world to defend certain operations or evade duties and obligations, but it becomes very difficult to see the main instigator, for so many obvious maneuvers of corruption, as a victim. There are infinite creative accounting resources and tricks to operate in a quasi-legal way (when not directly illegal).

No matter how usual these irregularities may be, it is still a criminal offence, even if everyone is doing it. In some countries, there are genuine schemes of fiscal manipulation around the industrial systems with the sole purpose of misappropriating public funds and/or money laundering. Usually, the production's low quality is clear evidence that business activities are used as a simple cover up. There are even some extreme cases of fraud and prevarication in which such activity has never happened. And that is not to forget all those artists and technicians doing the most, to not pay taxes like any honest worker must do.

These legal and financial issues are part of the reality of the film industry. It makes no sense to deny or try to hide them. Due to its public nature, laws in so many countries are changed every now and then in order to prevent such malpractices. And this is the first stone of many film industries around the globe. This partially explains the precarious work conditions of their workers and why so many of them are forced to abandon the profession, migrate to other countries, or just barely survive in such situations. In further chapters we will see, however, that there are indeed people who manage to live on this. We will look at the obstacles they encounter and the odds they have for success.

INTELLECTUAL PROPERTY AND COPYRIGHT

When speaking of intellectual property, it is always in relation to the illegal consumption of content, from fraudulent cable television to P2P (peer-to-peer) networks, and illegal ripping off of those old audio and video tapes. All of that is what we call "audiovisual piracy." And people actually do not know too much about it. Amongst other things, they do not care too much. But at the same time, there are important interests against people being too involved. It is not convenient that the public can reflect on the legal responsibilities of creation and authorship because the entire current trading system might end up turning upside down. The industry is already suffering to adapt to the black hole of the internet; the last thing they need is everyone's opinion on artistic creation, property rights, and legislative competences. It should be enough that ordinary people understand that watching a movie without paying is stealing. End of story (you know, let us tiptoe around the subject, just in case someone stirs things up unnecessarily).

The same happens when talking about copyright. Both terms tend to be used with excessive lightness, without knowing their definition or function properly; sometimes used even as interchangeable synonyms. Any debate about them results in a stalemate because no one has enough information on the matter. It is not a question of choosing one radical position or the other, but about facing the true underlying dilemma: The friction between what we understand intellectually and culturally as opposed to what we defend as property and capitalism. There are irreconcilable stances, due to the intrinsic contradictions of said concepts. The problem is compounded when international laws recognize and protect all these terms separately. And when trying to mix them, even the legislators who created these laws admit to looking the other way and applying sloppy fudge.

At the moment, the only way to enforce the laws is by putting some rights above others. It is that simple. But first things first. Let us start with theory. Every author has the moral and patrimonial right to be recognized as the creator of their project. This is dictated by the Universal Declaration of Human Rights (UDHR) and guaranteed by international laws of any democratic country.

An example of this is very simple: If you think of a painting, it all starts with a painter who has an idea and depicts it on a canvas, in the end giving us another concrete object. It is a unique piece that the creator gives a specific value to. The creator owns all the possible rights to it. Now, any country with intellectual property legislation must have an institutional organism or union where one can register any work they have created, giving the work legal validity. Because of this, the creator can defend the rights they hold on their work, if needed. (Registration is a preventive measure before any infringement occurs.) Moving forward, this morality of being publicly recognized as the author of your work is a right. So, you can decide to exercise it or not. This means that you have the right to use a pseudonym, even if your real name and ID appear in the registry. The intention of registration is to legally declare the real author of a work.

THE FILM AND AUDIOVISUAL INDUSTRY

Registering is the first thing you must do before anyone else can have access to it. That should be enough to show if someone's work is being passed off as another's, by both date of authorship and coincidence of content. Dates are not open to interpretation. (One work can only be copied or usurped from something that has previously existed.) So, disputes are reduced to one of three things: The possible negligence of the original author (i.e. not registering it or allowing a usurper to do it before the rightful author), the disagreement between co-authors (these things happen), or plagiarism. (Copying so much content from another's work that it can basically be considered the same.)

In any case, the simple act of registering a work does not imply that someone else will not copy or steal it. (It cannot prevent it in the strict sense, that is evident.) It just means that you will have a legal way of demonstrating that a particular work was created by you, on a certain date, if it is indeed copied. From there you would need to report a criminal offence for any misappropriation. Bringing the case to court is each victim's personal choice. It is not an automatic process. It will be necessary to prosecute and objectively prove that a series of subjective artistic contents have been copied from your work to the point of causing a concrete economic prejudice. It can be a hard task for you and your lawyer (it is not a bed of roses), but it is not impossible either. In very flagrant cases, substantial agreements are reached when the defendants are big production companies (including Hollywood studios because of course, they steal too).

All of this is related to moral rights but, with regards to proprietary rights... things get complicated. It is an intellectual right but, in turn, susceptible to being economically valued. Returning to the example of the painter, putting a price on a painting as intellectual creation is relatively simple. You think about the expense of materials, add the amount in which you value your creativity and effort, perhaps your possible cachet in the market, and finally, the buyer pays you that amount in exchange for the physical object. It is easy because there is only one object. But what about a novel? The concept of copyright comes in like this: The only ones allowed to create and sell copies of the original work must be those authorized by the author, provided that he or she is properly compensated for every single copy. Although they are simple copies of that original, a unique object symbolized by the painted canvas, they are legitimate substitutes or "official" reproductions, allowed by the author. And they must be sold at a lower, affordable cost since they are no longer exclusive objects.

Apart from making copies, authors have the right to do many other things with their work. Such as massive distribution, expansion per territories, public display, adaptation to other media, partial use rather than complete, and the extraction of content for promotion. They can also authorize someone to reuse the structural format, without using the original, specific content (which is the most frequent way TV shows are sold). Additionally, authors have the right to make generic licenses for ideas and characters (without needing any existing story, just their generic concept, look, or name).

All these rights belong to the author. Therefore, you are allowed to call them "the rights" or "all rights" if you refer to all of them. You cannot do this if you just mean a few of them in particular (for example, film adaptation rights). Property owners can voluntarily give their property to other people, or just permission to exercise said rights. And as a counterpart for the transfer, the authors can obtain an economic profit, strategic benefit, or whatever they demand when negotiating. Both the transfer and the sale of all rights may be given together or separately; as a whole or in part, exclusive or not.

In this sense, when talking about the film industry, we should mention the most famous of transfers, the adaptation rights. Many people do not know this, but the vast majority of movies are adaptations of novels, theater plays, short tales, comic books, video games, and even newspaper articles. However, due to the high speculative nature of the industry at project status (not in vain, it is officially known as "development hell"), it is normal to not directly pay for the adaptation rights acquisition, but only for an exclusive option of purchase. For a few tens of thousands of dollars, you can withhold rights for 1 or 2 years (whatever you negotiate), to guarantee that no one will be able to adapt the same property at the same time. Thus, in case any studio is interested in making a film, they will not be able to buy the rights directly from the original owner/creator because the preferential option of purchase was reserved by contract.

In fact, moral authorship is the only one of these rights that is inalienable and non-transferable. When you create a work, reality cannot be distorted; the facts are not going to change. In addition to transferring them temporarily, all patrimonial rights may be transferred by sale or demise. But that does not make the new owner of the rights recognizable as the author. There are big millionaire licenses that have been sold for life. Authors who have decided, for economic or personal reasons, to detach themselves over the control of the creation, in the buyer's favor. But that is not to say the author's name is just erased, the total transfer of the patrimonial rights does not mean the recognition of moral authorship is sold too.

Now it is clear that you should not say "copyright" without specifying the type of rights and their context. But it is a much more serious topic than the confusion it generates. Everyone in media (in other words, the industry tycoons) is interested in building a protective wall around everything involving artistic creation, so that no one asks too many questions about the contradictory parts of the subject. There is hardly any mention of it, but in those years when CD sales started to plummet (coinciding with the rise of the internet and the MP3 format), the controversy was on TV all over the world announcing the absolute end of the music industry and practically the apocalypse. You can see how right the wealthy industry representatives were with that pitiful victim story that did not convince anyone. Even today, when people talk about this, everything remains in relation to piracy, but the very conception of copyright is still blurred.

THE FILM AND AUDIOVISUAL INDUSTRY

Every time the debate approached a critical part, important interests misdirected the attention to the moral side of the law and creative aspect. No matter how many debates were made, the same excuses emerged once and again. Things like: "Sharing audiovisual works is stealing," "Even if big companies are evil, the artists also need to eat," "Celebrities are not going broke, but you have to think of the small artists," "Are business agreements with artists abusive or not?" "Is sharing profit percentages from CDs and tickets fair or unfair?" "Artists' real earnings come from concerts and not selling albums anyway," etc.

The truth is, there was never a public explanation about remuneration structure for royalties, and there still is not. The attention is always focused on artists, but only in appearance. It never delves into the real part of the business that affects them: The producer's and distributor's role in this and a detailed comparison between royalties collected and royalties distributed among the artists. This is directly related to the nature and internal functioning of the collective copyright management entities (which are demonstrating once more, how slow they are at reacting to the unstoppable new digital era).

These collective management entities were self-proclaimed as the flag bearers of copyright, since their creation in the first half of the 20th century. (As well as many successive imitations that arose around the world.) By being the first ones to promote the social debate, they were able to maintain control of the situation. That was a very clever move. If you adopt the defender and spokesperson role (with legitimacy recognized by the government itself), there is no room for any other "official" artist representation. But something does not work when the artists themselves do not stop to wonder how these societies work. Their operations are extremely opaque, when ironically, they define themselves as completely transparent. (Typical, right?) Whether artists receive royalties or not, very few professionals know exactly how these massive payments and collections work.

THE FILM AND AUDIOVISUAL INDUSTRY

No one explains or provides any evidence of the specific money origin, the collection process, the distribution criteria, or the destination of so many millions in royalties. The laws are dedicated to giving up responsibility to the collection entities and they write vague and onerous guidelines in their statutes; with tremendous legal and formal loopholes, while no one says anything (probably because artists are also not the best profiles to analyze or question legal documents).

Any artwork can be reproduced in a copy, as well as in a live performance (a song, film, play, etc.). We have seen the reproduction right belongs to the author of the work. And one may wish to transfer it to others temporarily, in exchange for compensation. This reproduction can be momentary access to the work (in a movie theater, a concert, the musical thread of any store, a television screen, etc.) or involve getting a copy to enjoy as many times as you may want (video/audio/download). Exercising that right generates monetary gains that must be shared according to the conditions agreed upon between the assignor and assignee (the author and the collection entity). An agreement that collection entities kindly provide, with no possibility of being negotiated and without any kind of regulation or mediation. (More than a few people erroneously think that royalty collection entities are governmental institutions.)

The collected money's origin is easy to understand. There is a part of each sale (book, album, movie ticket, theater play, or live concert) that goes to a common fund collected by the rights management entities. However, when it comes to understanding which amount corresponds with which author, how it is calculated, documented, and processed, everyone wonders how they can keep thorough control of each reproduction (in any city, any building, at every second). And the solution to the mystery is more than obvious: There is no such control.

At concerts and in events, radio, and television there is an official form that states the specific works played. Exactly like the number of copies put on the market of any musical album, DVD/Blu-ray, copies in cinemas, or number of performances.

But, is there any control over the veracity of those forms? Of course not. And most importantly, what happens to the thousands of bars, cafes, hair salons, and small stores with piped music or a television screen? Simple, they must pay a regular fee. A variable amount, depending on the condition of the place where the reproduction took place, as well as the specific situation and purpose. No one counts how many times a song is played, it is based on predictability, according to the "success" in measurable terms. Like the number of edited copies, days on the billboard, promotional campaign levels, and number of shows and tickets sold. That is the formula for distributing the collected money. The common fund is shared between the artists in proportion to their "popularity" (which is to say, their industry power and distribution extent of their published albums). And the most worrying part is that below a certain number of published copies (not actually sold but simply published), you have no right to any kind of sharing. It is that simple. Independent and small artists do not obtain anything. Anyone who cannot afford to publish thousands of copies on the market or be able to show an audiovisual work inside the system (local television networks are not part of show business by the way) just do not have the right to receive any remuneration. Let us say that they are not considered professionals yet. That is why the "system" exists. If we think about it, anyone could make a lot of money if their songs were played on local radio stations or television networks every day, no matter how horrible they were (maybe they have a little extra help from the inside). Understanding this is a very sensitive and dangerous topic. All of this is never recognized, clearly explained, or defended in an official way. And you will never see this written anywhere.

For example, small independent authors may find themselves in the embarrassing situation of having to pay, being their own producers/publishers, royalty fees to collection entities in order to publish their own music albums. They may also find another payment as promoters of their own live shows, which concert-halls or clubs will demand as compensation. (Clubs are forced to pay to the collection entities, but it is actually you who are paying for your own royalties.) All of that just to not be paid. Even if you are not a member of a collection entity, no one cares and the payments will be equally required by law. You can always politely ask for your rights (good luck), try to fight a case in court, and even sue these collection entities for a lot of uncertain procedures and numerous irregularities; but it does not help their nourished team of lawyers (and even judges). Anyhow, at the end of the day you could just accept the simple truth: If you are not receiving any royalties it is only because you are out of the system, which means it would be a small amount of money anyways. Trying to fight against a giant monopolistic for a fistful of dollars probably would not compensate the effort.

Apart from the profit generated by unclaimed rights, the real gravy train is the disconnection between the massive, indiscriminate collection and the limited payments among the members of the entity. A lot of money is paid, yes; but the real collected amount is not distributed. There is no control or justification for any of these two, disconnected operations.

Here comes the master political move, the international intellectual property laws guarantee creators the right to get paid for royalties. (Warning: that does not mean it guarantees payment, but the right to be paid, which is a very different thing.) On the other hand, it does not offer any kind of guarantee or regulation on how to enforce that right. In case simple artists ask for the money directly from television networks or music clubs, let us say that they will have a very small chance of success. The answer will be: "I already pay my mandatory fee to the collection entities, so join one of them and they will pay you."

That sounds fair, right? They are not going to pay twice. So you simply have to join one of these entities and demand your royalties for that show, album, or whatever (but as we have seen, this depends on your capacity and category inside the industry). With the law in hand, as an artist you will be within your full rights to claim in court from those who should pay. And yes, you might even end up winning your case, but does anyone conceive such nonsense where an artist must spend his life in court claiming his rights? The situation is very ambiguous around the world, and some countries' legislation even forces the author to belong to one of these collection entities. In some cases, by means of imprecise and vague wording, and other times in an explicit way.

Going beyond the real chances that you might have to operate outside the system, we are talking about laws that, for practical purposes, are forcing authors to give 10-25% of their income (supposedly for management costs) to a private company whose license is granted by the government and for ambiguous reasons (like everything at the highest political level). People who are indiscriminately charging the entire society, but are only paying to an exclusive minority of famous authors. Is that defending the artists?

Like any other right, you can exercise your right to claim for royalties. It is voluntary (such as the right to vote, for example). But nevertheless, collecting royalties for these entities is mandatory (in an impersonal way, on behalf of all the authors of the world.) It becomes a revolutionary tax charged for any type of musical or audiovisual content played in theaters, cinemas, live events, clubs, stores, and businesses of all kinds. Mainly because of the other big controversial detail. By just having one reproduction device in any place, (including just a couple of speakers) the laws assume the possibility of playing licensed content, which is enough to require the payment fee. And collection entities do not hesitate to automatically sue anyone who is not willing to pay. Therefore, it is the defendant who must prove that there is no licensed material being played in that place (and not the opposite as presumption of innocence states).

As we stated previously, the progressive decline of record sales (not the music business, but rather the physical albums) spotlighted these collection entities to the regret of the big fish of the industry and their efforts to focus on copyright fraud on pirate content (on the streets, in P2P networks and in illegal downloads of audio and video).

THE FILM AND AUDIOVISUAL INDUSTRY

Producers' and distributors' understandable, yet deceitful, point of view was defended tooth and nail. It was always from the rigid legislative argument, the hypocritical defense of the culture, and the stupid criminalization of consumers all rolled into one. They know how to take advantage of the basic contradiction that we mentioned at the beginning. By directly attacking the consumer, who just wanted to enjoy something as superfluous and easy-to-acquire as digital entertainment. The consequence was just the opposite: Intentional disobedience. (Like teenagers do, just a direct defiance with a deep conviction.) The battle against public opinion was already lost and quickly transformed into the eternal struggle between ordinary people and big corporations. It was quite surreal. Million-dollar, multinational companies were trying to make people feel sad by using the most well-worn clichés from the mouths of world-famous artists. (For example, they often mentioned the small independent artists, without means and resources, when we just saw how cynical this was.)

The arrogance of the powerful turned against themselves. It was clear that small artists would never support the same big industry that never did anything to accept them. So it was easy to imagine a new business model where the toxic mainstream system was not needed anymore. The internet was the perfect distribution channel for every small, independent artist. The world was within their reach, free of charge and was not controlled by anyone. The production resources were becoming more and more affordable every day and it was not uncommon for every musician to have a professional studio at home.

As it could not be otherwise, the collection entities were also affected in that time. Apart from allegations of some questionable actions, as a political lobby, they were publicly exposed. This came together with a whole series of criminal proceedings, totally gangster-style: extortion, threats, tax fraud, defalcation, abuse of power, and influence peddling. These kinds of controversies always have political consequences and international laws are constantly revised and updated in order to set a legal framework that is as fair as possible. But no matter how hard we try to have a greater control over collection and royalty payments, the real issue is that we are talking about trading with intellectual rights. The system currently used for commercial exploitation of the arts is clearly obsolete and pretty soon artists will not have to give anything to intermediaries. With a proper and centralized digital management tool for both collection and payment it will be more than enough. That is of course, assuming that the whole concept of copyright will stay alive for a long time.

THE FALSE PROTECTION OF IDEAS

It is very common to feel as if someone has copied your idea or simply be afraid that someone will do it. It may have happened to you. The question is: Is it a crime? On the one hand, the World Intellectual Property Organization (WIPO) states that any creation of the human mind is part of a person's intellectual property. But on the other hand, it turns out that ideas cannot be protected as such, therefore they cannot be owned by anyone.

Let us explain. Scientific discoveries or theories, for example, cannot be registered with ownership. However, it is possible to protect any physical invention that can be sold to the market; therefore, manufacturing plans are required. In regard to artistic works, they are more or less conceived in a similar way. They are the culmination of an evolved primal idea. The final artwork may be yours, but the original germ that nourishes the subsequent evolution cannot exclusively belong to anyone. The world of ideas and pure inspiration cannot be registered as property. Only your very specific expression of music, image, literature, or any other kind of practical work, in its final form, can be protected, but not the conceptual idea behind it. From a legal point of view, a work of art is understood as a specific sum of possible combinations, where certain concepts are ordered and presented in a particular way. Only that combination, with character and personality, can be registered. One particular unique text, drawing, photograph, video, or song.

These vague definitions are the reason for a high number of legal related confrontations. And that is considering that we all have an approximate idea of what copying is. When you copy something, you know perfectly well that you are doing it. But, is anyone going to notice?

Besides, the common saying is that everything has already been invented. The truth is that in this new era of overexposure to all kinds of content, copying anything is incredibly easy. Apart from being labeled as "unoriginal" or publicly exposed for being too blatant, the real consequences of this venial sin are minimal.

All intellectual property will enter into the public domain (which means people can reproduce it, adapt it, and trade it freely) between 80-120 years after the author's death. (The large margin is because it is not the same if one particular work or character falls into the public domain. Or, if it is a full collection of a published series that is available). Although it should be noted that this margin was 50-60 years until the "Mickey Mouse" law was approved in 1998. It was designed to maintain control over Elvis Presley's first songs, the first Mickey Mouse short-films, and the first James Bond novels.

To clarify the level of protection we are talking about, let us look at an example. It is clear that no one can have exclusive control over a character that is simply an ogre in a children's tale. However, you can own all the property rights for the look of a particular ogre that has been designed for a specific film and has also been given a full name. Anyone is free to write a book, song, or movie based on classical tales from the nineteenth century, since they are already in the public domain. Just like it is completely lawful to make a comedy parody of said tales. But now, if your protagonist is a green ogre with a talking donkey as a companion and he saves a princess from a curse that transforms her into an ogress at night; that idea has taken a very particular shape which is much more concrete within the inexhaustible world of ideas. The content is then more unique, recognizable, and distinguishable.

When the film's actions and dialogues are completed, the script is registered as a set of concrete ideas; just like the entire visual look of the work will be registered once it is finished. It is thus understood that the sum of all these individual elements results in the work's success. Therefore, the repetition of elements should achieve the same success. That is where the conflict begins. Who judges (and how) the difference between a generic idea and a specific expression that belongs to an author? The answer is more obvious than you think. By the jury, in a trial.

Intellectual property offenses are not considered as such by default. No matter how flagrant something is copied, it is only considered an offense when those offended parties consider their rights violated. Someone must formally prosecute another for using their property to make a profit. It is either literally the same work or so similar that it can virtually be considered the original material. The point is that you cannot use others' work to attract their audience to your copied work. You would be stealing another person's success and therefore, their economic profits. It represents an economic injury and perhaps some damage to the public image (depending on the specific copy and its context).

For example, laws are supposed to prohibit the selling of unofficial t-shirts, backpacks, or caps with pictures of the ogre and the donkey; as well as the selling of cheap imitations that can be deliberately mistaken for the original trademark (again, it would be exploiting another's success for your own benefit). However, even without making use of the ogre and donkey, kleptomaniac creators can copy or steal from others' stories, scenes, turning points, or even identical dialogues; and they do it with total impunity. Ideas are a dangerously ambiguous nebula and boundaries regarding homage, copy, and plagiarism are too easy (and tempting) to cross.

Let us say homage is the most "accepted" form of duplication. No one is bothered when you borrow camera angles, scenes, critical turning points, character profiles, or even exact sentences from classics as an obvious tribute. These are all considered grateful nods, as a sign of respect, to great films or directors that made a difference in their time. But it is different when, due to lack of talent, someone decides to use elements from another's work rather than creating something original themselves. It is a complete lack of inspiration and resorts to the simple imitation of what has been seen elsewhere. Basically, this quick and lazy solution saves a lot of the time, as well as the mental effort that artistic creation requires. Not to mention plagiarism: When there are enough detailed coincidences in a copy for it to be considered an illicit duplication.

It is difficult to explain what inspiration is to those who do not have said innate ability. But, according to the definition, usually given by the artists themselves, it could be a kind of competition between all the ideas in an artist's mind. From distant ideas that remain hidden in the remote past to the most recent one that emerged in a matter of seconds. A sort of selection, sometimes voluntary and sometimes subconscious, where the mind takes a little bit from here and a little bit from there. As any artist knows, everything is created from previously existing things. No act of creation is completely new or original.

Artistic creation is, in a way, the evolution of a primitive and subconscious copy of something we already know. And with respect to the line that separates a legitimate creation from a cheap copy, everyone agrees on the same key point: The effort. As we said before, a minimum amount of creative effort is required in order to provide what makes your work yours.

In conclusion, from a legal perspective, we said that violating intellectual property is a crime that is pursued. It is just because some people obtain an illicit benefit from using material that does not belong to them. There will be no offense without an offended party to claim it. And in fact, as we all know, reporting a robbery is not a guarantee for justice anyways.

There have been lawsuits filed against huge successful films and franchises based on unofficial books or other films, meaning they have been shamelessly copied or plagiarized. Completely stolen content where the names of the characters have barely been changed (the vaguest form of copying). The legal arsenal of big production companies and studios usually allow them to remain unscathed. However, a lot of these cases (especially the most blatant) are resolved with a substantial economic agreement in exchange for the victim's public silence. In fact, if it were not for the deals confidentiality, the reputation of several well-known international franchises would have been damaged.

INTERNET AND NEW TECHNOLOGIES

Before the end of the last century, the internet arrived. It did so little by little but we all knew that it had come to stay. The first modem connection used a slow speed, inconceivable in the present. The aggravating circumstance was that back in those days no one installed a new telephone line for internet (when mobile phones barely existed), so you had to use either your landline telephone or surf the internet; but never both at the same time. Taking the context into account, plus the relative usefulness of the early internet, you can deduce that the technology's first users were only computer geeks and business people who were impressed by electronic mail, which condemned old faxes and letters to extinction.

These users immediately perceived the inexhaustible source of resources that came with the free exchange of files, whether it was between friends or strangers. It was only a matter of time until some of these guys, with their technical knowledge and needed software, began to capture audio and digital video to share their favorite movies and songs with friends. They did not even need to buy blank or rewritable discs, thanks to the latest compression formats—the popular MP3, MPEG, and the brand new DivX (a more specific AVI video encoder). By using these file formats and a couple of very simple freeware (open software that you can use for free), anyone was capable of ripping off songs and full music albums in a few hours. Additionally, they could copy movies at a low, but acceptable, resolution within a few days.

THE FILM AND AUDIOVISUAL INDUSTRY

Once internet connections became more common and everyone had at least one email account, the market began to take the possibilities of electronic commerce more seriously. It has been known as e-commerce since then. The quote: "If you are not on the web, you do not exist" increased in popularity, and over the years even those who were the most reluctant to change, had to accept it. Apart from increasing sales, thanks to e-commerce, a simple web page provided the visibility and credibility for a business that only television could offer at that time (an unaffordable luxury for most companies).

The true internet business was consolidated by advertising. Similar to what happened with early newspapers and magazines, advertisers paid thousands of websites and portals (networks that contained other webpages and services within them) to include a simple link or a small banner showing their ad or logo. There was an advantage to being interactive, i.e. clicking the ad. This would directly access the advertiser's content. At that time, it was impossible for the transmission capacity of that first old internet to support video streaming. However, it was predicted that in a matter of years, television and the internet would fuse; as it is today. Once speculation turned into reality (it is impossible to forget the dot-com bubble), e-commerce and internet use were slowly evolving at user level, reaching what we all enjoy today. Children, adults, and even the elderly use it every day.

Moving forward, it should be noted that this new digital world inherited bad habits from the telephone market. This series of bad habits still continue today. Abuse from service providers, selling personal data, privacy violation, invasive publicity, and of course, scams.

In addition to finding copyrighted artwork and commercial software to download for free, most pirate websites contain many other crimes. For example, scams, data theft, viral attacks, or the promotion and sale of illegal products (even all of this happening at once). Free movies or songs are the perfect bait. In most cases, the content that they promise does not even exist.

THE FILM AND AUDIOVISUAL INDUSTRY

Many people cannot conceive that pirates take the time to create a totally updated catalog of Hollywood blockbusters. They use all of the promotional images, texts, trailers, etc. However, every link on their website is probably fake. All of this for the sole purpose of deceiving you in order to get your phone number, email account, or just direct access to your computer. They are in search of passwords, credit cards, and bank accounts. Needless to say, only being successful once would be worth it. But if there is something that causes even more bewilderment, it is that on their websites, along with illegal material, you can see ads for completely legal products from regular markets. Things like food, cars, or even household goods; just like normal ads that you can see on television. How is that possible?

This system is well thought out. Internet advertising is based on the succession of intermediaries; a countless number of big and small distributors and service companies, with no responsibility for the content they advertise. Huge chained platforms distribute ads through a series of automated codes, which millions of customers can use worldwide. It is a long chain that is intentionally obscure.

To put it simply, the advertisers pay for their banner or video to appear on a website during a specific time frame, a certain number of times, or within a particular parameter. But beyond choosing one specific website, these platforms, full of intermediaries, integrate the ads in an automatic global network. These ads are then displayed on any webpage in the world that wants to include each platform's specific code (in turn, these websites could belong to another, bigger platform, and so on, and so on). There is no control of where advertisements are placed. It is like trying to find a grain of sand in the statistical mountain of a million published ads across the web. Obviously, agencies and advertisers are not responsible for the internal contents included on any website that wants to advertise. It would be impossible to check the legality of every single website looking for advertising revenues. (There are more than 1 billion active websites with some type of paid advertising.) In addition to this, to provide service that has global coverage, a fully automated system has to be in place, which is convenient, right? It is a fact that most legal battles regarding the internet are lost causes. Beyond a few arrests and shutting down a few websites, (as a deterrent measure more than anything else) little more can be done. Anyhow, the truth is that although some global control is impossible in practice, it is not because governments or security forces cannot access the things they want. Let us remember that the internet was initially invented as a request, by the Department of Defense during the Cold War. It was then marketed because of its strategic nature as a surveillance system and apart from its obvious (and more than convenient) socioeconomic advantages.

The fun part is the limits established by Liberty, with a capital "L." Some governments, like the Chinese government, exercise such control in a very direct manner like limiting international access and censoring contents. But, in the territories that we know as The Free World (basically, the first world democracies), any kind of intervention has to be done with much more subtlety and a compelling need for justification. The U.S. Government, like any other country's government, can use national security, if deemed necessary, as an excuse to violate the rights and liberties of the people. This includes the internet. Taking into account that the entire planet will be digitally connected throughout the 21st century, governments consider the World Wide Web as "national territory." It needs to be protected (that is, at the end of the day, the whole point of it).

The key is the practical inability to prosecute every crime on the internet. Tracking, surveillance, shutting down each website, and detaining each offender would be excessive, useless, and require a lot of attention. Besides, you would have to repeat the process again and again, at an unsustainable pace. It is impossible to deal with the crimes committed every minute on the streets, so you can imagine in the virtual world. The time that any criminal needs to disappear (without a trace, if you are good) and repeat the crime is ridiculously minimal.

THE FILM AND AUDIOVISUAL INDUSTRY

A brand new website with illegal, downloadable links to songs or movies can be created in less than a minute. Although governments or any security corps shut down those websites immediately, you could instantly create a clone and let all your users know in just a couple of clicks. Even if you were to shut down again, you could just repeat the operation again and again. Governments understand that they cannot fight this effectively; and locations and punishments for users have been discussed. We are talking about a large number of people who, for the most part, would be minors. Should internet users be criminalized just because the criminal cannot be persecuted? In the music industry, the biggest players in the game had no other choice but to adapt their business model to the new reality; accepting the internet as the new, ultimate medium of diffusion and exchange of information. But they must continue investigating to find the most profitable way of taking advantage of it. Because do not forget, from a business person's point of view, as well as from the users', at the end of the day everything is related to money.

We are talking about paying for entertainment. It is good that people like to listen to music, watch movies, and read comics. But when the product is so expensive, it poses a problem for your personal finances; and on the contrary, it is so easy to enjoy these for free. Who is surprised at the amount of piracy that is consumed? Admittedly, it is just a little bit of fun; simple, inconsequential enjoyment. The money citizens have in their bank accounts is certainly relevant, just like these business people care about the money they have. For these industry tycoons, each consumer is only a number; a statistical element that makes sense en masse as a combined gain. But consumers are real people, each person has their individual and personal life with a specific financial capacity. It is not a coincidence that consumers of audiovisual entertainment are mostly young people. It is clear that their principles and priorities are different. And their limited purchasing power could justify the trend of consuming illegal content. But according to that, how would you explain how they are also the largest consumer of legal content?

THE FILM AND AUDIOVISUAL INDUSTRY

From their perspective, big companies are not improving their public image with the trite defense of million-dollar losses in the industry, while they proclaim to the four winds about the fantastic profits they earn each year. Besides, when some companies have losses or low moments, it is very easy to automatically blame the usual suspects: illegal contents on the internet, the comfort of home cinemas, movie theaters going out of business across the country, etc.

Over time, this message of ambiguity continues to perpetuate itself because one of the most important and worrying evils of today is meaningless information overload. If they continue to spread every possible message simultaneously, what you will remember will be the specific message that you have received. For example, losses or benefits, stability or instability, the golden age, or the time of crisis. Additionally, in the hypothetical case that someone with an interest in the subject notices all this, the only thing generated will be confusion and absurd arguments like: "I heard this," or "I heard this other thing," or "But they said this here," or "Ok, but they said that there."

From an industry perspective, we are enjoying a new golden age for movies, whether this is recognized or not. No matter how much they like to play this bipolar contradiction of victimized whining and triumphant arrogance. Since the 90s, Hollywood studios have had invariable multi-million-dollar benefits that have grown without stopping. We are talking about 30 years of continued growth and increase. From only the biggest, successful blockbusters of the year and their incomes, each major studio is able to pay off its global investment. Not only with regard to the cost of those films, but all possible losses caused by the biggest fiascos. And after that, making great profits.

We said that art in general (and entertainment in particular) is not the highest priority in people's lives. But there is, no doubt, a fervent attraction to audiovisual content. Not around everything related to it, but mainly the selfish enjoyment of said content. This form of communication brings together a series of qualities that make it ideal for human beings. Much more than reading, radio, music, or even talking with other people. We have established a worrisome dependency, almost like a vice. There is a very powerful engagement factor in audiovisual content caused by the immediate pleasure of being disconnected from reality (or if you prefer connecting to fiction as an alternative reality). An interesting disconnection which simulates the feeling of being connected.

As a recreational activity, a vast majority of the population considers going to the movies to be more fun than reading a book. Not just because of the film itself, but because of the ritual of going to the movie theater. It is considered a social act and a group activity. Teenagers want (and need) to be out of their homes and doing things with their friends. Young children have to be accompanied by adults (including their parents, each child means at least three guaranteed tickets). And, we already talked about the basic standard of going to the movies as a date. Much has to change in our society so that the film industry does not just survive for these reasons alone. Naturally, it will have to continue remodeling and adapting itself, but no more than any other industry; it is called progress.

That false fear of: "There is no longer a need to leave home to enjoy movies" is completely unsubstantiated. This could be true, in any case, if people's natural tendencies are to stay at home as long as possible; provided it was the most desirable place to be. But it is no secret that in today's society, only a small percentage of the population thinks so. Most people consider leaving their home a positive, desirable activity. The voluntary option of going outside to enjoy some leisure time is always more attractive (especially if you do not like your home or your daily routine).

The uncontrolled diffusion of copyrighted content may be impossible to avoid, but the only time that the amortization process could actually be harmful might be in the first weeks after the premiere. As long as it is still something new and fresh. And this is precisely why people are more eager to go to the movies.

THE FILM AND AUDIOVISUAL INDUSTRY

It is not a coincidence that in the first 2-3 weeks, the industry is getting all those impressive box office records that have never been seen before. Every movie has a limited commercial life. And once this has passed, every film remains as a simple back-catalog piece, with very low profitability, finally becoming a discontinued product, no longer available for the public. Anyway, very few titles are really successful nowadays, and movie collectors hardly suppose relevant revenues anymore. (Blu-Ray, merchandising and such.)

Therefore, we do not see a reason to be worried. By the way, has anyone noticed the vast number of full movies available on YouTube? How is it possible that on said platform you cannot find the latest Hollywood remake that has just been released but you can find versions from 40 years ago? They are not filing a copyright claim for the old versions that are perfectly available for anyone? Is it a marketing strategy for young millennials? Brand reinforcement? Nostalgic effect? Perhaps the new ad-revenue system on protected content might have something to do with it? All this is very easy to deny and the official stance will always be that it is not allowed or encouraged. As we said before, it is impossible to pursue each specific website or every video that users have uploaded, etc. But remember YouTube has a simple content ID detection system and claim process. It is 100% effective to remove the latest blockbuster premiere (because anyone can record a movie from the theater and upload it). But why it is not effective with versions from the 70s or 80s? It is simple, the effort is not worthwhile in comparison to the "damage." Instead of just blocking the content, they can earn money with ads from the illegal content, just like in regular TV. Not to mention, the free publicity that the modern version in theaters will get. Especially for the younger generation that do not know any movie prior to the 2000s, and who are no longer watching TV.

We can accept this new scenario with more or less resignation but, in global terms, the internet's effects are not as negative as they are positive. It is not a question of denying the crime, since we are talking about laws that have been created and modified expressly for making all this a crime. Nevertheless, this is a new scenario which has proved impossible to contain; so let us keep trying to take advantage of it, instead of playing the martyr. That is not forgetting that the root of the problem is much more complicated. The thorny subject that no one in the industry wants to hear a word about. We are in a new reality, where such lucrative works can be reproduced in infinite replicas and shared with the whole world in a matter of seconds. Does it make sense to keep talking about private property in the arts? Is there a real benefit for artists? Or just for big corporations, as usual? Again, the duality of art and industry causes headaches.

THE STUDIO SYSTEM

The Hollywood system was created at the beginning of the 20th century and laid the foundation for today's industry. In short, it is about having a very small group of big studios control the market on a large scale; both in content production and distribution. They are called "majors" or also "The Big Six." And thanks to extremely efficient planning and rigorous execution, these giants have been able to maintain control so far by always adapting themselves to the new times and markets.

Around the 1920s, when film became a profitable business with proper scalability, the oligopoly of film companies was even greater than the current one, in terms of control. Absolutely everything was owned by them, from sets to filming equipment. Even artists and technical crews were property of the studios as a fixed staff. This included carpenters, electricians, cameramen, actors, writers, directors, executives, and distributors. No one was hired temporarily in those days. But that was not all, they immediately realized the advantage of also owning the buildings where movies were screened. Therefore, they were always looking for expansion and were willing to buy more and more land and buildings.

Such a formula presented an obvious savings in cost and a high degree of business optimization. And all those who decided to invest for the flourishing film industry ended up amassing great fortunes, culminating in the famous Golden Age of Hollywood. In the 40s, there were eight majors in the system: Warner Bros., 20th Century Fox, Columbia, Paramount, Universal, United Artists, Metro-Goldwyn-Mayer, and RKO. By size comparison, Columbia, Universal, and United Artists were considered "mini-majors" (large production companies without the same power as the others). But the fact is, together they controlled almost 100% of that old industry. There was hardly any chance of making movies outside of this closed environment. Independent production was not even close to 4%.

But the oddest thing about this is the really ironic fact that all these businessmen began fighting against the perverse monopoly that prevailed in those times, the industrial trust owned by Thomas Edison. For those who do not know the term, a trust consists of joining several companies into a single one in order to monopolize a whole industrial sector (eliminating any possibility of free competition).

In the full "war of patents" Edison pretended (in fact, he did it for many years) that producers, distributors, and exhibitors had to pay a license to use each and every one of the materials and activities that were required at the time, in order to manufacture and trade with cinematographic works. Many critical voices raised against this trust and different acts of rebellion were gradually growing. Many of those entrepreneurs defied the status quo and even acted illegally. Mayer, Fox, and the Warner brothers all fought against the established system and were called "independents" until the government finally declared that Edison's macro company was illegal, according to the Sherman Antitrust Act which had been in effect since 1890. Other associated studios of a smaller size emerged, whose names may sound familiar to you (like Tri-Star, Orion, or Touchstone); but they were always owned, in one way or another, by the big studios through mergers, acquisitions, takeovers and such.

THE FILM AND AUDIOVISUAL INDUSTRY

Years went by and with such relevant business significance (in economic and social terms), after the monopoly conviction against Paramount Pictures in 1948, the map of the system we all know today was completed. When the government decided that the majors should not exert power of such magnitude, the only thing that could have happened, happened: A full restructuring of the system (so that they could continue doing what they were doing, but legally). In other words, do it as the government said.

So it was said and done. In the following years, several corporations of undeniable political power acquired the majors and restructured them, so that the new oligopoly could be appropriate for the country's laws, big markets, and global interests. Sporadically over the years, studios continued to pass from one hand to another. Sometimes, some responded to certain strategic interests while others to pure economic factors (remember, profitability is always the first of these interests).

Occasionally, there are still mergers between companies, as well as bankruptcies. But nothing that should be cause for alarm. The system demonstrates more than enough strength and efficiency, they are only punctual facts that respond to internal restructuring needs. Let us say that one of those unexpected box-office flops (the really big and unexpected ones) could destabilize, at worst, one large company and force it perform unwanted maneuvers in order to avoid bigger problems. But it will hardly affect the overall health of the entire system.

Thus, the current system remains ruled by this small elite of companies, now under the untouchable umbrella of the gigantic media corporations (which are at the service of political power, closing the circle). Unlike the old Edison Trust, this control is exerted under a much more organic and healthier structure. When politics entered the game, it brought some bad things and some good things, but it is a free market; which is the whole point of it. Competition is favored and new forms of association, financing, and even research emerge.

THE FILM AND AUDIOVISUAL INDUSTRY

Studios were prohibited from having absolute control over the industrial chain because this prevented others from exercising their right to compete. Now although anyone could produce what they want on their own, no one will have as much money as studios to produce. And even if they could, no one could prevent them from trying to screen their films in the theaters that they consider more convenient. In fact, taking into account that most theaters were owned by the majors, as soon as they could, they would try to build or buy their own alternative theaters. So, how do you take advantage of that scenario?

The first goal was to do what anyone who wanted to make movies would do. And in particular, those who prefer to do it for the studios. Anyone who is interested in filming anything could have the possibility of using the studio's money as an investment for a certain project, company, and/or producer (but all of them being external). The case was the same with distribution. Anyone was free to sell and screen their movie wherever they wanted. But, is it not more tempting to have the chance to distribute your movie around the world? Can any other option offer that? Only majors could do that. So that is how it was done. Needless to say, to this day, they are the ones holding the whip while negotiating conditions. Studios still control the whole process chain, but officially without a trace of monopoly.

Right now, the six major studios controlling the audiovisual market are: Warner, Fox, Sony (formerly Columbia, before they were bought by the Japanese giant), Paramount, Universal, and the very particular case of Disney. Apart from having recently acquired Fox, The Walt Disney Company earned its 'major' status by creating its own exclusive market: the children's market. (It is also worthwhile to mention the strength that streaming titans, like Netflix and Amazon, are gaining on their way to becoming majors.) At the foot of this Mount Olympus are a host of production companies, worshipping and paying tribute; some bigger than others. They offer production services in the most varied forms of association, with the sole aim of distributing their project worldwide, thanks to the omnipotent Hollywood gods.

THE FILM AND AUDIOVISUAL INDUSTRY

We are speaking of a strong and extensive industrial framework which, while not perfect, is pretty solid. It has had a surprising level of success, benefits, and sophistication brought by something as seemingly superfluous as simple entertainment. It is truly admirable; although, it is not always seen from that perspective. It is always easier to see it from the loser's perspective. ("I also want to be a millionaire but these m********rs do not give me a chance.")

How do you come to earn so many millions in this business? How does such a low-cost ticket turn into such a large mass of millions? It is obviously because of accumulation. So, revising in detail how the box office money is shared, all you have to do is some easy math.

To produce a film without dying in the attempt, it is essential to carefully study the balance between the expenditure that is going to be made and the expected earnings in return. Therefore, apart from ensuring that the quality of the product is something the public will like, the most important factor, from a pragmatic point of view, will always be the distribution scope. It is true that without a closed budget you cannot start your production (or you should not). We also saw that you cannot start your production without a distribution deal either.

This is a very difficult thing to accomplish for beginners and independents, but it is definitely an unacceptable risk to even think of investing money in a product, without knowing what is going to happen to it once it is finished. And no one, except the creators, will have enough confidence in a project to put money into it without a confirmed distribution.

Like it or not, the Hollywood production model is studied and envied around the world. In the 21st century industry, all nations know that they must be open to the international market if they want to take further advantage of their project. Therefore, elaborating a sufficiently universal product while being exotic at the same time, can get you fantastic results in foreign markets.

THE FILM AND AUDIOVISUAL INDUSTRY

On the one hand, if your movie has been a national success, it is normal that your domestic incomes are higher than those obtained in other territories. But on the other hand, it can also occur that earnings are equal or even higher abroad; especially because of volume. (Never underestimate sales in one territory, no matter how small it may seem. Like we said, accumulation is the key.) That is what happens with big blockbusters. Even after earning hundreds of millions of dollars in the US and Canada, they barely recover production costs although, they start to make a real benefit due to the massive success in the rest of the world. The global box office result is the only thing that matters, the return on investment (ROI). By recovering the production cost, your film will not be considered a failure, but it will not be labeled as true "success" until the income at least duplicates the cost.

From the majors' point of view, the whole system is sustained by the top successful grosses being able to amortize all the expenses of the year. This includes the most ordinary results of smaller films, as well as the losses from the fiascos that do not recoup their creation costs. And one of the fundamental premises to having this strategy be sustainable, in theory, is that every audience (even every minority) should have their portion of entertainment, specifically designed to their liking. (If all these products are not well conceived or executed, that is a different story.)

Besides, you cannot always be up to date with all the trends, fads, and sudden changes in people's tastes. That is one more argument in favor of trying to do a little of everything in order to test the results and monitor these tendencies with some empiricism. Logically, each producer will give their all to the projects aligned with their own interests, and will not focus so much on something that they do not care about (or cannot do properly). Likewise, the opposite strategy of trying to manipulate people's tastes, can also work. ("I will tell you what is cool and what is not, because you do not have a clue.")

THE FILM AND AUDIOVISUAL INDUSTRY

THE INTERNATIONAL INFLUENCE OF HOLLYWOOD

Which came first, the chicken or the egg? Another paradoxical question: Do we manipulate the tastes of the impressionable public so that they like what we want? Or, do we give people what they have demonstrated that they like, with the results in hand? The rule is a curious middle term, which can be given in two ways. You can either camouflage your interests within what the public demands or include things that they like into a story you want to tell.

Based on this thesis, it would also be stupid not to include those well-known elements that are already a guarantee of success, just to mitigate the risk of failure. We have mentioned how subjective the greenlighting process is for film projects within the specific interests of those financing, like majors, television networks, committees of public subsidies, and ministries or institutions. In the hypothetical case that someone wants to propose something new that has never been done before, it will have to be well justified as a strategic action against competitors. Although you cannot disguise the inherent risk in innovation. You can try to minimize the impact within a secure environment. For example, by not looking different on the surface. (Indeed, as we previously saw, this can be done to get the opposite: the same repeated thing masquerading as something different.)

Sometimes there may be a temporary commitment in what people are actually "interested in," like trends, as said before. But the most logical way to proceed is to wait for an appropriate amount of time in order to check whether any sudden "boom" becomes a future massive success, or if it is just a temporary, silly fad with no real profit. Considering the number of years needed to produce a film, it would be a disaster to release a film about something that no one remembers anymore.

We all know the main target in this industry is the younger audience because they are easy to mold and perfectly predictable. That is why it is possible to face an important social and moral dilemma: According to the heavy influence that show business exerts on the life and personality of youngsters, should not these products (films, songs, video games, books, etc.) instill desirable values and behaviors on our young society? Considering the privileged position of these products, it would be the most responsible thing to do, right? However, quite the contrary occurs, this useful or "educational" purpose is vilified and practically relegated to the children's arena, in a rather simplistic way (except honorable exceptions).

When children grow up enough to start spending their own money, even if it is their weekly allowance, the hunting season begins. Because of their inexperience in life, there is no easier prey than teenagers because they are kids who yearn to live as adults; the perfect combination. They must be pleased in all the typical desires of that age. The fulfillment of their wishes, the materialization of their dreams, the confirmation of their theories and reasonings, the flattery to their ego, social acceptance, the triumph of winners over losers, quick solutions to conflicts or mishaps (usually using violence) and, of course, anything related to sex. Just reflect their behavior on the screen and you will have their trust. As with any audience, success among young people is assured as long as they can identify with the characters' personalities, the story content, and/or the philosophy behind each action and reaction.

Although it is simple, fictional entertainment, every spectator likes to see indicators that the world works as they think it does. It does not matter how it works in reality, but the fact is, your own point of view is being shown publicly and something as cool as a movie is supporting your vision. That is why a film designed for one particular target audience will hardly be enjoyed by someone on the other side of the spectrum (again, think of teenagers as opposed to another age). Although many creators find this to be an aberration, writers and directors must take all of the above into account when telling their stories, usually against their own personal opinion. It is a basic industry standard. Any product targeted for young people always highlights a lot of ridiculous, adolescent behaviors; no matter the age of the characters.

THE FILM AND AUDIOVISUAL INDUSTRY

It is not that you cannot see adults behaving like that in real life (lamentably, you can) but, in broad terms, human beings should not be doing (use common sense) what characters in Hollywood movies are doing. This is called making the film "interesting." Sadly, you can extrapolate that to many other areas of the entertainment industry. The reasoning is that if fictional characters, actual singers, or celebrities of any kind behave in a rational, sensible, logical, and normal way, they would not be half as interesting as they are now (and not a fraction of how rich and famous they are).

But let us not deviate from the subject. Have you ever gotten angry while watching a movie? When characters do something so stupid that it ruins everything? That is what the author wanted (and we know it), but there is something in our brain that avoids such rationalization and it annoys us anyway. The audience's attention is so involved in the story that they feel powerless when these things happen. Once you have empathized with the characters, you will be frustrated if they cannot achieve their goal, or that their plans are not going as expected. These are all simple tricks that screenwriters do, traps placed right there to provoke the public's emotions; even at the cost of credibility or common sense. If you get the audience to feel certain emotions by using a few fictitious "facts," it means that you are doing something well. Fear, anger, frustration, etc. is the product of fulfilling a purpose: To entertain the audience.

Adults or youngsters with a certain degree of maturity get angry at that kind of nonsense. For example, there are many people who like music or cinema but hate a certain range of human behaviors. There are things they do not like to see or hear. There are people with a criteria that is different from the majority. They also despise specific art forms because of certain additional connotations involved (some styles of music, clothes, or other cultural features). This most demanding niche is focused on another type of literature, music, or cinema. However, they must accept with resignation that they are a minority. The mainstream production primarily targets the majority, which is totally unrelated to them. We have already seen that it is a simple question of profitability. Such a huge system cannot work to everyone's liking. You have to focus on the majority in order to make something profitable. It is important that the mainstream consumer is satisfied without thinking too much. However, those interested in the artistic part of entertainment should have their small portion covered. Their money is worth the same as everyone else's. The only problem is the gross income generated by them will be much less money than the majority's. It is that simple.

As mentioned in Chapter 1, the duality of art and the industry is inevitable. It is an objective fact that this is a pretty big industry. Many of you will have already noticed that almost all the peculiarities mentioned in this book are not because of the artistic side of it, but the business side. It is true that the entertainment industry has a certain social impact on our lives; but it is not as big and influential as many would like to think. It moves a lot of money around the world and, like many other businesses of this magnitude, politics rules in one way or another. The big fish of the industry (including stars as business people too) make their own economic contributions, show support, and participate in political campaigns. Even if quite tangentially, this industry is obviously related to government strategies of the highest level. Arts and culture, tourism, defense, industry, and labor. But the key takeaway is: "only quite tangentially." It is just entertainment. Although it can have some degree of influence on public opinion and be a useful tool of ideological promotion, it does not have any real and direct power to affect people. Nothing beyond the public transmission of messages and opinions (which is just regular propaganda). Their level of influence cannot even be elevated to the category of manipulation. They can obviously try (and sometimes more subtly than others), but beyond preaching to the audience, movies are just there to give people what they want to see. And this may include the ideological positioning of authors or just simple leisure and mundane entertainment.

THE FILM AND AUDIOVISUAL INDUSTRY

For a start, they are selling fiction, so their capacity to manipulate cannot be compared with the press or TV News. (Despite contradicting each other, the press is supposed to be selling reality, not fiction. As a result, someone is lying, if not all of them).

On the list of the 100 most powerful companies in the world, only one of them belongs to this industry: The Walt Disney Company. And it is not in a high position, despite being much more than a production and distribution company. (It is also the studio with the highest worth by far, but not as close to a trillion dollars like Apple, Microsoft, Google, or Amazon.) Nowadays, the world is ruled by the will of technological, financial, chemical, food, and transportation companies (without taking into account illegal markets, of course). Hollywood majors, like their foreign equivalents (the Chinese protectionist giant and the Indian Bollywood), may seem to be huge corporations with excessive power and control capacity; but moving several billions a year only gives them power and control over what they produce, which is entertainment content. They are private companies after all, and everyone works for someone. As stated previously, film studios (as well as the biggest television networks) belong to big news corporations: Time, News, Viacom, Comcast, and Disney (do not forget that they are the new owners of Fox News). It makes sense that every group would focus on their own task. Some of them try to change people's mindset while others just try to take economic advantage of the mindset that people already have.

There are also cases where the whole industry belongs directly to the government, as in China or India. In Chapter 2 we mentioned, in regard to distribution and exhibition, the idea that companies from all continents are beginning to collaborate with each other in a convenient symbiosis. Co-productions with a blockbuster spirit are totally compatible with both markets (doubling the potential benefits). Beyond the differences and similarities between cultures, it is impossible to avoid having the modernization of some countries end up "westernizing" their societies.

THE FILM AND AUDIOVISUAL INDUSTRY

The natural tendency of every film industry is to reflect its own society first, then look outside. And it is precisely in social transformations where the entertainment industry can contribute some of its influence. In society's small habits, in people's behavior, in the attitude towards life and in the aspirations for the future. Movies, songs, books, and art inspire us. It affects us and provokes reactions that we often did not even expect. In this new era of communication, audiovisuals serve to bring and merge different cultures, more than ever before. Perhaps through fiction stories on screen or due to the number of professionals traveling around the world to find a job in this business. As we begin the next chapter, we want to point out that it is truly difficult to enter such a complicated industry. But, even if the number of competitors multiplies exponentially, the range of possibilities is also extended to the whole planet, so the chances of success are higher.

THE FILM AND AUDIOVISUAL INDUSTRY

GETTING INTO THE INDUSTRY

If you are lucky enough to be one of the few professionals that will work in this industry, it will probably be after lots of trying. You may also have other, previous work experience in life. But, if you start working in the film industry very young, even as your first job, be careful, because things might become too difficult, too soon. Coping with everything at the same time is, as they say, what happens when bad meets evil. It will be even harder to learn, understand, improve, and, of course, succeed. Throughout life we all define our personalities little by little. As we live experiences, we set goals and interests and along the way, hobbies will rise and fall. Some try to make a living out of them, while others define their priorities on the sidelines.

Taking into account the fact that everyone needs a job to survive, many people are satisfied just having any type of job (one that is more or less pleasant, bearable, or even painful) in exchange for the financial support they need. No one will become a millionaire living like this, but sometimes one may not have many other options. In childhood we are often asked to think about our dream job. Even though there is a lot of childish naivety in those first reflections, sometimes you can perceive certain abilities that when well directed, can contribute to making your dreams come true. Unfortunately, there is a hard road ahead. At some point, all young people suffer with that inner struggle between the dreamer's optimism and the inherent realist's pessimism.

Much has been said about the major challenge that millennials are facing in the current job market. Just like it was discussed with Generation X and will be discussed with the next one. The generational replacement can never be generalized. Are all young people better prepared than the adults of their time? Maybe worse? Are they all lazy slobs who do not appreciate what they have? If that were true, how could humankind evolve faster and better with every new generation? It is not a coincidence that everything said about new generations has already been said before by those who support society at that time. That does not make the cyclical paradigm stop, but at least it means that there is hope.

Typically, young people face their first job with absolute ignorance, due to the poor information they receive on the subject. The little information they have is probably messy and confusing and what is worse is that the amount of distractions that bombard them prevents them from seeing the origin of the problem with clarity. We all grow up and mature at different speeds and the reality of the world is being presented to us in different forms. So, when finally playing in the real world, kids are completely exposed without any assistance. They are used to having everything already done for them, in their comfortable world of streaming tutorials and easy clicks. Life does not come with a user's manual, but it is also very easy to criticize the ignorance of a whole generation when no one takes the time to explain how something works and why. Your only option is to find out for yourself. This brings us back to the subject of this chapter and, ultimately, the whole book.

The relationship between the academic world and the work world is a good example of this. Having grown up under the promise that your studies will provide a good job, no one notices that even in university, the only thing you can do is gain knowledge. That is necessary to work in your future profession, for sure; but our education never includes clear information about how the real industry works inside each professional field. Firstly, because that is not exactly their primary function and secondly because no one wants to get their hands dirty with this issue. Why do we lie to children, young people, and society in general about how the world actually works? Because no one wants to be the one who destroy the hopes and illusions of people. Let each one see the truth of things when they do. So that no one is responsible. What is the result? Clean hands. Clear consciences.

It is easy to get used to having what you want, as long as others are paying for it. But when you must use your own money, things are a bit different. The employer is the one who has the upper hand because obviously, money rules. "Do you want my money? Well, work for me. And if you do not like the conditions, perfect. I will find someone who needs it more than you."

No company will change their workflow to accommodate you (much less an entire industry). You can believe that you are unique, an extremely valuable worker, and you may even be really good at what you do, but no one needs you as much as you think. This may hurt a lot. We have had two decades of advertising and marketing companies exploiting young people's ego, like we have never seen before (and it has been taken to the nth degree with social networks). To make matters worse, many are deceived by the reductionist idealism that big benchmarks promote. Multi-million-dollar companies allow their employees to arrive and leave at any time they want, decorate their work areas as they want, or stop working to play video games whenever they want; not everyone can do this, so the debate would ask the question: Is this motivational or frustrating for other companies? The corporate culture responds to its own logic, where everything has to do with productivity, i.e. performance results. But economic profitability is, above all, a direct consequence. Feeling at ease and relaxed at work can make you more productive, but every passing hour is an attack against profitability (the company spends more but gets less in return). Any expense that is not strictly necessary to developing activity is a waste. In that sense, it is a miracle that companies even have free water or coffee machines. So you should be careful when expecting a game room with a pool or ping-pong tables, a foosball machine, and a super fun slide instead of elevators.

We said that believing you are special, better than others, or absolutely essential, is a deadly trap for the workers of this new millennium. As mentioned in Chapter 3: "Economy and Law," the audiovisual industry generates few and mostly temporary jobs; so getting a job may be pretty hard (imagine a good one). We highly recommend doing some deep soul searching before facing this complex professional world. Above all, you must thoroughly revise that capricious and arrogant attitude that today's young people boast about as if it were valuable. There is a big difference between self-affirmation and an excessive ego. And do not forget, if there is anything we have too much of in this industry, it is ego.

The number of applicants is higher than the number of jobs available, so competing is the only way to make it. It is not exactly a fierce battle but, as in any job offer, when someone covers a vacancy, it means that everyone else loses an opportunity. Logically, for positions with greater responsibility such as directors, actors, or screenwriters it is more difficult to compete, unlike profiles that are based on the conformation of larger teams. Many more opportunities are given to technicians, supervisors, designers, animators, task managers, or assistants.

The more successful you are, the more work you will get. And as long as you keep guaranteeing success, it will not stop. This is how the wheel works for the lucky few who can manage it. However, given that even consummate professionals may be waiting for years to work on a movie again, you can imagine the number of available opportunities there are for new talent.

THE FILM AND AUDIOVISUAL INDUSTRY

The competition is such that most applicants, in all areas, are reduced to beginners who achieve nothing and only a few professionals that are gaining experience with independent productions. With some luck, they stay active in the audiovisual sector, which means a lot. Because there are very few who can finally enjoy that maximum level of recognition with huge salaries, parallel business, luxurious comforts, and the VIP treatment. (That coveted standard of living that is definitely above average.)

Take it one step at a time. Before anything else, you have to make it clear who needs whom. Any professional, artistic or not, could argue that companies are nothing without their workers. You could extrapolate that to the entire sector and beg the question, who will produce movies if no one is there to make them? (The basic concept of a strike.) However, reality immediately imposes itself. Employment is an essential condition for adult life. It is the professional who needs the job to survive (ideally a permanent job or something sporadic but lucrative). On the contrary, any producer or executive has a great job and, in many cases, does not need it because of their high purchasing power.

To think that employers are the needy ones is tempting and naive. They may need actors, screenwriters, directors, technicians and the such; but never forget that there are hundreds, thousands, and even millions of perfectly capable applicants out there, just like you. Why choose you? You may actually feel lucky just appearing on a possible shortlist.

Among the mass of beginners, some give up because they cannot find a way to get into the industry; but among the ones that do, sooner or later they realize that nothing is what they expected. It has always been said that it is important to maintain a positive and optimistic attitude (as any beginner does). The problem is, being optimistic because you are naive has no merit at all. And once you find out that your dream is not what you thought it was, it may not be worth it.

THE FILM AND AUDIOVISUAL INDUSTRY

As we discussed earlier, these professions are usually vocational (so the terms "dream" and "desire" are often used when talking about them). It is easy to daydream and see yourself succeeding, but it is just a reverie. We see celebrities that we admire or envy on TV and replace them with our own image. Simple. But all that must happen so that the dream can materialize is not that easy, because we often do not know what to do to get there.

We always talk about that "opportunity" that someone has to give you and it seems that everything comes down to waiting for it to happen. It is typical for successful people to say that the most important thing is to never give up, to keep trying tirelessly. Taking into account the tremendous effort that this entails, it is true. It will be even harder to get anything without some initiative and real passion. But that has nothing to do with the fact that a few fortunate people can reach the highest fame and recognition comfortably and effortlessly. There is no need to hide this. Some people get lucky. People who are offered work in this industry without looking for it, and even without being especially interested in it, are just lucky. (As much as there are many people who reject such offers, it is not that crazy).

No one has said that everyone here is competing on equal terms or has the same possibilities. Quite the contrary. There are prejudices, favoritism, compromises, and subjective selection factors, plus might we add, simple coincidence. There is no magic or scientific formula to apply. It is best not to delude yourself, effort may imply a reward, but it has never been, is, or will be, an automatic guarantee. The closest thing to the formula for success is the famous quote: "Being in the right place at the right time."

As we will see in later chapters, the only factor that can be measurable is how much your specific profile is aligned (or not) with the particular requirements that the industry demands, depending on the job. And regardless of what your background and previous experience say, your professional and interpersonal skills will be put to the test. Because not everyone is cut out to work in such a "special" industry.

THE FILM AND AUDIOVISUAL INDUSTRY

Assuming the best possible scenario, imagine that people from the industry start calling you because they want you for this and that. We are sure that you remember watching a movie or television episode where there is a classic situation of a young character who has dreams of being some kind of artist. There are always two variants for this. The first is that the character is looking for representation (it is the artist who has the need) or it is an agent or manager who offers their services to the character because they are attracted by his or her talent (it is the talent-hunter who sees the opportunity to make a profit from artist's skills). In this chapter we will see how this double path works and how it is actually only one-way. The industry has its own mechanisms to get to you, if they want you, but you have no way of interacting with them—if you are not invited to do so.

Of course, you can send your resume and a "demo" with your work to the most important agencies in the country (just look up their email and addresses on the internet). They may call you and sign you up with them. Then you may pass an audition and get the job of your life—all in a few weeks (yes, this could actually happen). Nevertheless, the agency will be the one to call you, offer something for you to sign, and give you work. Let us highlight the contradiction: Managers and agents may work for you, but you cannot go out there and "hire" them. Each of them, even the most mediocre, is more inside the industry than you. They will decide if they spend their time representing you, or not.

AGENTS AND MANAGERS

To begin with, it is essential to clarify the difference between an agent and a manager. Most people do not know the difference and often use both words synonymously. We will see that there may be situations where the tasks of one and the tasks of the other intersect; to the point where both jobs can be performed by the same person. But it is important to understand what makes them different.

THE FILM AND AUDIOVISUAL INDUSTRY

These two professionals are the most basic units of the team that any artist might have throughout their entire career. We will mention other possible members of their personal entourage but, no matter its size, communication and understanding between all parts are fundamental, especially since none of them are physically working together in an office.

At first, it may seem that having many people around each artist may be excessive or unnecessary, but creating one of these teams as soon as possible is the first thing to do with each newcomer. Otherwise, an artist cannot focus on the real work and at the same time, always be available as a point of contact for the industry. But not only that, let us dive deeper into why these "public relations" profiles are so necessary, starting with agents. They could be considered the most important members of the team because they are usually the ones who get you jobs within the industry. (In fact that is the exact definition of their job.) It is not that unknown artists who are just starting their careers cannot be compensated for a job they found on their own (an independent film or a television show through an open casting). But when someone's talent really draws attention, the most immediate effect is that one starts receiving calls from various agents offering their representation services. If you are good enough to find an agent, then other companies or projects will not offer you more jobs directly. Everyone will begin asking who represents you. In fact, most likely it will be someone from that first job (even from the casting director themselves) who will recommend you to an agent from their trusted contacts.

Over the last hundred years, the industry has been developing a structure too large and convoluted to be able to operate with simplicity. And one of its most efficient achievements, adopted from the business world, is the perfection of a communication system that provides a guaranteed reliability, organization, and margin of discretion for all parties involved. Fundamentally, this means that there is a certain way of doing things. Conduct codes, procedures, and best practices that you must learn and respect.

THE FILM AND AUDIOVISUAL INDUSTRY

But do not expect to find them in a manual or any wise and dedicated master guide. We are talking about the famous "unwritten rules." A series of formulas to communicate that will make things run either smoothly (or not) from the beginning. Something that can only be learned based on experience and personal ability.

As in many other industries, an essential part of these professions depends directly on the interaction with others. Direct treatment and informal "proximity" are not the most appropriate (or safe at a physical level) ways of dealing with certain issues. For these things, distance is always advisable and necessary. Many people may tell you the opposite in person, but it is only one of the many contradictory fallacies you will have to hear if you are invited to this crazy circus. (You will see a lot of people hugging, smiling, and praising each other while you know that they hate each other.)

Agents have a double function. They work in both directions. They bring the industry closer to the represented artists, while at the same time, build a wall between the artists and people of hierarchy. Do not forget that the art world is one of the most elite circles for excellence. In the golden age of Hollywood, a new and peculiar hybrid between two very different circles of influence was created. A hybrid between artists and intellectuals and businessmen and investors.

To visualize this, let us look at this example. One of these snob executives would never call an artist directly to communicate that he or she has been chosen for a project. Just as an artist does not pick up the phone to call this type of executive and ask if they have something to offer or how the project is progressing. There must be intermediaries dedicated to doing all that. People who pave the way and relax the tense competitive relationship implied in this complex job search. It may not be very pleasant for an artist to lose a great role at the last minute, after months of conversations, trips, meetings, and after having rejected many other roles for this one. Would you like to call that artist or deliver such big news in person?

Ironically, regarding this prevailing snobbery at the highest levels (also millionaire, influential or trendy stars), there may be some interest, convenience, or personal whim that makes an executive make such a phone call in person. At a certain point it might happen that they want to add this factor of closeness. Eating with a star (consummate or rising star), inviting them home, or enjoying the same possible hobbies. Even if they are pretending, the strategic interest of that close relationship could be the key to having the star in your production and on board.

This could mean a difference of many millions in benefits. However, although personal phone calls may occur at the highest levels of fame, it does not mean that artists can negotiate work directly, without any representation. No matter how famous actors, screenwriters, or directors are, agents are the direct contact of any artist for the other side of the industry, and that is mandatory. Artists cannot represent themselves.

Agents are a fundamental piece in any artistic career, even if you look at them as a mere communication bridge. Their job is to make your name known at the highest levels. To show your work and make sure those who make the decisions know who you are, remember you, and consider you as an option among the many other possible options (all with their corresponding agents doing the same for them). This is a constant competition and, as we see all the time, subject to many determinants that escape you and your agent's control.

It might be interesting to mention that agents usually do not work independently. The most profitable formula is to have an agency, that is consolidated as a company, have several employees or associates. That way an artist is exclusively represented by the agency and can be assigned to one agent or another (usually the same one who brought that artist to the agency). Even beginners and agents working at modest production levels often resort to this partnership formula as soon as they can.

THE FILM AND AUDIOVISUAL INDUSTRY

The most traditional model of the old, independent agent continues existing even at the highest level outside of the United States. In countries with smaller industries it works in a similar way, however less organized. There are also a few agencies, but independent agents are just people who, for whatever reason, have all the necessary contacts to introduce and keep their represented artists inside show business. They can make recommendations, bring members of the industry in contact, and even act as a direct influence on important decisions. This power can be given by personal friendships, favors, or just simple convenience like making a casting process faster or easier. We will not discuss the more reprehensible reasons, but it is interesting that now everyone can finally fearlessly comment on how show business people are doing certain things in exchange for favors (some of them are consensual while others are non-consensual).

In small industries with fewer people working on this, everyone knows each other even closer than they do in Hollywood. In fact, it is very common for independent agents (here and anywhere in the world) to be quite eccentric. Fully aware of their privileged situation, they can afford the luxury of carrying certain stigmas and acting in certain ways. In some cases, they transform themselves into true media celebrities (something that eventually ends up affecting their careers and the careers of the artists they represent).

As for an agent's compensation, the standard is usually between 10% and 15% of any income obtained by the artist, usually with a maximum fixed by law. Each industry has its own standards and regulations. Within the legal framework, agents and artists can mutually agree on all the conditions in writing. And if you are wondering, when there is no income, there is no payment commitment either (exactly, there is no cost in being represented). Actually, the intriguing part is, how do you know if your agent is actually working for you? Is he fighting for you? Is he or she a good agent? Unfortunately, it is impossible to get answers to these questions. Even if you have not been working for a whole year does not necessarily mean that you or your agent have not been actively looking for jobs. In fact it is quite the contrary, both of you may have been fighting tirelessly for them.

The norm is to sign a contract with exclusivity for a specific period of time (1 year, 3 years, or 5 years). It may happen that artists are tempted by other agents that try to make them change their minds and switch. It will be considered a dirty move, but this practice is part of the game. Besides, in case your agency is really interested in not losing you, these situations might even put an interesting counteroffer on the table.

Here are a few different reasons to change your agent (no matter if you are a beginner or a star): Because you want to share a smaller percentage of benefits, because you think the lack of jobs is your agent's fault, because of a bad streak of low-quality offers or jobs, the suspicion that other artists from the same agency are being favored over you, perhaps a bad relationship between both parties, or maybe the promise of more and better jobs (this typically happens when they already have a specific offer on the table which tempts you to change). As a "dirty move," the decent thing to do would be for an agent to recruit an artist knowing that they are not happy and that he or she is already thinking about changing agents or agency.

It is true that Hollywood's great productions always look for talent at the most prestigious agencies (there are not many big agencies anymore because so many of them are disappearing or merging). These companies are already taking care of their own interests, by making sure that they have the best artists working with them. As well as the biggest possible number of new faces. New talent that suddenly rises. (They could be young or old, inexperienced, or bring relevant success from other countries or the independent scene.) The most common thing agencies do is prepare and offer, to the production companies, a complete package of a director, screenwriter, and actors for a project. The more you can include, the more facilities you are given from possible investors and executives of the studios. Although, no one blames them for trying to put as many artists from their agency as they can in the same project, sometimes the proposals do not make much sense.

And now let us talk about the manager's work. In general, managers are people who have knowledge of each and every one of show business' ins and outs, not only in regard to work; therefore, they represent the artist in a much broader sense. Thanks to their personal experience, they offer their services as a spokesperson, counselor, and manager to the most diverse aspects of the artist's personal life; as long as that area can be affected by working in this peculiar industry.

Considering what "representation" means, managers can primarily speak on behalf of the represented artists. So we can say, in short, that the manager-agent binomial is a joint force created to manage the artist's career, acting on their behalf within the industry. Like we said before, that mandatory distance between members of any business conversation must work in both directions. Like two sides of the same coin, it can be in favor or against the artists, depending on the moment of their careers. When an artist receives hundreds of calls and offers, it is the representation team that manages, organizes, and passes them on to the artist in an orderly manner, according to priority and convenience. Nevertheless, in cases where the artist does not receive offers (although the manager and agent both work for the artist on paper), there is very little an artist can do about this; except change representation, as we stated before, if the artist thinks it is their fault.

Managers also demand to represent artists exclusively. Even if they are also often associated with partnership models, like agents do, in this case, the independent profile is more common. In many cases it is to the extent that they are relatives or close acquaintances with a more or less knowledge of the industry. This may lead to not doing their job as well as a guild professional would, but it is not completely pointless. These responsibilities are related to the daily personal life of people, and how it is affected by the industry itself (mostly because of fame and money). Sometimes it is about professional issues and sometimes it is personal, so it is also very useful to know the artist's life very well (their relationship with their manager is closer, so the closer the better). As a result, depending on the type of life the represented artist decides to live, and how much the manager decides to actively be involved, work can either be hectic or relaxed. The responsibility of a good manager is, at least, to have enough knowledge and experience to advise the artist wisely, in the most convenient way for his or her career. If they are also able to avoid problems or solve them as they occur, the artists will be more than happy and will feel as if they are in good hands.

Strictly and legally speaking, managers should not be able to get a job for the artists; since that is agents' job and could be considered an overlapping intrusion (unless they obtain their own agent license, of course). But as long as there is proper understanding and tacit consent, it is not bad for the manager, and even the artists themselves, to try and find as many jobs as possible (intentionally or not). There is no problem, as long as every new opportunity is transferred to the agent when it becomes official. In other words, when it comes time to convert that into real work, via a regular workflow. Everyone on the representation team will be obtaining their corresponding percentage from the future incomes of the artist. So, with this system everything is fine, right? Provided that respect and collaboration limits are appropriately established among the team members, the more active and dynamic they are the better. (By the way, the percentage of a manager is also negotiable and usually involves the same standard as agents).

Being pragmatic, an agent or manager that is not very well known or who works alone will be quite useless to newcomers (and this is without mentioning if they are legit industry workers or not). Fortunately, nowadays it is very easy to inquire information about the person you are dealing with on the internet. Things like their past achievements, represented artists, and even financial solvency. It is easy to know the reliability and position of any professional in the sector and, fortunately, it is more difficult to be a victim in a typical fraud or abuse cases, in regards to the early stages.

Contrary to what many people think, you actually do not need a manager when you are outside of the industry. As an amateur or semi-professional artist, you do not have to worry about finding representation, because you do not have a decent professional career to be represented yet. When you grab the industry's attention, they are the ones who will find you. And if you are good, you can be sure they will find you.

Managers can represent a very small number of artists at the same time (maybe only one), while agents can represent many more, especially when they are associated with a large agency and have their own assistants. In fact, when artists think about all this, they usually find the classic dilemma of a conflict of interest. What happens when agents have to favor one of their artists over another? By default, they seek to have customers with the greatest possible variety of profiles. However, taking into account the thousands and thousands of projects trying to get produced every year, and the minimum amount that become solid job opportunities, it is an unlikely coincidence that such internal competition may happen (and in any case, it would be just one of those things that is out of your control).

We stated before that agents and managers can be the same person, especially at a local level. But it also happens quite often that the artists must have different representatives in different territories around the world. Experience dictates that if an artist has to choose between an offer coming from an American production company or any other offer in the world (including his or her own country of origin) they will usually prefer working in Hollywood. It is the most reasonable option due to money (obviously), but each artist is free to decide their own professional strategy, thinking of their career.

In fact, for an American representation team, the percentage of income they would get for such small productions would not compensate for the effort (and time) needed to invest in positioning themselves in foreign industries. Places where, to begin with, they would be considered intruders by the elite circles of each country.

ENTOURAGE

There are many other additional activities that artists have to delegate to third parties. Due to the specificity of the field, at a certain level of fame and money, it is impossible for a manager (or for the artist themselves) to manage.

An attorney is a classic example. It is evident that entertainment attorneys are specialized in film and audiovisual laws, as well as in a majority of matters related to the "busy" life these artists are living. Apart from advising, supervising, and negotiating the conditions of the contract for each project, they are prepared to cope with divorces, debt claims, defamation complaints, image rights, and anything else you can demand financial compensation for (or avoid having to pay for). There is not a defined percentage to be shared, and it will have to be negotiated. Attorney services can be offered per hours of work or income percentage; which can range from 5% to 45%, depending on how useful that person is in saving your ass (so the prestige of both parties in their respective area could be a relevant factor).

In business, everything is about making contacts and everyone is connected at some point. So on the representation team, even the attorney can get a potential job opportunity for the artist. He or she can be an indispensable member of the team although, ideally, apart from the standard contractual consultations, it will be a good thing not to have to use your attorney often. The downside is that, in this industry, problems arise where and when you do not expect them.

THE FILM AND AUDIOVISUAL INDUSTRY

There are people who think that large, million-dollar studios will never delay a payment, will make a mistake in accounting, or will break the clauses of a signed agreement. And you can be sure they will. That is the time to use your attorney. No one wants to pay for a lost lawsuit because you do not count on a specialist in the sector, right?

Artists can also delegate money management, tax payments, and all of their assets to their attorney or the attorney's law firm, as well as hire a personal accountant. This is especially useful if you also have separate assets or companies, or when you start to handle significant amounts of money. On the other hand, everyone understands it is not easy to put your professional career (not to mention your personal fortune) in the hands of so many other people. There is always a dangerous, potential risk of losing control, little by little, over life itself. And there are many who feel too much pressure, insecurity, and fear in this regard.

When achieving certain levels of stardom, other activities that should be delegated to specialists are your public image and publicity. Although managers can find and coordinate interviews and publicity coverage of the artist in general, with some degree of success, there comes a time when a publicist will get better results in an easier way.

Of course, you are also free to choose the way you dress and your haircut or hairstyle, as well as you can be advised by your manager or your publicist. But you can also choose to hire a professional stylist with celebrity experience. As experts on the subject, they will be more aware of the impact caused by your decisions in your public image and in your career.

In short, artists will have to start surrounding themselves with a greater number of people, as long as their popularity is becoming more powerful and influential. There are many other minor tasks that managers can do for their artists, depending on how close and committed they are (either by being a rising star or precisely for having already succeeded). For example, they can travel together, attend important meetings together, do personal favors, errands, and appointments, drive them here and there, etc. Although all that is what personal assistants are there for, there are always artists who like to keep doing things by themselves. But once you have a certain economic solvency, it is tempting to have others work for you.

This is exhibited in the television series *Entourage*. The series exploits a typical premise in the entertainment industry. We watch beginners' dreams materialize. (Actors, directors, singers, etc.) The main character enjoys success and fame while he is young, accompanied by a gang of friends. Regardless of the position assigned, it is true that your family and friends can be your personal assistants, your driver, your manager, your publicist, your stylist, or whatever you want them to be. Everyone wins with such a lifestyle. Close family and friends are the most loyal employees you can hire. And at the same time, it is the perfect way of consistently seeing the people you love if you were to become successful and your life were to change forever.

Entourage is fiction, exaggerated, and superficial with some details, but the series' content reflects how the Hollywood industry naturally functions in a fairly reliable way. (This was the goal of its creator and producer, the A-list actor Mark Wahlberg.) In order to be interesting for the audience, the series shows the protagonist's perspective. An artist with desires and illusions, like any other professional in the sector. But the key to understanding how hard the early stages are, is hardly found in the series. It is the correlation between the active role and the passive role that artists play in their own careers. This character's story is supposed to be a story that every student or beginner should be able to identify with. The show begins with the protagonist already inside the industry; however, it does not explain how the character got into the industry, how convenient.

Nobody in the industry is ever going to give you real, specific details about how they got into the business. Firstly, because it is probably not an interesting or funny story (more likely, it is a boring or really long story, maybe a little depressing), and secondly because it would just involve too many explanations and clarifications about how this "special" industry works. How incredibly subjective, capricious, unstable, and surreal it can be (basically, what this book uncovers).

We already said that one of the biggest problems in the industry is the number of artists and projects that decision makers have on their tables every day. So, let us examine this from the office side. The place where even the biggest stars are just one more piece of the puzzle inside the puzzle factory. The decisions made are complex. All of them will end up having consequences and there is a lot of money at stake. However, at the same time they are simple. In the case that one piece does not fit, just try it with another piece and that is all. And if it is still not working, after many attempts, (exactly like a spoiled kid's tantrum) they can always throw the puzzle away and pick a new one from the desk. After all, that is why their drawers are full of puzzles, puzzle pieces, and anything else they might need. (That is also the advantage being puzzle factory owners, right?)

To conclude, we will mention the relatively recent case of "internet celebrities." This new trend that caught everyone by surprise, looks like a great alternative to the old way of understanding show business. They enjoy the freedom and autonomy of doing and saying what they want, provided they respect the rules of the online platforms where they publish their videos. But the reality is, if average Youtubers, Instagramers, and similar influencers want to reach "the next level" (having similar revenues as entertainment idols and stars), they need artistic representation, just like any other artist in the industry (even if the market window is internet only).

With a little luck and a good strategy, it is relatively easy to gain a considerable amount of fame (however, primarily among younger audiences, that is also true) and obtain decent incomes from advertising. But these revenues are still at a level far below what the real world of entertainment can manage. Many may be satisfied with such earnings, at least until the business model or audience's tastes change again. (There is no doubt that that will also happen to them at some point.) But who would not want to get to the next level if you have the opportunity?

When these "artists" are unknown, to be successful they have to draw the public's attention directly. However, in the case of the traditional industry, you only have to draw the attention of a small circle of people who make a distinctive decision. Thus, by controlling the media (cinema, television, radio, and written press) you can decide who is popular and who is not. You decide who is chosen and the fate of their careers. But, what about this new kind of celebrity? Those whose fame comes from regular people. Everything is about rewarding homemade reality: It is immediate, random fame that may occur overnight and is impossible to predict. You cannot have any control over what the public likes or dislikes. There is no selection filter. No intermediary between the author and the audience. The only thing the industry can do, is not to grant these regular people access to the next level of fame... unless they want it.

Only, in case it is decided that the internet celebrity has enough potential to be next-level famous (potentially profitable enough), the internet would act as a springboard. But from a contractual perspective, it would just be an exchange of sides. Hence the importance of taking them to the "right side" as soon as possible. This is done so that these new celebrities do not develop excessive independence. As usual, it is important that no one challenges the established order and it is even more important that internet stars do not challenge it too much (you know, just in case).

At the end of the day, it is not complicated to tempt any of these kids to change their side, since money can buy everything in this world. Plus, the internet and social media contribute to the reach and influence of traditional entertainment much more than causing damage. At an artistic level, this fame is not even based on any concrete quality work, but rather the creator's natural charisma.

THE FILM AND AUDIOVISUAL INDUSTRY

This phenomenon is closer to the television world. Any kind of additional income will always come from advertising and sponsorships (remember that television and the internet will continue to coexist separately for only a few more years, until they are pretty much merged). Money always comes from the same place, the business sector. So to conclude this section on artist's representation, no one from the elite division is going to talk directly to one of these teen Youtubers. No matter how much ego a kid has. It will be a mere speck of dust compared to the egos of the people who will pay him to advertise their brand, no matter what kind of business it is. For that to happen, a talent agency must first contact the kid (probably even his parents) for them to be professionally represented with proper negotiation. And if everything goes well, they would be able to get the Youtuber other forms of income that on their own, they would never had known existed.

Because it does not matter what kind of artist you are, everything depends on that call. The official confirmation that you have been looking forward to. You could be looking for months or even years for the next job, asking around everywhere for opportunities and negotiating hundreds of possible deals without a break. And still, no victory call. Then on a day like any other, the phone rings and someone offers you that perfect job that you were not expecting.

COMMUNICATION: THE MEANING OF WORDS

Everything is connected in this industry. And the biggest advantage of this is that any possible path that you could have possibly taken, has already been taken and has been optimized over the last century by hundreds and hundreds of people before you. Everything has been standardized in a totally natural way, so that everything flows easily, almost automatically. All artists choose their own, individual paths that is presented in front of them. Not everyone knows how to walk down each path though.

THE FILM AND AUDIOVISUAL INDUSTRY

Considering the lack of guarantees in this sector, when we think of a "stable" job in show business, it is assumed that we are talking about payments that are equal to any other good salary, in any other area, except condensed. (You can earn half a million dollars for a movie, but wait six years before filming the next one.) The only ways of getting a full and sustainable livelihood are permanent positions in solid companies or big opportunities of fame, which can only come from film and television. And, in order to maintain decent continuity, it is absolutely essential that you maintain the level of quality in your work.

In any other circumstances, it is really hard to consider any job in this industry as truly stable. Even working sporadically but with certain frequency, it is easy to get stuck with a low relevance profile: small parts, commercials, and low budget productions. That is why the most common thing is to have other alternative sources of income, to make a living or simply to live better; actually, even some renowned artists do this.

The truth is, the deeper into this industry you get, the more you move away from a normal life. It is inevitable. Success in films and TV is not compatible with having the same regular life that normal people have. A clear example of this is how basic human interaction can drastically change. Take communication for example, speaking clearly and concisely is obviously the best way to interact with others. Understanding and being understood. Emitting and receiving messages. Pretty basic, is not it?

Likewise, truth is understood as something tangible and verifiable. According to its literal definition, truth is: "Those affirmations in concordance with the real facts about a situation, event, or person." It is not in vain (according to all the etymologies and interpretations for the word "truth"). In past and present cultures and philosophies, truths are "reliable" because they can be verified in reality. Even if some facts coincide, or not, with what you were told about it. Keeping it plain and simple, anyone can tell you that truth always comes from concepts like honesty, good faith, or sincerity. So then, the first question would be: Could we deduce that lying starts from the opposite concepts?

THE FILM AND AUDIOVISUAL INDUSTRY

As we have seen page after page, the first step to understanding this industry is to accept that you cannot apply the criteria and value judgments you may have from your previous life. You cannot judge some particular mechanics from a partial and incomplete view, without first knowing exactly how it works and what the purpose is; or without knowing the points of view and objectives of those people using said mechanisms. Once you know all that, then you are allowed to judge as much as you want. Show business' falsehood and fickleness is well known to all. It is something that, in turn, derives mainly from social classism and personal vanity. Envy, hubris, and grudges have always been a fundamental part of life in the upper social classes. They do not know any other way to be.

The imperative need to always be above others and to have more things than others (even if it is only pretend), is complemented by the self-demand of being idolized, desired, and envied by others. That haughty superiority that is innate to the rich and powerful comes together with the most sophisticated forms. Excellent formal treatment, cordial and affable, which does not really mean anything except what we already pointed out: The simplistic ostentation of their status. Before a new member is allowed to enter these select circles, it is necessary to confirm the candidate's acceptability. It is essential to make sure that his or her behavior matches with the rest.

If there is any doubt, cordiality is the law in business. It is the only language that you are allowed to use for business, as in any other working environment. No matter what kind of personality people may have, anyone trying to do business with the show business elite is expected to use a calm, respectful, and polite tone. If possible, with a halo of glamor, sophistication, and elegance that proves that you deserve to be among them. Interestingly, due to the egos, quarrels, personal problems, and miseries that many celebrities and rich people have, (since they are just people like you and me) it is not rare to find some of them going from sophistication to eccentricity and overconfidence to abuse.

THE FILM AND AUDIOVISUAL INDUSTRY

There are many people who take the liberty of speaking and acting abruptly and unpleasant, making others feel uncomfortable. It is classic that whoever has the money and power is the one who behaves inappropriately, loses their way, or crosses some line. And needless to mention, are those who display inappropriate sexual misconduct with young actresses, just to give a popular example. These are things that everyone has been silent about, and even tried to justify (for a whole century), as a "classic" abuse of power. Sadly, it does not help erase the thin red line that separates these abuses from the dirty gray area of consented sexual favors (as they exist in many other areas of our society, whether we want to admit it or not).

Nothing justifies certain behaviors, especially the criminal ones, but one way or another, this behavior is about letting you know who the boss is at all times. That is the deal. You do not get the privilege of getting into the elite unless someone from the inside invites you. You can get kicked out as easily as you got in. If there is someone in particular that you do not want to have anything to do with, there are always ways of dodging them while you wait for other job opportunities, right? Easier said than done, no doubt. "What would I do under certain circumstances?" That is what you should ask yourself if you want to enter such a sketchy business. Because once the game of lies, reasonable doubts, half-truths, and infinite excuses begin, it never ends. And do not forget that it works both ways. Endless falsehoods and ambiguity can work against you but also in your favor, if you know how to do it. It is a valuable (and risky) double-edged sword.

Once you enter the dark side (if that is your choice) you will have to play by their rules. Never forget that they own the game board. Rule number one is to make sure that it is not you who loses your manners. The most important thing, above all else, is to never offend anyone (never ever). If you are going to say something about someone in this industry, you better say good things. Otherwise, it is best to say nothing. If you pay attention, most conversations are always positive and hopeful; full of promises, good intentions, and great news (at the very least informative, but never completely bad). This should mean a high percentage of successful collaborations, right? But nothing could be more untrue. Only a small percentage of hundreds and hundreds of conversations held throughout the year will materialize into fruitful business. Make no mistake, cordiality and positivity in conversations are not signs of anything in particular. It is just a healthy standard, that is all.

Imagine if artists, agents, and executives were to constantly show their subjective feelings about the uncertainties of their job. Or if they were to scream, cry, insult, threaten, or take vengeance against others. It is fun to show all of that in the movies, to make them interesting. But, yelling at an executive or crying in front of them would not be very smart. We have already insisted several times that only a negligible number of projects on the table get the go ahead. As a consequence, all of the hypothetical jobs that must be created per movie (including yours as an actor, director, or whatever else), depend on that same green light. So, this is one of the first things every beginner will gradually realize. Everyone else in the industry knows perfectly well that if your chances of getting the job are so small, why should you have a negative attitude in every conversation you have, for every project? It is also necessary to understand that in the moment, in one simple conversation among many others, no one can know what will happen to a project over time. Maybe it will become a top box-office attraction and make everyone happy. No one knows yet. Uncertainty is applicable by default.

No one will know for months or even years. You could receive good news at any moment. Perhaps they greenlit your project, bought your script, or gave you that role that you were fighting for. It is always nice to pick up the phone and talk about things like that. But you do not want to receive bad news, and definitely no one in the industry wants to give you bad news. So, what do you do? The answer is simple: remove the bad news. That is the most basic unwritten rule of the business.

THE FILM AND AUDIOVISUAL INDUSTRY

Always keep a positive attitude to make everyone feel more comfortable, even if it is fake. Everyone in this business has the intention of making films. Movies are what this industry produces, so it is not about rejecting projects just for fun. Only a few of them are selected while many others are not. It is the slowness of the process and the dying hope that makes it impossible to predict the future status of any project.

The cluster of circumstances and coincidences needed to succeed are extremely complex and random. Therefore, once you have done all that you can (as a tiny piece of the puzzle), the only thing you can do is wait for that last phone call. That call will give you all the information you need. Either the project is going to be made or it will be canceled, it will either move forward or backward, and you will be in or out.

Usually you get this kind of news several weeks or months after your first conversation about the project, so the impact is never that strong, making it less painful. Accumulating and attempting projects cause a relative sensation of movement. Like you are doing a lot of things or at least trying to do them. Although, it is also true that facing such erosive working conditions day by day, makes it inevitable to wonder if there is something you should not have said at a certain occasion. Or the opposite, would it have helped to say something that you have never said?

The strategic thinking of when to show your cards and when not to, is a fundamental part of any negotiation, and it is very useful in this profession. The power is always on the other side of the table but there are also some strategies that you can follow to improve your options. In proportion to the advantageous position that each side may be in (who needs whom, etc.), any conversation can be guided in different directions. To gain a specific advantage, to position yourself as different from the rest, to be remembered in the future, or maybe just to focus on listening and to keep learning. Failures, mistakes, and hard decisions (whether they are good or bad) always teach us important lessons and make successes even more valuable.

THE FILM AND AUDIOVISUAL INDUSTRY

The traditional trial and error procedure is always the best way of knowing the dirty core of any business because that is how you can see the authentic facets from different angles.

Since we have revised the basic behavior and cordiality, let us now address another of the main principles regarding business people, the relativity of truth and the emptiness of words. Every industry member has the commitment (if not the duty) to speak, to some extent, both publicly and privately about how the industry works. Public appearances, statements, promotional events, interviews, etc. Looking at everything we have analyzed thus far, you can imagine the thin margin they have to dodge all the uncomfortable truths that they have to deal with in their daily lives. Consequently, it is essential to rely on a series of standard formulas, sound bites, and playing to the gallery. (Always keeping the expected, glamorous halo.)

You can say half-truths, omit things, beautify anecdotes, invent details, or directly lie. It is up to you to decide how to use your words in order to fulfill what is expected of you. As we have already stated, the more irritating part of show business is the fact that everything is part of the show. It is all neon lights, props, and makeup, all the time. Nothing is authentic.

In our real life, we all face different degrees of honesty and disloyalty with family, friends, at work, and on the street. Humans are imperfect and use lies and manipulation every day. We all know that. But at least within the universal convention, this is a reprehensible action; something against society's ethical and moral code. Liars are considered dishonorable figures, despicable people, and are socially rejected by society (although we all are liars to varying degrees). However, is it not ironic how people admire their idols meanwhile, most celebrities live in toxic environments where the truth has no value at all? It is an interesting coincidence that every single celebrity looks like they are super nice and charming and that their lives are so awesome all the time, right?

THE FILM AND AUDIOVISUAL INDUSTRY

In any case, we are not talking about an abuse of lying, like a malicious sense of deceit; but more like the simple fact that words have no meaning anymore. As if they were stock value, words may have some value in the real world... or they may not. The value of words is always relative. In the stock exchange, everything is in a purely speculative language. And the same happens with words. You cannot expect for everything to have real value, but rather a relative value (depending on how convenient something is for people's interests). If we should highlight one of the unwritten rules of show business, above all others, it would surely be this one: remember that anything anyone tells you, in any conversation, may not be true.

Nothing else should matter, if we start from a false premise, right? It is not that everyone is persistently lying for no reason. We are talking about a certain kind of reasonable doubt taken to an excessive extreme. Almost paranoia. It may sound too cynical for some or just one more truism for others. However, take into account that everyone is pretending and hiding in this business. They are doing it in front of you, the entire industry, and in front of the public. Every person is a world unto themselves and within this ephemeral microcosm of shooting stars, nobody needs higher motivation in order to sacrifice their principles, personality, or behavior. They will conform to the rules of this hard game where they have a lot to gain and a lot to lose.

As we said, it is not about lying with bad intentions or with a perverse purpose. Rather, it is about protecting and maintaining the collective appearance of success, as a shared comfort zone. As long as there is no intention of harming others (thus reducing the chances of being harmed by others), it is not necessary to lie to be protected. By using polite words and rhetorical formulas, you can carefully get what you want. The main problems you will face are other people who are doing exactly the same thing. (Usually the people with power and control of the situation.) As we were saying, you can use truths and lies in your favor. Ambiguity is your best ally, but it is also theirs.

THE FILM AND AUDIOVISUAL INDUSTRY

Once you are in the spiral of subtle nuances, subjective prisms, contradictory opinions, and biased information, it becomes increasingly easier to modify reality however you like. You just get used to it. Compulsive liars have admitted that lying with impunity is too tempting and too easy. And as time goes on, you gain better and better control. (Actors, for example, have an advantage in pretending that lies are real or detecting when people are lying to them.)

This need to keep up with appearances by forcing the idea that everything is fine, self-censoring real opinions, denying facts, and hiding reality ends up justifying any kind of lie for the common good, to protect each other and maintain the status quo. No matter what you say, whatever it is, it is always going to be something positive and nice to hear. As a baleful consequence, words no longer mean anything.

I can tell you that your project is already gaining momentum, that you have a lot of possibilities, that I will call you in a couple of weeks, or that I will pass your message onto someone—but none of that matters. Maybe some of that is true and will happen or it is absolutely lost in the oblivion. Those things may also happen to any of us in our everyday lives, for sure; but not all the time. Not in any single conversation we have.

In this business, you can risk your whole future on one meeting. It could be the most important opportunity of your life, after years of hard effort and personal sacrifice. But for the person on the other side of the table or phone, it may just be a completely irrelevant, routine meeting. Remember, every meeting is like a job interview. And, within the long list of candidates for the position, you are probably the one with the smallest chance of being chosen. In fact, it is possible that you are not even on the list, so you may not have any chance at all. Maybe this executive accepted the meeting just to get to know you better, or to test you. Or even as a personal favor to your agent, your manager, or someone from the studio.

THE FILM AND AUDIOVISUAL INDUSTRY

At this point, beginners usually start questioning: "Really?!" Coping with such frustrating situations, everyone asks themselves the following questions: "Why would they do that?" "Would it be easier to not have a conversation or meeting, especially if it is going to be useless?" Again, saving appearances is everything and talking is the only thing most people do in the business world.

Like many other industries, a lot of decision-making and intermediate leadership only have the function of a pre-selection filter; which is absolutely subjective and kind of pointless, since they do not have the required skills to do it correctly.

A prestigious master's degree in Business Administration may not be very useful for this position in a Hollywood studio; however, it is "highly desirable" to have had an executive position in a large company (no matter which company it was). And surely, you will not have to explain and train this person about classism, forms of conduct, ambiguous communication, and unwritten rules. As mentioned before, it is essential that there is always one or several of these intermediaries in order to lengthen the hierarchy chain, so that there is greater distance between degrees of accountability. It is always good to be able to say that the person responsible for something is the boss of his boss of his boss. The situation's visibility is reduced and it is even more difficult to understand what stage anything is in.

A project that should start filming in a couple of months may suddenly be canceled for any unexpected reason. And reasons or explanations do not matter very much. You may or may not ask or you may or may not understand them. It is completely irrelevant because you already know the golden rule: whatever they tell you, it probably means nothing.

This may sound too nihilistic for some people (especially for those who are more sensitive or those with a more positive attitude to life), but this is just one of the many reasons why so many people voluntarily decide to get away from this industry. Not only because of the frustration of not getting into it, but also because once they achieve success they realize that they cannot continue living this way much longer.

THE FILM AND AUDIOVISUAL INDUSTRY

It is sad to mention this, but it is no coincidence that there are a large number of artists and technicians, in all branches of the sector, that are victims of depression, anxiety, and many other psychological and physiological ailments caused by how difficult it is to deal with living this way. The constant pressure and uncertainty generated by this means of communicating, every day, all day is just too much.

If you ask those who are "lucky" to live this way, many will tell you that it is equally hard to confront the fact that you get used to it, that it becomes addictive. You end up losing any kind of connection with reality and the few people who can stay close to you, such as your family (if it is not one of the things that you have already destroyed).

Who has never heard of all those artists who end up ruining their lives because of their addiction to drugs and alcohol, or in extreme cases, committing suicide? Some are really young and in the full swing of their careers. Others are not so young and have enjoyed a long career of success. Even counting on the respect of everyone in the real world (and apparently inside the industry too). We know nothing about the parts of their lives that you cannot see. They might look joyful and happy most of the time (this is especially worrying when we are talking about comedians, but they are normal people too), but when these sad things happen, a lot of uncomfortable questions arise.

Can anyone feel so alone that no one notices their unhappiness? Or is it that nobody cares? Of course, in a world where all your success and fortune come from the need to save appearances, what can be real? Once all words have lost their meaning, how can you communicate with others for real?

THE FILM AND AUDIOVISUAL INDUSTRY

SCREENWRITERS' REALITY

Everyone can write. As foolish as it may seem, that is the first big issue that a screenwriter must face (actually, any writer). The problem is not about recognition, since awards and good reviews bring you prestige. This job is generally considered well paid, around $100,000 (final version and revisions included), probably double or triple if the film is greenlighted (if you negotiate well), or even one million dollars (or more), if it is a huge success.

The problem is, people usually think the task of writing is, by itself, simple to do. And perhaps it is. The difficult thing is doing it in a professional way with proper quality. That quality that makes Hollywood buy your script. Literature is a complex, neat, and demanding artistic activity. Those trying it, without having the required knowledge or talent, end up realizing this on their own. For sure you know a lot of people who have said: "I have a great idea for a movie."

Any good synopsis must expose the idea, the premise, and the essence of the story in a clear and seductive way. And nothing else. A lot of people can find an inspired combination of elements that many others might consider interesting.

THE FILM AND AUDIOVISUAL INDUSTRY

But that does not necessarily mean that it is a million-dollar idea or that everyone is a creative genius. Rather it makes clear that having an idea for a film is not the complicated part.

In the 16th century, Shakespeare realized that, in fact, there are only seven types of stories: Boy meets girl, poor becomes rich, hero defeats villain, someone is on a quest for something, murderer kills victim, someone's overcoming something or has a rebirth, and adventurer goes on a long journey. Starting from there, you can make as many variations and combinations as you want. The voyage includes a return or not, the adventurer goes alone or in a group, the character to be reborn is young or old or handsome or ugly, the villain is monstrous, the hero is divine, a father searches for his son, a son searches for his mother, boy cheats on girl, girl cheats on boy, son lies to his father, father kills his daughter, son kills his father, boy meets villain, father kills villain, etc. The possibilities may be infinite, yes, but somehow, they are always strangely familiar.

The next thing you have to choose in the writing process is the genre, which is how you decide to tell the facts. The same idea and even the same story can be told in a thousand different ways. The genre is basically how you decide to approach the facts. You can expose the events in a crude or delicate way or at a lively or leisurely pace. You can convey a crazy or reflective attitude or use a serious or funny tone. All of these are depicted by the genre.

And none of it defines the quality of the script. Any kind of story is capable of resulting in high quality work. A hilarious comedy, a heartbreaking drama, or a scary horror film. The writer's ability and their mastery of the genre will end up defining the quality of the writing. Therefore, we are applying two different quality standards: An objective one, depending on the literary correction of the writing, and a subjective one, depending on the audience's tastes.

That explains why some mediocre works become huge successes. It is because of the massive connection with their potential audience. Since the beginning, they have taken the specific tastes of the target audience into account.

Likewise, the opposite may also happen. When there is a very polished, sophisticated, and well-written script ... but no one is interested. In order to make a script that connects with an adolescent audience, without greater pretensions, the only thing you have to do is sort through all the subjects that interest such audience; to think the way they do, using their same mentality.

This is not to say that the formal structure or quality of the script must be lower. Teenagers deserve a good, consistent story as much as children do. The tricky thing is, by default, they are a less demanding audience. It is tempting to justify a bad script with the excuse: "It is for teenagers and you know, they are not very smart." As we said at the beginning of the book, screenwriters with great skills will be able to write (if they want) less ambitious works; but it does not work the other way around. Writers with limited talent may never be able to create top-quality, complex stories. No matter what their experience is with lower complexities.

THE SCRIPT FORMAT

We mentioned in Chapter 1: "Art and the Industry," that scripts are just work tools. But they are not only technical writings though. They must avoid an elaborate, ornate literary style, the way novels have. When we talk about the objective quality or the artistic nature of a script, it has nothing to do with the formal beauty of the writing style. With regard to writing, it is automatically assumed that the use of grammar and spelling must be absolutely professional and correct. The peculiarity of the film script is that everything has to have a practical utility to be filmed. But, for example, you should never describe environments in detail, internal feelings, or conceptual conclusions that are not going to be expressed with something the audience can see or hear; as well as anything that can be considered an unnecessary intrusion into the future work of the film's director or the different teams: Costume, scenery, music, photography, etc.

The script must focus on describing the events, apart from dialogues, of course. In terms of narration, it is about mentioning the overall actions (never in excessive detail) needed to understand the story in words. It is not its function to delight the reader with flowery language or fussy, detailed descriptions (whether visual or emotional). One of the main tasks of the film director is to visualize the story and provide the narrative. Think in pictures and endow them with emotional significance. But all that must be worked out during the making of the film, not in the script. The script must be much more pragmatic, focusing on the essentials. Its magic is in the evolution of the events and the impact of the dialogues. As a literary work it does not pursue beauty in itself, but the appeal of the narrative to be potentially transformed into an audiovisual work.

There are differences between a professional script and other types of writings, that beginners often do not know about. In turn, they may ignore their importance. Firstly, there are a few formatting details that must always be fulfilled; such as margins, alignment, spacing, font size, etc. Nothing special that any specific software cannot provide, or a myriad of free templates that you can find on the internet (how different this was a few decades ago). And far from being a whim, they are important details that must be respected for various reasons. To begin with, they make the reader detect at first sight whether you are a real industry professional or a novice. As a beginner, imagine somehow that you got someone relevant to read your script, you do not want to run the risk of being rejected by the first page, without needing to read it, because it is immediately noticeable that your script is out of format. But such automatic rejection can also happen by reading just a few lines.

The first grammatical rule of screenwriting is that the script must always be narrated in simple present tense and third person (Events happen and people do things, right?). Actions must be described in real time, as if you were describing what is seen on screen (so forget about that regular past tense from novelistic narratives that a lot of beginners use).

And we must say that none of that is for aesthetic reasons. Such a page format contributes, as a standard, to the approximate equivalence of "page-per-minute." If you have not heard about it before, it may sound hard to believe, but it really works. At least as an orientation. Usually, novice screenwriters' narration includes too many descriptions (and too specific) of costumes, characters, environments, actions, and detailed movements. Again, as if it were a novel. Or even worse, like wanting to indicate that something should be filmed in some specific way (a typical writer-who-wants-to-be-a-director mistake). And the same happens when the scenes or dialogues are too long. Whoever is going to be the director will have to remove or rewrite said issues to provide a proper narrative sense, without killing the pace of that scene, or even the whole movie.

This is an important detail to highlight. Many inexperienced rookies do not understand why the dialog columns in the script format are so tight. Firstly, it is easier for actors to read and memorize their lines that way (an interesting lesson learned from newspapers). Secondly, it is also a good indicator that a dialogue is perhaps too long. A lot of newbies believe that such limited width is ruining their page per minute standard, when it is precisely helping them to compensate for other factors of maladjustment in the opposite direction. Like natural silences, which do not happen when reading but they are consuming time in the finished film; or the time it takes for our eyes to read and follow the narration, while things happens faster on the screen.

There are people who try to justify themselves by criticizing the inaccuracy of the format, rather than recognizing that they do not dominate the functional writing standard yet. The format is the same for everyone, and it has proven for decades that everything ends up naturally compensated when it is professionally written. If the standard is working for everyone except you, perhaps you should accept that you do not control the technique yet. But do not worry if that happens to you. It is not the end of the world, just keep on practicing.

CRITICISM AND SELF-CRITICISM

As with any other artistic profession, self-criticism is an essential part in the career of any artist. It is also one of the main indicators of personal and professional maturity. It is everyone's responsibility to face their own limitations as best they can. First of all, every screenwriter (established or beginner) should be aware of their status within their professional career, and act accordingly.

Screenwriters with technical or artistic limitations that fail to get good quality results can react in two ways: By accepting it or denying it. (You may continue to think that your work is very good, although nobody likes it because after all, every critic is always subjective, right?) A third option would be to avoid the type of writing that gives you trouble (you can be very good at writing horror movies but have no talent for making comedies or social dramas). Actually, in the fourth and last place, you could choose to devote the time and effort required to overcome your weak points, until you can finally improve your skills.

Because self-criticism is not something to be applied only to one specific moment in your career, but rather during the whole process of creation. In every single work, rewriting is, in fact, something essential to the habit of writing. We are not going to talk about the most basic knowledge that every writer should have. There are hundreds of books, courses, and workshops where anyone can learn anything about the three-act structure, the turning points, and all the keys to making interesting characters, hooks, climaxes, and the like. What we can do is highlight one absolute truth that you should be aware of which is, knowing the rules that govern a process, whether basic or advanced, does not mean that you have already mastered the matter. Creative writing is the most important thing, of course, but before that, it is assumed that any writer knows how to write well. Spelling mistakes, incorrect grammar, inconsistent verb tenses—all of these details reveal an amateur or bad writer.

THE FILM AND AUDIOVISUAL INDUSTRY

As obvious as it may seem, it is often forgotten that writing a script correctly, does not make it a great script. And even good writers can get frustrated by that. For example, artists who can write well but are not especially good at writing audiovisual scripts. This is because it is about literature, yes, but it is also about film making. It is a different type of product with its own nature.

In the art of writing, form and content are equally important. But when writing movies, apart from the story you are telling and how you tell it, it is also crucial to decide what makes sense to show on screen, as much as what does not. Your visualization skills are paramount. Screenwriters have all the tools, resources, and writing tricks at their disposal in order to seduce the public; but in this case they are not popcorn eaters yet, but rather executives, producers, and directors. The quality of the final product will end up depending on all of them, but the script is the basis on which everything will be built. You have to be sure of its strength. It is always preferable to get stuck at some point, solving any problem you find rather than writing a complete work without a break or without finding any obstacles. When there are no problems along the way, it might mean that the story is not sufficiently developed. It may mean that you might have fallen into laziness or, much worse, complacency. Probably you are not a genius who writes with astonishing ease, but most likely a lazy, simpleton writer who approaches writing without personality or passion; without a proper voice.

The perfect example of this is that simplistic and cheap trick used in narrative that every writer knows well: The "deus ex machina" (Latin for "god from the machine"), which basically means that everything goes. ("As a writer, I am the divine creator here and things happen as I want them to happen.") In short, to resolve situations in a sudden, unlikely and barely credible way because you do not know how to get out of a messy, unsolvable situation that you previously created. The term's origin comes from the Roman translation of the ancient Greek theater where gods were usually characters coming down from the clouds (using a rustic machine of ropes and pulleys) just to solve conflicts in a capricious and unexpected way. Of course, things happen because writers say so, but they also decide if things happen in a logical way. Not to mention, the public will judge their decisions later. Where is the line between something original (unexpected, in a good way) and something simplistic and too convenient? (Just lazy and stupid.) Everyone has an opinion on this, and to this day you have probably noticed that Hollywood usually pushes the limit too much; considering that the craziest, funniest, or most spectacular options are always the best ones.

Which brings us to another great question. Should you write for yourself? Or for others? The debate is intense. You can draw many conclusions and divided opinions, depending on who you ask. This is a very hard job. What authors think about their own work can be very different from what others think. You have to be realistic about the possible criticism and the fact that even if your work is good (in any sense), that does not mean that people are going to like it or that you are going to be successful. It also does not mean that your projects have a higher chance of being produced than others. It may sound incomprehensible to beginners and certainly frustrating for the professionals, but that is how it works. There are great, amazing scripts in Hollywood that go from one office to the next. Some of them are expensive to produce and others are much cheaper. Some of them are more artistic while many others are quite commercial. As we have seen, nobody says that the quality of a script is the guarantee of a green light. But there are also a lucky few who make their debuts quite easily. At the end of the day, someone may fall in love with your script without warning; or just with your idea. Or maybe they do not like any of them, but your style and quality draw someone's attention, who then makes you an offer to write something new from scratch. As in any other profession, your vision of how easy or difficult it is to get into the industry depends on how well you do in the beginning. If you have just arrived to the city and some producer or studio buys your first script, you irremediably will think that everything is that easy. As simple as it seems: "I write and others pay me for it, this is great!" But then you may have another thought: "How come my last script is suddenly not interesting to anyone? This one is as good as the other, perhaps even better, so why is no one able to see this?" Since you never had any previous relationship with the classic feeling of frustration, it will be even harder to accept it. You might choose to go on a desperate hunt, knocking on every door in Hollywood. However, your script would be cursed forever. As soon as it is known that no one wants that script, people will be even less interested. They will not waste their time reading it, because that is the idiosyncrasy of the system: "If they do not want it, I do not want it either." Miracles happen from time to time, and one visionary might decide to invest in something different that nobody else wants to do, going against all the odds. (It is hard to believe that this happened to movies like *The Matrix*, is not it?) But also in those cases, the potential risk of being a total fiasco is still there. Even if production never happens and pre-production is aborted at some point, everyone will begin to talk about the problematic project. The people involved will be considered "less trustworthy." They will not be guaranteed success. Within an industry that always seeks the maximum possible guarantees, it may become an issue for your career. Even if the reasons why the project was canceled or why it flopped at the box office had nothing to do with your personal work on the project.

Continuing with the subject of criticism, when judging a finished film (the last audiovisual form of the script) the viewer's opinion can be simplified into three generic possibilities. In the worst case, too many elements of the story are bad, so all the attention is focused on the defects and weaknesses (to the extent of losing any interest). It also may happen that none of these elements are engaging or special enough, focusing all the attention (if any) on the sensory stimuli that the audience perceives more directly: Photography, music, costumes, etc. And finally, the events and/or dialogues may be so captivating (especially for viewers with some literary knowledge), that people are able to perceive the extraordinary work done by the screenwriter (even standing out above the more immediate audiovisual elements).

THE FILM AND AUDIOVISUAL INDUSTRY

The best professional recognition screenwriters can receive is keeping the public glued to their seats, completely immersed in a story and admiring and recognizing its quality—even if they do not have any screenwriting knowledge at all. Luckily for everyone, that is the purpose of awards, is not it? Awards are there to make the mainstream audiences learn the difference between good and mediocre scripts. So on second thought, perhaps the best professional recognition you can receive is an award.

Remember, it does not matter how good you think you are or how good you actually are. Even as an acclaimed, prestigious screenwriter, the whole world can consider you a genius, but only a few will decide if it is worth hiring you or buying any of your scripts. The first option will always be better because you will get paid for writing, regardless of whether the payer likes what you delivered or not. Sounds good, right? (But you better write well if you want to work again.) After these first judges, hopefully the audience is next, and they are the strictest jury you can face. Millions of people will decide, with the money used to buy their tickets, if you are going to keep working on this or not. And keep in mind, what people say about the quality of your script on the internet has no relevance. The only thing that matters is what their money said to the producers of your movie. This is the only way your success will be measured.

BEING A PROFESSIONAL SCREENWRITER

We just mentioned the two ways of generating income. Selling any personal, previously-written work or being hired to write from scratch on demand. In both cases, you can be paid for an idea, an elaborate plot, or a longer treatment (which is a fully developed story, without needing dialogues yet). You can even be hired for your special ability to write characters' lines. (It is very common to have experts who specialize in dialogues, especially in TV series.) Finally, we must also mention "revisions."

THE FILM AND AUDIOVISUAL INDUSTRY

They can go from small tweaks here and there to major changes in structure, character arc, dialogues, or some part of the whole script. Revisions are always made with the intention of polishing a story (supposedly, to make it better). However, it is too often only applied as an automatic measure, as part of the basic philosophy of rewriting. The universal artistic truth that no work is ever totally finished and can always be improved. This means that no matter how good the work is or the internal reviews the script has suffered before being in the hands of a studio. It will most certainly continue to undergo several more revisions, even if they do not make much sense. That is correct, the number of changes previously made is not an indicator of the objective quality of a script; nor of its chances of getting greenlit. It may be closer to being approved, as much as it may be more and more confusing. So every time decision-makers read it, they like it even less than before.

After many revisions (of course, revisions are also paid, they are part of the deal), it is perfectly normal that scripts are rejected in the end. They may still not be meeting the desired expectations. This might mean another indefinite delay of the project, until producers decide to create a new script from another perspective, with different writers. They may even cancel it, regardless of the time, money, and effort spent up until that moment (perhaps several years). And that is without mentioning the deplorable practice of splitting a script into separate pieces and copy/pasting it into other scripts owned by the studio.

In every decent industry, screenwriters must be paid for the act of writing, and not because their work is finally produced (as pointed out before, in that case they should receive an extra bonus paycheck for that). It is no less true though that as artists they live with that bittersweet feeling of frustration throughout their career. When an idea, story, or complete script is acquired by any studio, independent company, or producer, screenwriters know perfectly well whoever is going to buy it can do whatever they want with it.

THE FILM AND AUDIOVISUAL INDUSTRY

On the other hand, the more opportunities you have to get your scripts produced into actual films, the easier it will be for you to find new jobs. There is no doubt that the public exhibitions, via films and television, is the best way to demonstrate the reliability of your talent, in a tangible way. But even enjoying success, it is quite frustrating to see so many parts of your script (probably your favorite parts) being removed or modified by other writers or film directors that you do not like. After so many people touching the scripts, even their original creators may have no reason to be proud of them.

But far from the starry skies on solid ground again, let us come back to the foot of that big wall where the beginners crowd, desperate to receive their long-awaited opportunity. How can unknown "nobodies" show their first job? Reading a script takes time so, how many people are willing to read a hundred pages written by a perfect stranger? With no previous information about the author? The risk is too high. What if it is incredibly boring? Even if it were a decent but ordinary script, its reading would have already been a waste of time. Let us say, if it is not a resounding and immediate success, transmitting a gold mine feeling from the beginning, (which is very, very unlikely, according to the statistic) nobody will have interest (much less the need) in reading a newcomer's work. But then, how are we going to know how good or bad it is if nobody reads it?

This problem is common to all kinds of writers. And just like in the publishing world (and not only for novels), there are people whose only job is to read manuscripts. These readers may be hired by studios and producers or may be external professionals who present their reading reports. They are probably not the first audience that you would like, but it is better than nothing. They are the ones who take care of the initial sieve, so that big fish end up reading only those scripts with better potential. These first filters may discard scripts during the first pages if the story is boring from the very beginning, or the interest takes too long to appear, or it is absolutely predictable.

THE FILM AND AUDIOVISUAL INDUSTRY

Due to their extensive experience in the field, they are more than aware of every stereotype that beginners repeat over and over again (we are much, much less original than we would like to think). We will not be discussing the profile and background of these people, but it is suffice to mention that it is not an issue exempt from the debate. Are they writers? Have they got a wide judgment and discretion capacity? Were they screenwriters? Are they right now? Do they take advantage of their positions by stealing ideas? The controversy is served.

Anyhow, the procedure is not as simple as sending your script to everyone. The only professional, industrial way to do this must be, of course, through an agent. (Read Chapter 5: "Getting into the Industry" if you have not done so yet.) And by the way, it is not enough for a friend or relative to pretend to be your literary agent. It is totally assumed that your work is good enough to sign up with a real agent from the industry (someone who insiders may know or ask about). But above all, what you should never do, under any circumstances, is approach a producer in person.

No matter how often you see this behavior in the movies, (let us notice the irony) unless you have some kind of personal or minimally professional relationship (in which case you might have this person's approval), these are extremely sensitive situations and you should never, ever invade another person's personal space. Firstly, out of politeness and respect and secondly, because of that distinct classist attitude we have talked so much about. If you do not want to cause too much of a scene, try not to talk directly to any big fish in the film industry (or any other industry, actually).

In the best-case scenario, you may get an arrogant indifference that will leave you in exactly the same place as before. And, even in the hypothetical case that someone decides to be kind to you at that moment, the chances of them actually reading your script are very small. Few miracles happen in these cases, because intellectual property issues are a very serious matter.

THE FILM AND AUDIOVISUAL INDUSTRY

In that regard, "unsolicited materials" can be an important and unexpected nuisance. No one wants to run the risk of things getting messy because of an innocent manuscript coming into their hands. The industry standard way of proceeding exists for a reason, it offers a series of minimum guarantees (not perfect though) to everyone involved, sufficient to make the process more secure, especially from a legal perspective.

Producers may be reluctant to consider manuscripts from strangers and, even worse, take them in person. However, is the writers' fear of their work being stolen not worse? It is not exactly an unjustified fear. It happens more than we all would like to admit. Mainly because stealing ideas (and even full stories) is much easier than it seems and doing so is not necessarily even committing any crime. There are examples of it everywhere. All the productions you know include petty thefts or blatant copies of something. You just do not know or remember the copied works (like most people around the world), but you can be sure the authors of the copied ideas do.

Everyone steals from everywhere. Forgotten old films or theater plays, novels of unknown authors, TV ads, video games, students' short films and, of course, scripts that were never produced (and this one is definitely the most painful for the victim). It does not matter whether they are beginners or other professional writers. From the very moment that producers (independent or working for a studio, it makes no difference) find something interesting in a script, they will always have two options: steal it or buy it.

It is not even a difficult decision to make. There is an unwritten rule to apply in these cases: If the whole script is special (meaning, its quality and global content make it valuable), it is bought as a viable product. The buyer will then continue with the next steps, which are marketing analysis, budget and profitability, rewriting, negotiation with the author, etc.

If there are only a few interesting moments or ideas in a mediocre script, they just apply them to any other project, transforming them a little (perhaps even without transforming them too much).

THE FILM AND AUDIOVISUAL INDUSTRY

In fact, that is what we call inspiration: the influence of others' ideas, as a starting point to creating something new. In short, depending on how much you transform your script, by taking ideas from other people's works, you may have copied or been inspired by them. We saw in Chapter 3: "Economy and Law," that ideas cannot be legally protected. An idea is only a determined structural concept. It is posed and developed in a unique and specific way, in certain scenes of one particular project, and it is only the finished version of the project that can be protected.

Now, scenes can be very well developed, even though the concept is nothing out of the ordinary. But the opposite may also occur: All the grandeur of a scene or set of scenes resides in the concept, the idea itself. Since it is an abstract structure, this "great idea" can always be adapted (for better or for worse) to any plot, situation, environment, and set of characters that you want, without a hint of illegality. The key part is proving that a screenwriter did not have a similar idea as someone else when writing his or her own script. Although it would be a tremendous coincidence, it is perfectly plausible; and that is the only thing that matters in a potential litigation. There must be a lot of evidence (and very good evidence) to prove that you suffered an intellectual property robbery, instead of a mere creative coincidence. When you win one of these cases in court, the number of coincidences has to reach such an extreme, that it cannot be considered reasonable that two artistic works could be that similar by chance. Besides, there has to be conclusive evidence that the defendants had direct access to the original work. Hence the importance of following the appropriate business processes. Things like proof of certified mail, a script request, (remember unsolicited materials will probably be returned without being opened) a purchase receipt of the copied novel, or the legitimate protection offered by the intellectual property registration in your country. This is the ABC of writing and should absolutely be well known to everyone. Although, all this does not mean, of course, that screenwriters must live in a constant state of paranoia.

THE FILM AND AUDIOVISUAL INDUSTRY

It is true that there are as many thefts as true coincidences. Maybe there is a unique and special idea that you have been working on, completely alone and privately, (therefore it is impossible for anyone to have known about it) while a writer in another part of the world may have written something incredibly similar at the same moment or a few years before you. Perhaps they were using the same source of inspiration as you.

But it is not the end of the world. Although this might be ruining the unique, distinctive element of your idea, and now you are not the first one to present it, (now you might be the one who looks like the thief of ideas) at least you are sure it was not a robbery. These things happen.

To conclude, let us look at the different ways in which screenwriters can allow their work to speak on their behalf. How can I attract the industry's attention? Through reading the script, an expert eye can already detect the writer's capacity to capture and evoke images and sounds on paper. For some people it is an innate ability, for others it is gradually developed and for the majority, it is never achieved. It is like spatial vision or the sense of orientation—some have it and some do not. There are many things that can reveal a writer's abilities such as, the organization of discourse, the pace of narrative, the effectiveness of descriptions, or the fluency of dialogues.

This brings us to the second way of standing out: Letting others talk about your skills. It is definitely a good sign when someone out there might be talking about your script. The more your name is heard, the better your future; and the more people that talk about your project, the better it is for everyone.

And finally, we cannot miss the most effective way to draw attention, given the nature of this profession: The finished work in audiovisual format. The advantages are obvious. On one hand, it takes less time and is more entertaining than reading hundreds of pages (which usually takes a couple of days minimum, since no one is that interested in reading it in one sitting).

THE FILM AND AUDIOVISUAL INDUSTRY

But on the other hand, there is the great inconvenience that someone has to produce it. Therefore, the final quality will totally depend on the category and talent of the production team, director included. The director and actors might make your script better or worse, but you cannot be there to clarify: "I did not write that detail" or "That part is not mine." So you will have to learn to live with that, no matter if you are a beginner or an A-list writer.

By the way, when producers want to avoid direct impositions and unnecessary tensions, they usually prefer to hire a new and different screenwriter to do the required changes, instead of extending the commitment with the previous writer. And just to mention, at high levels of stardom, it is true that directors and actors are given the privilege of introducing their own modifications, as a sign of confidence in their talent (in some cases even required by their contracts). This is a very creative and artistic approach, but also a huge risk, contributing even more to the dangerous "Frankenstein's monster" effect.

Needless to say, these ways of draw attention are perfectly applicable to amateur-level and short film filmmakers. Thanks to fantastic digital video technology, you can tell great stories in fifteen minutes or less, at a very decent and affordable production level. This amount of time is more than enough for good writers to demonstrate their talent through the eyes of others. If someone is not able to tell something good in less than half an hour, it will have nothing to do with the running time used; it will have to do purely and simply with the ability to tell a good story.

THE FILM AND AUDIOVISUAL INDUSTRY

THE DIRECTOR'S JOB

In audiovisual works, the director is recognized as one of the three creative authors, together with the screenwriter and the music composer of the soundtrack. However, directors are the only ones who can tell other team members the direction to follow (hence its name), so that the final work is what he or she wants. Everyone is at their command and they are considered the highest authority when filming. Although, they must be held accountable to the producers, who hired them with absolute confidence in their talents. So much confidence that producers put the daily spending of large amounts of money in the dangerous hands of directors, without physically controlling them (although there are ways to do so, of course).

That is precisely one of the main arguments that directors wield against artistic restrictions on their work. If a producer is already interested in hiring a specific director, we might allegedly assume it is because of the quality observed in previous works. It is assumed that that person should be perfectly capable of providing the same quality for a similar project. So why so many restrictions on his or her creativity?

THE FILM AND AUDIOVISUAL INDUSTRY

In Chapter 5: "Getting into the Industry," we talked about the peculiar use of language in this business. The first thing that directors hear from producers is that they are more than "interested" in your work, and that they are "excited," "passionate," and even "in love" with your project. If that were true, should not the confidence in the artist be blind (or at least greater) in terms of creative decisions?

When shooting the film, as director, you can actually organize your team and apply your management style with relative freedom. (The only major thing is that you must stick to the plan, keeping schedule and budget under control.) But there are a lot of key conceptual and production decisions, previous to shooting, where producers are not willing to cede their authority. (Like disagreements on casting or opposing views on critical parts of the script.)

As we will see in the chapter about producers, from the director's viewpoint, it is clear that artistic quality is fundamental for their public image (both professionally and personally). While from the producers' side, the artistic vision of directors always means an uncontrollable risk. By being so personal, it is dangerously subjective and will most likely not fit the thoughts of the majority. This is exactly the initial purpose of any film, to connect with the public as best as possible in order to succeed. That is why the power of the director's actions must be limited and controlled.

Interestingly, when the studio system first began, the director was little more than a technical chief who would manage the film crew. It was a young theater director named Orson Welles who prepared the ground for artistic recognition of the director as an artist, dictator, and main creator with *Citizen Kane* in 1941. He was also a pioneer in the tense relationship that exists, by default, amongst the producer, director, art and the box office.

Welles recognized himself as a great admirer of D.W. Griffith (who is considered the father of American film), Robert J. Flaherty (the creator of the first documentary in history), or Jean Renoir (son of the famous impressionist painter), who was the main influence of the famous "Nouvelle Vague" (literally, the French "New Wave"). This is relevant, because this peculiar collective from the 60s pushed strongly for this image of the film director as author. Therefore, they gained the right to express themselves freely; taking the audiovisual experimentation a little further, in both form and content. With such affinities, it was easy to foresee the continuing difficulties that Orson Welles would suffer throughout his career. He also held expressionist German directors in high esteem. These directors decided to leave their country (fleeing from the ascent of the Nazi party) to work in Hollywood in the 30s. They were under the rules and methodologies of the American studios now, completely abandoning their previous way of making movies, very dark but also highly aesthetical.

Quite ironically, his favorite director was the prolific and successful John Ford, who never had a single problem with his responsibilities and obligations to the studios. We are talking about a man so old that he witnessed firsthand the beginning of American movies. He worked on set even before he was of legal age. He directed his first silent Western film in 1917, when he was only 22 years old. This had a lot to do with his viewpoint on the studio's standards. Since his entire family was working in the new business of movies, he spent his adolescence helping as a crew assistant in a lot of the first silent American films. What is more, the Western genre was fairly unpopular at that time; and thanks to the little interest that studios and directors had for such films, this talented young man faced a completely virgin territory, waiting to be exploited under his own rules. The whole genre had yet to be defined, which indirectly provided him such margins of freedom, impossible to conceive 30 years later. Becoming a master and enjoying great success in the box office, Ford always received the highest respect from the industry, therefore, he had no reason to respond in a different way.

Things were very different for Welles. He only received rejection from the industry, with regard to any attempt at genre or language innovation (which meant a potential risk of failure).

Due to his constantly different personal struggles and his defiant attitude, the legendary director greatly contributed to increasing that distance and mutual reluctance between director and producer. A producer sees box office failures as more than enough justification to not trust a "doomed" artist. However, anyone can understand the frustration Welles had to have felt as an artist, considering that many such failures were his magnificent Shakespeare adaptations or the film noir masterpiece *Touch of Evil*, which even starred Charlton Heston (who pushed the producers to hire Welles, despite his combative reputation). In addition to deficient distribution, part of this failure was due to editing that producers did without Welles' approval. They even filmed new scenes with another mercenary director. In 1998, through notes and indications of Welles himself (jealously guarded by Charlton Heston for years), the original director's cut was finally published and distributed.

This is one of the best examples of "final cut privilege." Once shooting has finished, the editing process begins. And editing can critically affect the film's quality. Including, the specific shots selected (directors film the same scene several times from different camera angles and distances, and editors choose the best ones later), the specific takes selected (among the number of times actors repeated the same lines, for each shot), and the specific order of these pieces. The quality is affected not only in artistic terms, but in how viewers enjoy and understand the film. This privilege is controversial because by contract, the director has the right to make the last and definitive edit of the movie, according to his or her criterion. Producers are obliged to distribute the director's cut, even if they don't like the final result. Under normal circumstances, producers could just do whatever they wanted. But because of the final cut privilege, they are not allowed to change the content after the director's approval. If they really hate the film, the only thing they can legally do is boycott their own product (for example, not wasting money on big distribution or a promotional campaign for something they do not actually support).

THE FILM AND AUDIOVISUAL INDUSTRY

As we just said, movies are filmed in short pieces (shots), without following the chronological order of the script. They shoot what is technically convenient first, from a production perspective. Within those fragments, actors must repeat everything multiple times with different artistic approaches (or because of bloopers), as well as from different camera angles. This is so the shots can be organized and linked with the best possible narrative during editing.

This is where editors come into play. You might be wondering: "If editing affects the film's quality that much, is it the director who cuts and pastes these fragments?" Originally, editing was done with a device known as a moviola. A kind of similar technology to a film projector, but focused on the free reproduction of the filmed material in both directions (forward or backward), as well as the speed that the operator may want. The purpose was to detect the exact point in which every shot should finish, cut the film roll, and paste each strip consecutively, in the final master. (The master copy is the first original you use to create the rest of the copies.) This type of editing is called linear, because it forces you to follow the final order from the beginning by choosing which shot should be the first one of the film, then the second one, then the third one, and so on, with every shot. Finally, "The End" title is pasted after the last shot.

The evolution of technology allowed for the improvement of the rotating system, followed by the cutting and pasting process. The invention of video made editing much easier by introducing the possibility of working in a nonlinear system. At the beginning of this century, the digital revolution removed the need for an original master film and celluloid rolls to shoot; nothing but digital data is used now. Something that many people do not know is that the famous "clap" of the clapperboard is used to synchronize the audio source with the pictures captured by the camera since image and sound are recorded with different devices. Currently, clapperboards are also digital and communicate directly with cameras, sound devices, and anything else you want, because data is transmitted electronically.

The resulting files contain a series of internal metadata, with which you can quickly locate and relate any visual shot and frame with any audio minute or second.

All this has caused a lot of directors to decide (if they are allowed to) on editing their films by themselves, on their own personal computers. The comfort and control obtained this way cannot be compared to any other option. Although, as said before, this is only possible for independent filmmakers. The norm inside this industry is that the editor must be a different person, expressly hired for that role (maybe even with one or several assistants).

In the past, the editor position required technical knowledge of the moviola, in addition to the manual dexterity of carefully cutting and pasting celluloid so as not to damage the film. Besides, even today it is still considered a boring and repetitive task, despite the obvious advantages of digital editing. The situation can be compared to the large painting workshops from history. From the Renaissance to the Baroque, all the great painters had, once they were considered masters, their own workshop full of workers and apprentices. This allowed them to undertake a large production of simultaneous orders, reserving only the supervision tasks and the correction of paintings for themselves (if needed).

The relationship between the editor and director might be similar. Depending on the amount of freedom granted by contract, the director can personally edit, be present in the editing room to provide indications, or not even have the right to participate in the editing process at all. In the case of having sufficient power, directors have to draw a few master lines of language, pace, and significance to be used, defining those key guidelines to follow, according to their own style. And from their side, editors must know and understand the director's style, ensuring that they are making proper use of the filmed material from all the shots the director previously selected as useful. A lot of these decisions are made, as we will see next, during the shoot itself.

THE FILM AND AUDIOVISUAL INDUSTRY

DIRECTING A FILM SHOOT

In this stage, everyone understands that the director is the person in charge, and the rest of the crew must align with his or her vision. But there is usually a very fuzzy perception of how that alignment is actually produced. Few people know or understand what a director really does. Let us try to explain.

At the organizational level, the production team starts the day before anyone else, making sure that all the essentials needed for the day are prepared.

This begins with the crew's most basic maintenance and logistics needs. (It is a bad sign if everything is ready except for breakfast or what you need to move everyone to the shooting location.) Once the crew arrives on set or to the location, the technical team will prepare everything necessary to shoot, under the management of the assistant director. Before filming each scene, more and more technical details are properly set up and checked within each area, such as the camera and lighting positions. For this boring task, stand-ins are used. A type of body double, with a similar complexion (and more or less similar facial features) as the lead actors. In the meantime, the actors will be going through makeup, hair, and costumes. Once the heads of each department approve their corresponding parts, everything must wait for the final approval of the director. Thus, the process described in the paragraph above repeats over and over again throughout the day, shot by shot and scene by scene.

It tries to follow the shooting plan designed in the previous phase (pre-production), as well as the technical script, where the director has defined each shot with essential and practical notes (without needing all the unnecessary literature included in the script). This goes together with the production breakdown sheets (which includes everything that is necessary for each scene like times, names, phone numbers, addresses, props, costumes, vehicles, etc.). The work of the script supervisor (also called script boy/girl or just continuity supervisor) is especially remarkable.

They have to take care the pickiest details between scenes so that the look is always consistent on screen and within the logical chronology of the script (scars, wounds, stains, rips, accessories, decorations, and so on). So, as you can imagine, this is crucial when it is imperative that scenes be filmed on different days.

There are always additional needs and contingencies on the go, whose minimum expressions are the repetition of the same shot (this is called "takes," as we saw). Normally, they are just small tweaks, but any stop longer than usual may require a thorough overhaul of costumes and/or make-up, like a lunch break or any change of scene (which refers to the group of shots in continuous action, until the story's place or the temporal moment changes). But there are situations where the risk of unexpected problems is too high. For example, shooting in too remote of a location (like jungles, deserts, and those sort of places), the impact of weather (if you put both together you can imagine the chances of disaster), or the sudden indisposition of any element of the human crew or mechanical equipment.

This brings us to the daily activities. Production managers must carry out a daily report and send them to the producers. There is also a daily crew meeting, where problems and solutions are discussed. These meetings usually take place during lunch or at the end of the day. At the end of the day, the production team can give a better measurement of how the shooting plan is going. Once the stress of the shooting day is gone, it is the perfect time to review the footage that was filmed throughout the day, discard useless shots, and take note of which ones are the best. So, the days pass like this until the whole script has been filmed, using as many shots per scene as the director sees fit.

Now given that context, if there is one way to summarize what the director's job is in film production, it is pure and simple: He or she is the person who has to answer all the questions. In order to convey to others what they have in mind, they can make some storyboard drawings but it is impossible to explain the logic behind each decision. Therefore, everyone is working "blindly" most of the time. Assuming (and hoping) the director's indications will make sense in the end, so they can focus on getting what they have been told to capture.

It is not necessary to understand what directors are looking for, it is more important to try and give them what they are asking for. They will approve or reject the take according to what the on-set monitors show. (It is the cameraman who looks through the viewfinder. However, not too often nowadays, due to the amazing display screens that current cameras have.) It is the director's responsibility to give instructions on how to improve every detail that needs to be corrected. (That is why understanding each other is so important in a film crew.) Beyond the professional quality of each worker, there is an immense subjective ocean in which all the technicians and artists involved are adrift. As captain of the ship, the director is in charge of taking everyone to their destination, along with other responsibilities that are equally important. For example, doing it all within the planned schedule and existing resources, while taking care of the crew's morale. That is the only way to prevent the ship from sinking.

Unfortunately, it is not a pleasurable trip and the proper metaphor should be a warship, not a peaceful cruise. Every day is a tireless battle and a struggle for survival, come hell or high water. As we said before, in this exhausting war of attrition the director has to answer any question that crew members might ask at anytime. And all of them need these answers to be able to do their job. It is also important to understand that, at the same time, directors do not have to justify their decisions.

This dangerous, double-edged blade can be a serious problem when there is not enough understanding. A crew member may need more information to understand the director's needs (always asking with the best of intentions). But it would be creative suicide to waste time explaining the reasoning behind every decision. What is more, the problem might not be the lack of information, but the personal disagreement with the director's decision or intention. In that case, it does not matter how many explanations and instructions that the director gives, things will probably go wrong if people do not understand why they are doing what they have been told to do. This might lead to losing even more time, engaging in open discussions and trying to propose alternatives. That would mean a horizontal teamwork hierarchy; however, a vertical hierarchy is the only practical one in audiovisual production.

This point is crucial to understanding the real function of the industry: The necessity of working as a team is undeniable, everyone knows it. The sum of individual talents generates this community of professionals that contributes to the success of a particular work. However, due to the artistic (and therefore subjective) nature of audiovisual works, the hierarchy must be structured vertically. The crew has to be directed literally. These creations cannot work in other ways. The diverse opinions, characters, mentalities, and capacities of each individual makes any "democratic" decision-making impossible. When beginners attend their first shoot or work for the first time in their sector (whatever type), they are full of questions, doubts, and eagerness to know how everything works. At first, the novelty is fascinating and the more you know, the more you want to deepen your knowledge. But obviously, beginners are not the center of the universe and the purpose of professional productions is not so that rookies can learn. That is reality. Not to mention, the deeper you dive, the darker the waters become.

Part of the problem is the double standard we always apply in our society. First, we promote curiosity and the logic of rational knowledge in children. We frame "asking questions" as something positive that denotes interest in learning (always within a relatively fake environment, made of white lies, for their own protection). Then comes the manipulation of youngsters, with tons of standard lies for all these new questions caused by the first contact with the real world, the functioning of adults' society. And finally, at a certain point, adults are clearly aware that regarding certain subjects, it is better not to ask if you do not want to get in trouble.

So, is it wrong to ask questions? Or can you ask too many questions? And, how do you know what should be asked and what should not? And when? What is more, when anodyne answers are insubstantial and insufficient, you realize that you are being treated like a child, in that first stage mentioned above. So, is it actually beneficial for you to keep asking questions? Reaching that level of self-awareness is a very valuable lesson along the way. An interesting turn of events that gives you to an inevitable change in approach: Do I need to ask questions to learn how things work?

As in the case of military hierarchies and disciplines, the ultimate goal is actually known and understood by only a few. And the only thing others must do is simply obey orders. From the perspective of those who ask the questions (actually from the other side too), there should be a clear difference between the questions relevant to do the job and the questions coming from personal interests. For example, "I want to learn" or "I am curious" vs. "I want to know the truth." As you know, information is power. And, in the case of beginners, apart from the imperative need for relevant information, you must add learning and training issues. The youngest members in a film shoot always tend to ask more questions than usual. This is because they are also full of that understandable insecurity that prevents them from thinking or acting with clarity. Prudence and respect are the best weapons to counteract that natural "stage fright." They are as fundamental as humility, taking into account the crazy festival of egos that is involved in audiovisual production.

Besides, directors tend to command respect. (The good ones should inspire confidence.) Even at amateur levels, everyone tends to admire, envy, or detest the director. But the director is never someone who leaves others feeling indifferent. Any crew member, even with a minimal knowledge of movies, is capable of understanding the heavy burden that falls on their shoulders. Even if directors do not have the obligation of knowing, in detail, how each specialized task works when filming, it is mandatory that they are absolutely clear about what they want, so that the rest of the team can help them to make it happen. Hence, the more knowledge they have, the more insistent they are on the way things must be done (more often than not, this is contrary to what an expert in the field might recommend).

All this is especially serious in the case of first-time and amateur directors. Because of possible knowledge gaps, young directors may not be prepared to handle such a flood of questions and find proper answers for everything (this is one of the first ways of detecting talented directors with potential among simple "wannabes"). If you are a beginner in a professional environment, fortunately, the rest of the crew will know what to do. But in case the crew is full of people without proper knowledge or experience, it is very likely that no one will know what to do or how to do it, even with specific instructions. Aside from that, newbies and amateur collaborators know very little about the ins and outs of the profession, but want to know everything. So, indeed, it is exhausting to constantly instruct and satisfy the curiosity of laymen. (Especially when they are friends and family, lending their inestimable and selfless help.) On the other hand, it may be useful for novel directors to be aware of their own knowledge gaps, as well as their ability to stay focused and calm in adverse situations.

So far we have intentionally said nothing about the most commonly known task for a director: Directing actors. Everybody knows this, but you should not think that it is a simple duty. In Chapter 9: "The World of Acting," we will see that we are talking about artists who must also be respected professionally. The director must not only value their work, but also understand it. Directors always run the risk of treating actors as a mixture of a mannequin, which is dressed and posed in a showcase, and a trained monkey. A kind of robot that obeys their orders, as 3D characters obey the animators who manipulate their skeletons. So, it is important to keep in mind that, besides professionals doing their job, actors are human beings first.

Sometimes, finding the balance between what a director wants and what an actor proposes is a complicated task; since what an actor knows or does not know comes into play, and what the actor is physically capable of doing. As we will see in Chapter 9: "The World of Acting," actors work by controlling their bodies, which is more difficult than it seems. It may happen that a director expects an actor to do something specific, that he has imagined or seen in another movie, but this does not mean that every actor is able to do that. Besides, if a director is asking an actor to do something that he or she has already done in the past, for that very reason, the actor may prefer not to do it. As professionals in their field, actors may want to try something new and different.

There are many physical and psychological challenges that crew members must face during a film shoot. And dealing with one another's egos and whims are some of the worst—until you get used to it. You might think that these are personal issues, not professional ones, but that is exactly the point. We are talking about something that, no one can deny, is a substantial part of the profession. It is completely intrinsic to this business.

THE BEGINNER FILMMAKER

Directing a film is complicated work, but the first real challenge is getting the job. As we have already seen, the need to choose a director starts at the very moment it is decided that a script "might be interesting enough to consider the possibility of its real production at some point." (Note the uncertainty of the hypothesis, in case the quotation marks have not shown irony enough.) To draw up the first list of options to consider, studio executives or producers send the script to the possible directors (actually to their agents) to check their potential interest. Likewise, directors can expressly show interest in a project that they already know or are pursuing. (Like an adaptation of something they like, the remake of some cult movie, or the latest work from their favorite screenwriter.)

THE FILM AND AUDIOVISUAL INDUSTRY

One of the most widespread desires is always the option to pitch a personal project. But the chances of success are really really low. (Actually, making a pitch presentation is not that difficult, but getting results from it... that is another story.) Great acclaimed directors try all the time and although some do manage to produce their dream project (less than you would imagine), it is always after years and years of perseverance, infinite patience, and having to make an excessive number of concessions here and there; which is inevitable if you want to make it happen.

That is the spiral trick. A hurricane that is so hard to escape from, once you are trapped. Imagine that you succeed in making a couple of movies as a newcomer (even with mainstream intentions). You manage to build your own personality and style. It is assumed that personality is precisely what brings you success, prestige, and perhaps even impressive box office results. A chain of events that lead you to be a director in high demand. What happens next? Once you have finally been able to prove your professional worth, the industry suddenly wants you to direct products aligned with the most conventional standards, forcing you to minimize your own personality as much as possible. Your movies must look like they are personal, but they are not anymore. When you are really successful, you are no longer in charge of your own movies... the studios are.

Many of you might be thinking that this is the same thing that happens in the music industry. And yes, it is. The compensation is usually so attractive that it is hard to resist the temptation. Obviously, any professional's first priority will always be to put food on the table. And once you have enough food, all the luxuries of the world might be nice second priorities. So, as we have already stated, the more commercial successes you have, the more mainstream jobs you will be offered. And while your work continues to guarantee success, you will not lack good offers for lucrative jobs. It is designed to be a vicious circle. So in the end, the long and exhausting process of trying to finance personal projects (which are potentially risky for everyone involved) is relegated to the background.

THE FILM AND AUDIOVISUAL INDUSTRY

A lot of people do not know that professional directors (including top directors) are not personally connected to most of their movies' conceptions. Directors are called and offered a finished script to direct and they can accept the job or not. Obviously, they try to get projects that are more or less consistent with their own interests and personality. But the truth is, for renowned directors that are accustomed to success, it is frustrating to fight (as hard as beginners must fight) for so many years to attract investors to finance a really personal project. And it is no coincidence. That is how the industry prevents famous directors from believing that they have more control and influence than they actually have. Producers and studio executives always want to make sure that directors understand who is in control of the business. So, even the most powerful directors must make many concessions for the real owners of the product (producers first, and studio executives later), if they want their movie to be finished and properly distributed worldwide.

Let us return to the early stages now, before a director is world-famous and can rub shoulders with the rich and powerful in Hollywood. We have said several times that these jobs are conditioned by strong competition due to supply and demand. However, the digital and multimedia society that we live in today offers a huge and varied number of jobs for audiovisual creators, related to their skills. Such as marketing and advertising, multiple needs for digital video, and the multimedia revolution of the internet (online video games, audio/video streaming, audiovisual interactivity, and much more). As a matter of fact, any creative person with professional aspirations can survive the day-to-day with an occupation that is more or less related to his or her interests. Shifting high and personal ambitions, probably not too realistic, takes a mature attitude; but not all young people are willing to do this. Realizing that you should not bet everything on such an uncertain and maddening profession might be a smart decision, but it also means that you will end up having less time to dedicate to that ideal occupation that you dream of.

That is why most wannabes quit. One day, they start realizing that there is another priority much more important than their dreams: Their real life.

Once again, self-criticism makes its appearance. Apart from fighting your own ego and arrogance, it is also very useful to identify where you are on the road. The first thing you should know is the length of the road, in order to calculate how much is left. Unfortunately, this confusing road is always covered with fog, and you can barely see anything in front of you. We have already pointed out that each person will get their own vision of the road as they go. So, it is also true that nobody knows (literally) how far someone can go, including yourself.

Since childhood, we are irremediably conditioned by our family's particular situation. Even the city we live in depends on your family. The same goes for young adults, whether they go to college or not. That is to say that not everyone has the same means to start a career (economic means or otherwise). In fact, when you plan to make your first movie, it is essential to be fully aware of the production means that you can count on. No matter how modest they are. Whatever you can use for free or very cheap is probably better than nothing.

When cinema began, only businesspeople of the rising sector and a few wealthy individuals were able to buy cameras and film rolls. Back in the 1920s and 30s, the pioneering company Kodak began selling 16 and 8mm rolls, cameras, and projectors as more economical adaptations of the defined 35mm standard. But it was not until 30 years later that Kodak decided to put this technology into the hands of the average consumer.

In the mid-60s, the improved Super 8mm format was conceived to allow the wealthy middle class to record their own home movies, things like trips, special occasions, and memories. After a decade of sweet apogee, not even the new Super 8 with sound was able to curb the immediate popularity of video and therefore, the video camera. Breaking into the market like a sudden hurricane, this new technology offered the possibility of recording in color and built-in sound, on a magnetic tape that did not need photographic exposure or development of any kind; and at surprisingly affordable prices.

Following this, the democratization of cinema took its first steps. During the years of the millennium change, computers and non-linear editing software made recording and editing audiovisual pieces possible for anyone with a certain level of professionalism. And nowadays, all of the above is irrelevant because it has just become audiovisual history. Cameras are no longer photo or video cameras, but they all are multifunctional. Any smartphone on the market captures moving images with surprising quality; and there are a lot of cameras and devices that record at 2k and 4k (movie theater screen resolutions of 2,000 or 4,000 pixels horizontally), being sold at prices reasonable enough for beginners who can afford to invest in equipment. Besides, it is not expected for this technology to become obsolete as quickly as DV (Digital-Video) tapes had in the first decade of this century, due to the fast evolution of memory cards.

We can see that the recording system is no longer a problem. So there are no more excuses. The important thing is the content. To this day, anyone can show their greatest talent with a smartphone. But let us qualify this, so that it does not lead to confusion. We are not saying that you could record a movie with any cheap cell phone like you could with a professional camera. The recording device's technical and visual limitations affect the image's cinematography, of course. But many other elements will not be affected at all, like the script, the editing, the narrative pulse and pace, the actors' performances, screen geography, and many other artistic intentions that have nothing to do with the camera's quality. Every professional director, screenwriter, and actor would be capable of remaking any of their successful films or scenes with conventional video cameras, cell phones, or tablets. And, to many people's surprise, they would look pretty similar. Many achievements would remain intact and, above all, this experiment would be narratively identical.

THE FILM AND AUDIOVISUAL INDUSTRY

The obvious differences could be: Lower definition, worse quality in colors or contrast, much less visual depth, more digital noise, or poorer sound. But in any case, it would still be far superior to what any amateur crew could do with the same means. This is something that very few beginners understand and/or accept. Talent and work done well has nothing to do with the production means your budget can afford. It would be useless to put 60 million dollars in the hands of someone who does not master audiovisual language or has no previous experience (that would mean that even the personal relationship with the crew might be a total disaster).

What is much more important is what happens in the opposite case. Even when working under precarious conditions, expert eyes could detect outstanding talent (that is the basis of talent hunting). As it happens, one of the main consequences of such technological democratization means a saturation of young creators who, even recording with more notable resources, are not capable of making any special contribution. Nothing relevant. It is difficult to draw the industry's attention with such an expendable material devoid of any personality. Then one might wonder: What other things determine the quality of an audiovisual production?

We could start with the quality of photography, one of the outstanding subjects most beginners tend to ignore. It is difficult for people without artistic knowledge to understand the importance of lighting and photographic treatment when shooting. So, the options you have are: Learning on your own, calling another beginner who wants to be a director of photography, or maybe asking a professional photographer for help. Even without specific experience on a film shoot or with movie photography, the visual and technical knowledge of an actual camera expert will significantly improve the final look of your work. For example, with solid visual compositions, appropriate color balance, the correct usage of depth of field, minimally decent lighting, and other things.

THE FILM AND AUDIOVISUAL INDUSTRY

The vision and final word come from directors, but in regards to capturing the story in pictures, directors of photography have to know how to compose with the use of light and the behavior of the camera, in terms of technical matters. They have to contribute to the aesthetic beauty of the film, but firstly making it technically correct. That is why the more artistic knowledge directors have, the better it will be for everyone. The greater understanding directors of photography and art directors have (if there is one of these, it will depend on the production's size and ambition), the better communication will be in each phase of the film. And therefore, the better results you will get in the end.

It is important to emphasize that when we talk about the use of photography and color, many think of something very elaborate and demanding, of artistic content rather than technical. But it is not enough to know a couple of tricks about the symbolic use of colors in sets and costumes. That is the easy part, the obvious one. May people think that filming with a very natural, "real" look simplifies things, eliminating the need to worry about lighting or photography (and yes, they are wrong). The importance of photography is something that you simply cannot avoid. Light behaves in a particular way and the cameras and lenses that you are using will capture the colors and tones they receive in a very specific way. Depending on your choices and settings, everything will look brighter or darker, softer or sharper, pinkish or bluish, and you can avoid or provoke burnt whites, yellow skin, unwanted halos, untimely reflections, noisy textures, and filled shadows.

In order to deal with said issues, each and every object in front of the camera must be properly tested and might require modification, if necessary. For example, dyed cloth to obtain the subtle, exact tones required, spotlights and panels to generate light sources and shadows, screens and color filters to correct or create chromatic effects. And all that for shots with a static camera. New complications would be added for shots filmed with a moving camera (for starters, neither spotlights, cables, nor any other production equipment can be seen on screen).

THE FILM AND AUDIOVISUAL INDUSTRY

The choice between static or moving shots may seem irrelevant to amateurs, but it might mean serious changes in the narrative meaning, the photography set, and the production planning of the whole scene. Lighting conditions must always be taken into account and adapted to the needs and means you count on.

There was a lot of investigation throughout the 20th century to overcome photographic film sensitivity. However, because of the arrival of the digital era, the current cameras used in movies are already equipped with sensors with a light sensibility that was absolutely unthinkable years ago (now if you record in the middle of the night, almost in total darkness, the footage seems to have been shot late in the afternoon). Technology continues to advance every year at an unprecedented pace, but the technical purpose of the camera (capturing light) remains the same.

You still have to keep working each scene, so that nothing seen on the screen looks casual or incorrect. A good example is the appearance of light sources in the scene, meaning literally within the story of the movie. On one side we have the real light sources, positioned in certain ways to illuminate the set and the actors (that are always behind the cameras, never visible to the audience), and on the other side we have those lights that explicitly appear on camera. For example, when filming a bedroom scene, imagine a lamp on a night table. We would have a dozen people behind the camera, surrounded by several spotlights, with different orientations, intensities, and tonalities.

Those are the real elements that define shapes, volumes, colors and, in short, the formal and aesthetic look of the shot. But within this fiction (inside the reality of the story), viewers can see a lamp on the bed-side table which, in theory, is the source of all that aesthetical (but fake) light. It must be on, of course, but this bulb cannot be a normal one, as any bulb we may have in our homes. Any light of that intensity would ruin the luminous and chromatic balance that you have prepared. So, for these types of lamps, spotlights, streetlights, and any general light source that cameras are going to capture directly, you must use special bulbs with variable intensity, exclusively adapted for these purposes.

It may sound excessive, but in night shoots, you have to turn off street lights if necessary and change every bulb, or even create a whole new lighting system, perhaps just to shoot one scene.

Now it is clear that the lighting in a scene gives us the shape, volume, and color of everything in front of the camera. But there is one concept more advanced that must still be taken into account: The texture. This falls more directly on the shoulders of the art director and director of photography, but as previously said, directors should know the most relevant parts of their work. And this is an element typically unknown (and ignored) by novice filmmakers without an artistic background or training.

In summary, every work of art has a number of material properties. In sculpture, it is obvious that the basic texture is shown by the material itself (marble, stone, wood, clay, etc.) but it is also affected by how the artist decided to use it. The tools and techniques used by the author have ended up giving the work a specific polished finish (as a whole, but also to each part). In painting, brushstrokes are accumulated in embossed layers of different thickness (not to mention when modern artists started to include non-pictorial objects on their works). It also goes without saying that the sum of materials and textures is implied in architecture as much as melody, harmony, and rhythm generate a myriad of nuances in musical texture. And at last we come, logically, to the photographic texture. All objects, every single material in the world, have their own texture. Including human skin and hair, or the iris of our eyes. And, to no surprise here, there is something extremely characteristic and magically captivating in these details when we contemplate them through the eye of the camera.

Textures not only show the three-dimensionality of everything that surrounds and composes us, but they also have the quality to evoke, without remedy, the sense of touch, taste, or smell (because of a brain trick called synesthesia). Skillful filmmakers will always try to use textures in a smart way to convey sensations.

Indeed, everything influences the final look of textures in a film like costumes, decorations, lighting, and even casting. (It is said that the face is the mirror of the mind, right?) But the decision to enhance, soften, or ignore texture in a film, ends up being the personal decision of the authors.

Another fundamental responsibility of the director, that is also shared with the photography team, is deciding on the visual composition of the frame in every single shot. This is something that beginners usually neglect, but it is also the first thing they correct when they start to find out what filmmaking is about. Even if it is not possible to have a professional cinematographer on board (or a photographer who contributes the most basic knowledge), unconcern for the visual composition denotes a lack of attention to detail that is completely unacceptable (the camera is the eye of the director, never forget that). The formal concern for camera angles is another interesting detail that can detect talent (or the lack thereof). So, beyond the basic types of camera shots, which any beginner knows, directors who do not demonstrate enough interest in getting the best camera angles to tell the story, will prove that they still have a lot to learn.

When filming one single shot, the camera can be positioned in thousands of places and aimed at several different points. The so-called geography of the screen is determined by the set of said placements, meticulously calculated. Where is the camera? Where is it aiming? And where are the scene elements positioned? The answers to these questions define the exact image that appears in the viewfinder, shot after shot, along the whole scene.

The main purpose of a skillful handling of the screen geography is placing the audience correctly. They need to understand each element's location. This helps to avoid getting lost during the course of actions, which have been shot separately, and incessantly cut, with actors moving around the set. A virtuous mastery of space and using the camera, is actually as important as timing in editing. Both things together is one of the most relevant skills in talented directors.

THE FILM AND AUDIOVISUAL INDUSTRY

An interesting detail that allows you to instantly differentiate amateurs from professionals (or amateurs with a little more knowledge) is "crossing the line" or "jumping the line." If you have never heard of it or have had the natural ability to deduce it by yourself, it is difficult not to make this common mistake. It is a small error in practice, caused by the lack of theory, which immediately reveals what your preparation level in audiovisual direction is. And it is coincidentally related to what we were just talking about: the choice of where to place the camera.

The theory is simple. Given the spatial distribution of two elements within a scene, you can establish an imaginary straight line between them. For example, a dialogue between two characters; however, this is also valid for objects. The point is, in order to allow the audience to see every action correctly connected and perfectly understandable, the camera must be positioned on only one side of that straight line. The camera must also always be within the 180-degree arc (that is why it is called the 180-degree rule) or the viewer will be disoriented.

In the very first silent movies, it was observed in the editing table that if this rule were broken, the characters switched places or seemed back to back, looking at or talking to unknown places and people, and so on and so forth. It may seem like a very small detail of little relevance, but it is one of the most basic and important audiovisual conventions of narrative language, and it should never be underestimated.

Once understood, it looks simple, but respecting said axis is actually limiting the number of shots you can use to make an interesting scene. Let us imagine the case of a long conversation. Some of the most important decisions that directors make regarding camera work, are related to how they solve the complex equation involving the following: Duration (if the scene cannot be shortened, they must avoid it being boring), the number of characters (having only two is easy, but it also limits their creative options), the environment surrounding the characters (it is always good to insert a long shot or master shot), other elements of interest (close-up shots of objects in the scene, characters' bodies, and similar details), the subjective shot of a particular character's point of view (it is allowed, since the characters are the very limits of the axis), and, finally, inserting another scene. (In the script phase you would have noticed that this scene might be too long, so you may want to change the axis to the other side when coming back to the scene later.) It is also true that you can change the characters' positions by just having the actors walk while shooting. And that will always be the best and most elegant option to create variations on the axis, as well as moving the camera position through the set in a dolly shot. As long as there is no cut in editing, there will not be any aggressive break for the viewer; and just paying attention to the screen will avoid any possible disorientation.

Therefore, it is not the same to jump or cross the line as voluntarily modifying it in a fluent and conscious way. What is more, you can even break the 180-degree rule and cross the line on purpose to create confusion as a narrative resource. This is what gives you those recurrent scenes that we all know: A maze of mirrors, a violent shooting, and a nightmare or paranoid vision. These are situations in which the viewer is deliberately deceived or confused.

As we said, jumping the line is a mistake mainly made by self-taught beginners or careless amateurs with little experience or talent. But it can also happen on professional productions. This is due to the careless philosophy of filming material from all possible angles, as a mere routine, and not with specific, artistic purposes. Without a real criteria and just filming with a mechanical attitude, this excessive unconcern usually causes the entire crew (including the director) to have such little interest in what they are doing. So much so, that once at the editing table you might find the best shots (or even the only decent shots) are not on the same axis.

You can try to save the day with some of the tricks mentioned earlier, like inserting shorter or longer shots (typically filmed as part of the routine, to cover your back in these cases). And actually, in a lot of movies you can notice some shots where suddenly, the image is horizontally flipped in post-production (like reflected in a mirror). This is a cheap solution (and does not always work) to correct the axis when the 180-degree rule has been broken. By doing this, if you are lucky, you can see everything in the correct direction. However, this can also lead to small continuity errors, because of the asymmetry in the actors' faces, hairstyles, costumes accessories, the scene lighting, or objects in the background. If you pay attention to those details, you might have the odd perception that they have been relocated to different places. But it is also true that even in such cases, the chances of viewers noticing something is much lower compared to the possibility of leaving the line of action broken. In fact, you can actually cross the line and leave it in the final cut. (It is not that unusual.) In a normal conversation between two characters it might be too noticeable, and it is impossible for true professionals to make such a mistake. But in unimportant scenes, some filmmakers (not good ones) may decide to use some shot just because they like it more (or do not care at all), even if they break the 180-degree rule. Except for very extreme cases, this error happens in such a subtle way that the average audience does not even notice. Your brain may perceive something weird for a few seconds, but you are supposed to be immersed in the story and your mind prefers not to lose attention. It may be easier to notice it in amateurs' works, because in productions of such low quality, no one really gets involved in the story. In general, this is because the visual appeal is poor, the pace is slow, the script is boring, the dialogues are bad, the performances are lost, and yes, the camera probably jumps the line. (Everything is connected.)

One of the greatest virtues that all good directors have is handling of the "invisibility" of the camera properly; what we call the fourth wall (the side of the filming crew is the side of the audience too). Good directors are those who manage to transcend the screen as a window to a different universe, immersing you inside the story. A good story told with mastery even makes professionals forget about the industrial cinematographic elements and enjoy the magic of film like any other viewer.

THE FILM AND AUDIOVISUAL INDUSTRY

It is no coincidence that another of the most relevant elements to measure directors' talent is their sense of narrative pace. If we think of any narration, whether oral or written, it must be told in some way engaging for the audience. Every story has several crucial moments, surprises, and unexpected turning points, but also many parts of a more basic development, which must be interesting enough too. Otherwise, the viewer will get bored. The content of each shot derives from the intensive work of a large number of workers, directed with a specific intention to reach a certain ending. Besides, when editing, the specific concatenation of all the shots will provide the definitive form and pace to the story. But also, when shooting, and even since the very initial planning, directors should know (if you will forget the repetition) the specific direction to follow at every moment of the narration.

Each filmed shot contributes to create a series of images, displaying the narrative facts described in the script. And at the moment of shooting, every take already possesses, within the seconds that it lasts, its own pace which includes different intensities, tones, movements, and significances. However, to complete the whole story, you need to give each shot a specific position with respect to others, a hierarchy order. You have to assign a new meaning to it within a more global harmony. Whether hastily or leisurely, nervously or quietly, the impulse with which events occur will provoke a very specific chain of emotions in the viewers. Their level of satisfaction will depend on the subjectivity of each of them and the ability of the filmmaker.

Apart from the strength of the script itself, the important thing is to maintain and modulate a solid consistency in the intensity, tone, and rhythm of the succession of shots and scenes. That is, the pace of the narrative. This includes the solidity with which the viewers move forward throughout the story, and how easily they can do it.

Directors can manipulate the stories and play with their elements as much as they want, provided that they do it with firmness. Inexperience, lack of expertise, or an excessive amount of experimentation cause filmmakers to get lost along the way, forgetting or getting confused about what they were trying to tell or how were supposed to do it. From the viewer's side, it is the difference between feeling confused (or bored) and having that gratifying feeling of being engrossed in a great narration. Whatever they are telling you or however they are making you feel, directors with a good sense for narrative pace will take you throughout the whole story with proper fluency—almost without you noticing. This is also done without interruptions or any other thing that may take you out of the set of emotions they want you to feel.

Changing the subject a little, we cannot fail to mention here the importance of production design in movies. The real reason that so many films are engraved in our minds and hearts. This is what actually sets so many stories apart and make them good and visually memorable. Although the production designer is also subordinated to the director's global vision, they are the ones who define the overall look of the film. The complete artistic style in visual terms. This person would be, at the same time, directing the whole art team, all the people that transform the conceived designs into reality. And depending on the size and category of the production, one or more art directors might be needed (the person in charge of directing all the specialists in different areas, like set makers, carpenters, or sculptors). More modest productions cannot afford (nor need) both positions and that is why, for example, outside of Hollywood it is much more common to count on only one person as the "art director," which is what they call it in Europe.

It is not that imaginative directors like George Lucas, James Cameron, Tim Burton, or Guillermo del Toro have no merit on the eye-catching staging of their films, it is again, an established game of hierarchy. (Exactly how costume designers have their area of freedom, provided they follow the guidelines given by the director.) A production chain less centralized than is often believed, which is also why it is more efficient than people think. Most of the visual achievements of big blockbusters (especially period, fantasy, or science fiction productions) may be conceptually imagined by the directors and approved according to their criteria, but are specifically defined by the production designer, and executed by the large pool of anonymous artists working on the art team. Professionals who, fortunately for them, usually have great recognition within their areas of expertise, while enjoying quiet anonymity before the public.

Finally, we could also mention the exceptional cases where directors are allowed to write their own scripts. To be a good screenwriter is not a mandatory requirement to be a film director. And, in fact, except for some very personal projects created by themselves, any renowned director understands the convenience of taking an existing script to screen (that is, indeed, the director's job definition).

The opposite is even more unusual, screenwriters who develop enough skill to get behind the camera. What is more, most of the screenwriters who discover what directing is really about, usually lose interest in it. As soon as they find out that imagining a story in pictures is not the only thing you need, they realize how complex and strenuous the director position is. Many are terrified of the multitasking, the artistic-technical, and the multidisciplinary capabilities required. Not everyone is able to handle that pressure. Also, as a professional challenge, it is not particularly attractive for people accustomed to doing their jobs as writers in the quiet of their home or, literally, anywhere and anytime they want.

The thing is, in Hollywood, the process of making a movie is not designed that way. Writing a script is a completely separate process from shooting a film. As we have seen, the norm is that scripts are rewritten several times by several different people, until the screenwriter has (supposedly) the best version. Even after the final approval, the script is nothing more than one more phase of the process. It is never a final product by itself. A script is just a potential movie. Both the director and the writer have their own peculiarities.

THE FILM AND AUDIOVISUAL INDUSTRY

Writing and shooting separately is considered more productive. And this way, producers and studios have greater control of their films. It gives less centralized leadership to directors as "absolute creators." On the other side, directors' maximum aspiration is always to have total creative control (or at least, as much as possible). In other countries' film industries, it is more common for the director and screenwriter to be the same person. This is because most of these industries do not derive from the American model. They were created differently, at different times, and by different causes. They all evolved according to their own local situations. Additionally, if we consider the small size of these industries, we get a very limited number of people who are allowed access to that small "creative elite" of each country. (This also explains why it is so hard to find a real genius. You can find some good directors writing poor scripts, and some good writers who have no talent as directors).

To conclude the chapter and to complete the picture, let us talk about that crazy possibility of having a director decide to produce his or her own film. On paper, it may sound like the perfect solution for anyone, but there is a worrying number of factors, nothing simple, that make it one of the riskiest decisions that you can make in this business. For beginners, it is obvious that risking everything you have (perhaps even more, if you ask for one or several loans) can either work well or it can destroy both your career and personal life. But in the case of consecrated directors, must we expect it to be different? You might think that celebrities can easily convince a producer or studio executive to bet on their personal projects. But the truth, although it can be easier to get some of the elements needed to make a project interesting, the process is no different for them. Absolutely everyone, no matter how rich, famous, or talented you are, suffer the unspeakable to raise funds for their personal projects, if they ever make it.

This industry does not want anyone being more relevant than anyone else. It is no coincidence that there was only one Orson Welles or one George Lucas.

THE FILM AND AUDIOVISUAL INDUSTRY

Everybody wants to repeat what they have done. What no one expects is that, whenever any of these personalities revolutionize the industrial landscape in some way, the sector reacts to minimize the impact and takes immediate action to prevent similar cases in the future. Especially personalities or behaviors that are "inconvenient," problematic, or uncontrollable in any sense. After all, unpredictable consequences are never wanted, and Hollywood majors must ensure that nothing escapes their control. It may seem like a shocking statement, but money cannot buy everything.

With regard to producing with your own money, if you have "x" number of millions in your checking account, you will not want to risk everything on something as uncertain as producing a movie; or at least you would not want to simply waste it. You will want a guarantee of some kind and you will inevitably start to think like a studio executive. You can decide to invest part of your personal savings instead of everything. Okay, but as much as you value your confidence in the project, there are still a lot of crazy stories being told out there, discouraging you from doing it. Obviously, you can be totally sure about your project's quality, but the reality for rich people is still the same. Very few people in the industry have the power to decide what is going to be produced and distributed and what is not. And there is nothing you can do to change that, no matter how much money you have.

Even if you want to film your own independent production, spending your personal fortune. Do you have any guarantee that the studio system will be willing to distribute your product? Are you sure you will be able to provide the same quality as the mainstream industry? (In other words, do you know how to spend a fortune in making a good movie?) As we saw in the first chapters, it is not easy for independent companies to produce and distribute on their own. So many other questions arise. All of them are related to the same dilemma: Consider that the system itself practically controls all of your distribution and exhibition options, why would you insist on trying to operate out of the system? Instead of adopting a collaborative attitude?

THE FILM AND AUDIOVISUAL INDUSTRY

At this point, you have probably noticed that the entire industry is based, from beginning to end, on these kinds of paradoxes. The final conclusion (if any) would be that trying to raise funds for an independent production does not guarantee that you are going to make it. Because even if you finish it, that does not guarantee that it will be distributed. In addition to this, there are a lot of things the industry can do to destroy your movie. (Including the common practice of buying it but never distributing it.) Do you think you would be the first to try to operate outside of the system? Good luck. You are going to need it.

THE FILM AND AUDIOVISUAL INDUSTRY

THE FILM AND AUDIOVISUAL INDUSTRY

MEETING THE PRODUCER

Everyone has heard about producers. It is well known that they are at the highest level of film production hierarchy. But for those who are not sure of the types of producers that exist, we will talk about it. Generally, the producer is the main person who makes the film possible. Mainly in the aspect of economics, but also in many other areas. The producer is the first one to bet on a specific project, as well as deciding whether to continue with it until the end. This means that they are also the main person who has the authority and ability to cancel, delay, or modify the project at any time, regardless of the progression. This is not very common though because the natural thing would be to not start a production that you do not have total confidence in. If we take into account that this industry moves millions of ideas annually and only a negligible percentage of those ideas are produced and released, this would mean that most projects spend most of their lives in office conversations and will probably never go anywhere. Statistically, it is quite unlikely that it will pass through the barrier of presentations, explanations, handshakes, pats on the back, and the promising smiles and positive meetings that are full of good intentions.

THE FILM AND AUDIOVISUAL INDUSTRY

The challenge is attracting interest from the few who have their fingers on the green light. Those who have access to money and/or the possibility of finding it, aka producers. It is not a simple challenge, given the curious paradox: To achieve success and conquer the mainstream audience, you must connect with ordinary people; however, those who have decision-making power have a completely different lifestyle that is really far away from how the majority of the population lives. They do not share attitudes, reasonings, concerns, or needs. The most obvious essence of a human being is always there, of course, but what about the details? The industry's goal (which is to earn as much money for the company as possible) goes in the opposite direction of the content's goal (which is to be liked by ordinary people). This is a clear subjectivity that everyone is aware of. After all, it is something that is in the producer's favor, so there is no reason to hide it. On the contrary, producers prefer to emphasize that they are the ones with the strongest position. (Who can blame them?)

Inside the industry, the producer will be the first and last person responsible for the product's final quality; therefore, they have the power to intervene in the matter of artistic content; apart from forming an opinion on how appropriate or not that content might be. The producer has a voice and vote from the very development or initial acquisition, throughout the manufacturing process, and in the last detail of its completion, including its future commercial life in distribution.

They also have absolute control over the screenwriting process. They are the ones who decide to pay for a complete script or partial items like ideas, treatments, dialogues, or revisions. They decide whether to produce one script or another, and look for all the alliances needed to reach the most appropriate magnitude for that production.

With regard to the film shoot, it is difficult to control what directors do since they are operationally in charge of said environment. But never forget, directors are also professionals hired by the producer. Although you cannot know exactly what the director and the rest of the crew are doing every day, there are some things that the producer can do, remotely, to supervise and maintain some control over what happens while shooting. In a bit we will talk about the different delegates producers have on the field, but let us say, for the moment, that no one has any reason to be alarmed as long as the production is within schedule and budget.

So, what happens with artistic concerns? Producers can actually check filmed material whenever they want. Although this footage is still very raw in appearance and totally disorganized (in short, incomplete fragments with no global context or image processing), there are certain expectations for quality work and one can decipher if this has been achieved or not. With the revision of this material and the information that their delegates provide, producers can detect if the director has been filming exactly what was planned and agreed. In the past, rebellious directors with defying attitudes have given studios serious problems in that regard, but currently it is very rare that something like that will happen.

This brings us back to the famous debate over the film's creative control, only now from the opposite point of view. Directors have every right to claim their artistic vindication as authors of the final product, but for many, the debate usually ends for a devastating reason: producers decide if they will move forward with one project or another. This is because the producer decided to contribute and/or collect the money needed for everything to happen. Therefore, no one would have their job if it were not for them. This includes the director, who was the producer's personal choice within a long list of candidates (and no one is saying producers cannot regret and change their choice on the go).

The one who pays has the right to do whatever they may prefer, and that is indisputable. Any other role in the assembly line is just doing a job, exercising a profession in exchange for salary. Because this is 100% clear: Talking about producers is basically talking about money. And, as in any other industry, the most important thing is always money (spent and earned).

Being the ones with the maximum amount of responsibility, producers have the burden of finding, managing, and administering the budget. It is commonly thought that producers pull that money out of their own pockets, but that is not always the case. What does happen in all cases, is that they have the responsibility of having the money available—no matter where it comes from. And more importantly, they have the additional obligation of ensuring that it is used wisely. In other words, every dollar must be used the way it has been planned, without any wastage.

Obviously, there are always some margins of flexibility, different alerts, security measures, and emergency plans, but the most desirable scenario is to not have to resort to any of this. There can always be causes of force majeure that end up affecting production, such as natural disasters, political conflicts, accidents, deaths, and the like. But it is true that any economic problem in a project will always tend to look like the producer was not able or good enough to manage the situation.

So, let us start revising the different, existing roles in the field. Someone who assumes no active role in production operations, but just puts the money on the table, is actually called an associate producer. This is essentially an investor. It can be any person willing to invest a certain amount of money; no matter where it comes from. For example, venture capitalists, businesspeople from other industrial sectors, or just any rich person who considers, for whatever reason, that movies are an interesting investment.

Even if they are film enthusiasts, not very different from the rest of the public, they usually do not have any special interest in the production process beyond some sporadic "touristic" visit to the shoot. They want to be part of the business to make money. Associate producers understand the inherent risk that they are facing, but obviously, they hope to regain their investment. In fact, losing everything is always a possibility, so you have to be willing to accept it (like many other millionaires who lose a few millions in Vegas, during one of those crazy weekends).

On the other hand, the executive producer is more complex and always surrounded by a certain level of ambiguity. It does not help that the role has different responsibilities, depending on the sector you work, like film, television, music, theater, or video games. In short, we can say they are usually in charge of organizing and managing the office operations at high contractual levels. Executive producers (and usually a whole team of subordinates, depending on the size of the production) are directly responsible for properly distributing the money and searching for all the necessary resources. Depending on their interest and involvement in the project, they can also contribute with capital or not, and be more or less active in the search for additional funding.

The executive producer is usually an executive from one of the studios or an external producer that the studio has assigned to the project. The film's writer, director, or lead actor might receive this title as well. The executive producer role is, in fact, a title that is often shared among several people. Defining the term exactly as it is in reality, is a difficult task. In an approximate attempt, the meaning of "executive producer" could be: "Any person who is essential, in a decisive sense, in making the production possible." The specific reason can be varied. For example, attracting investors or getting an A-list star on board, or perhaps just contributing to the rights of the script, instead of being paid. (You are acting as a minor producer with a small percentage, but you are also essential in making the film possible.) It is clear that this essential contribution may happen in the most random situation. Like, a conversation at a party or brunch, or on a simple, casual phone call.

As we can see, this title tends to be more related to public relations than real business. In fact, to be credited as executive producer is a coveted recognition (besides its economic remuneration, of course). Actually, you can be credited or not, depending on how relevant the collaboration was, how hard the contribution was from your side, and many other subjective factors.

THE FILM AND AUDIOVISUAL INDUSTRY

Since there is no specific regulation in this regard, there are quite a few problems regarding if someone deserves the executive producer title or not. It is true that the Hollywood game creates friends and enemies very easily, although, the good players already know that. And ultimately, it is more about accumulating points here and there, rather than a game of fierce competition to the death. One of the smartest ways to gain and amortize those points is to "pay it forward." In this industry, everyone owes favors to someone and a new game starts at every moment. There is no rest—24 hours a day, 365 days a year. So, everyone agrees that positively contributing collaboratively, so that it can be returned to you in the future, is much better than feeding negative, unnecessary quarrels, right?

One of the most common questions among amateurs and beginners is: "What should I study to be a film producer?" Well, by simply being a millionaire, the doors will open as an associate producer (just bring the money and wait). Starting from there, if you want to go further it will depend on your social skills and your interest in learning.

If you want to be in your fancy office reading scripts, pressing the green light button, and putting together the pieces of the puzzle to earn a few million dollars, it is not that simple. First of all, in every country with an audiovisual industry there is a lot of academic formation in film production, including higher education. There are graduate degrees in communication, audiovisuals, and film business, more than enough to learn the most general theory about all of your organizational and administrative responsibilities. But the truth is, the only way to learn for real is in real production, with real money.

Master's degrees are helpful and studying at a business school will not hurt you either. However, no academic training will guarantee that you enter into Hollywood's privileged elite. Coming from a certain family or circle of influence will always be the easiest and most direct way to make it.

THE FILM AND AUDIOVISUAL INDUSTRY

But this is not to say that sending a good resume to big production companies and studios is useless. If you are lucky, you could receive a job offer from Sony, Fox, or Warner and start your career as an assistant. In fact, the audiovisual industry has been publishing online job offers for executive positions for years. A few years ago, these types of jobs were inaccessible and the possible vacancies were not even publicly available. But nowadays, the unstoppable social revolution of the internet is globally transforming important areas like employment.

We stated at the beginning that the producer role implies different functions and responsibilities, depending on the medium. In television and music, it has a more direct and unilateral influence on creative content. In video games, it has much more to do with organization and direct management of resources. The accountability for the budget is always implicit but, in these cases, the budget already comes from previous deals like distribution/sales agreements, or different types of licensing, or just from the production company's revenues (since we are talking about lower amounts of money). However, in theater and more generic events, the producer is a very centralized and totalitarian figure. All these profiles are merged into one single figure, having the sole power of decision, control, and supervision for everything.

Coming back to film production again, let us clarify any doubt regarding the polysemy of the word "production." Depending on the context, it could mean any one of the stages of filmmaking, i.e. pre-production, "production," post-production, distribution, and exhibition. But perhaps you are referring to the "production" team or "production" department, which are among the various teams existing on a film crew (for example, production, art, costume, and lighting). Or maybe you are using the word to mention the project as a whole. For example, using "production" synonymously with "film project in the process of being manufactured." Let us see all this put together.

The production stage is considered the main part of the entire process. It is where everything starts to take shape. This stage does not necessarily begin the first day of shooting, but maybe long before—just as soon as you start to spend money on the first element needed for shooting (such as costumes or decorations). From this term derives the previous executive and administrative stage (pre-production). This is where the conceptual decisions are made and all the technical, logistical, legal, and financial aspects are placed in the calendar. Post-production received its name in a similar fashion. It is the stage where the final footage is assembled, embellished, and properly finished (for example, this is where music or digital effects are added).

Well, throughout all these phases there is a transversal department responsible for all this happening: The production department. It is the team that follows the executive producer's orders. They are a larger or smaller group, depending on the size of the project, working tirelessly at the headquarters, office, or shooting location (even if it is a small mobile unit, someone from the production department should be there). It is the part of the team that manages and coordinates the operations that must be done to make any shooting possible. (Anything purely operational, different from artistic or technical content.) They make sure that everything is in the right place at the right moment.

Within this team, the first person in charge and the direct delegate is the production manager (they are the communication bridge between both worlds: executive business and filmmaking). Sometimes people call them "producers" on set because unlike the purely executive producers, production managers are usually present during the shoot, as the highest authority in terms of production. They are only subject to the director's orders, but also have a higher power in financial and logistical decisions.

Next in the hierarchy, is the head of production (which is, at the same time, managing the heads of each team). This relativity of hierarchies happens because film directors can make risky decisions that may have a strong impact on the fundamental competencies of the production manager, like affecting the planned schedule or budget. When there are important differences between these two, the conflict can transcend and become a major setback for the shooting plan. If you like production, pay attention now, because we are going to summarize how to break down the production of a film, step by step.

FILM PRODUCTION BREAKDOWN

Everything starts with a script that, after a few first revisions, should have real potential for success. This first stage is essentially endless conversations and meetings among agents, directors, actors, studios executives, other producers, and any person or company related to all the financial, legal, and labor issues involved. At this stage, producers must invest their own resources, while pursuing the green light for a major or minor distribution agreement. In the case of independent productions, the more interesting things you can get for the project, the more chances you will have of making a deal. Aim for things like A-list actors, renowned directors, interesting locations in other countries, fiscal discounts, and benefits.

A theoretical shooting schedule is then outlined and the first budget is calculated to judge its viability (figures that will vary depending on the evolution of events). Every project has the possibility of dying right before the production stage begins. However, in case everything goes well, the next step is to proceed with hiring the rest of the production team. Prior to shooting, the production team makes deals with the corresponding technical and artistic guilds. They also search for locations; which can be an odyssey, depending on the film's size and content.

Each location can be worlds apart. Besides the geographical and climatological conditions, it is important to consider the economic impact and the fiscal, social, and even political conditions of the regions that you are traveling to.

The authorities also need to be contacted and the production team must foresee the location of the base camp for each shooting area. This could mean office rentals, language interpreters, local consultants, and negotiations with services and businesses that can supply the production. This even includes interiors, whether they are natural or need to be built on set. They are always a headache in your own country (availability in the calendar, additional costs, special needs, etc.) so you can imagine what could happen in a foreign country.

Although there is an entire casting team, producers have the final word (in favor or against the directors' preferences) when it comes to selecting actors, specialists, doubles, and extras (background actors). Their only interest will be centered, logically, on the most visible faces and main roles, but they have the power to veto any particular proposal that is considered problematic for filming, harmful to the image of the film, or for any other subjective reason (as much as they can impose anyone they like).

There are many topics that producers can discuss with potential candidates. This is done through the long process of negotiation, no matter if they are actors or directors. However, what you never talk about is money (at least, not directly). In these "job interviews," empty conversations with executives only serve to get the frame of mind of the person you are interviewing. By observing the soft skills (i.e. personality traits, overall temperament, social and communicative abilities, habits, and vices), you can draw a few first impressions about what it would be like to work with this particular person, in relation to previous experiences. So, the more years you have in this business, the easier it will be to recognize personality and behavioral patterns. (We, people, are not as different and special as we would like to believe). It is the same from the other side: Even if you are never selected, the more experience you accumulate in these interviews, the better the next ones will be.

THE FILM AND AUDIOVISUAL INDUSTRY

As the final cast is selected, the terms and conditions of each contract are negotiated and closed through agents and lawyers. These extensive agreements do not only include salaries, of course, but also contain a lot of important confidentiality clauses and conditions regarding conduct, medical check-ups, insurance, eventualities, and even personal requirements from eccentric stars. There is always room for some tug-of-war before the final signature, (again, it all depends on who needs whom more) but as the shooting date gets closer and closer, all the elements necessary for filming must be fixed as soon as possible. Sometimes this happens even in a hurry, due to sudden last-minute changes (including starring actors, hence the importance of the famous list of options).

Once the director, the production designer, the artists for the art department, and the teams to start design and make-up are hired, they must test costumes, makeup, hair, scenography, camera, and lighting. Anything that will be used for the shoot must be tested before the first shooting day. From vehicles, furniture, and portable accessories, to office supplies, mobile phones, security systems, or a simple lantern. In terms of action on the ground, all the producer's delegates must supervise the corresponding set or location on a daily basis (as well as in advance). They must also attend daily production meetings at the headquarter's office and/or on set. This is where they review daily and weekly expenses and planning reports. They also prepare the post-mortem retrospectives (to analyze the relevant issues that happened in the previous days, and learn from them). Additionally, if necessary, they must adjust schedules on the go and together with the management team, watch and analyze the filmed material from the day (this is called dailies or rushes).

Meanwhile, marketing and publicity will begin to intensify in the middle of the production phase, at least in the case of large productions. The expectation for these films is enormous and many of these tasks begin in a very speculative way, without having definitive, polished material (but using mockup images or raw footage and working on conceptual decisions).

THE FILM AND AUDIOVISUAL INDUSTRY

In fact, a production continues to lose money after shooting, with apparently irrelevant details like sending actors back to their respective homes or the famous "wrap party" (this happens once the principal photography has been concluded, so most of the cast and crew are no longer needed). You also have to decide what to do with decorations and costumes, as they could still be needed for last-minute changes or emergencies. Even after they are totally done with them, you must consider their destruction, rent, sale, reuse, or storage for the future (each option has its own advantages and disadvantages that should be weighed calmly).

In post-production, you have to continue being careful with the latest expenses, especially with all the CGI (computer generated imagery) additions and digital effects. Currently, all the scenes in a movie might contain digital images, and more and more often we find entire shots without a single real element actually shot. In addition to being very expensive, from the production perspective, they are quite complex to do, although fortunately for producers, these are external services that are always outsourced to specialized companies. So, the only concern is actually negotiating the budget and schedule.

Once the movie is completely done, the only thing left is the technical part which is allocated for obtaining the final master. For example, recording the soundtrack, the possible need for dubbing, the design of every promotional image (static and moving) as well as the final cut, which is often affected by the results obtained from the famous test screenings (confidential preview screenings for a selected cross-section of the population, providing feedback through a questionnaire).

Now, with the finished product and all the statistical speculations in hand, it is time to gamble and decide on the scope of the distribution: To set the opening dates, number of screens per territory, and the overall strategic approach, according to the product's seen potential (always from the studio's subjective viewpoint, of course).

THE FILM AND AUDIOVISUAL INDUSTRY

Obviously, smaller production sizes mean fewer people to hire, issues to manage, and problems to solve. But regardless of this, there are a number of qualities that producers are expected to have: Knowing the market, understanding the audience's taste, trusting their delegates, being diplomatic and polite, remaining calm in adverse situations, and above all, being convinced and excited about every project they do. Regardless of whether they have these qualities or not, what is true of any producer in the world, is that they themselves are convinced that they have them.

THE GODS OF OLYMPUS

Producers have never been as rich and powerful as in the golden age of Hollywood. Although, a lucky few enjoyed that coveted status at the beginning of the new millennium (before the last economic crisis), thanks to the huge success of spectacular digital effects and the momentary apogee of the DVD format. The situation is very different now, but producers are reluctant to abandon the appearance of this status. Currently, the most important thing is that the producer's name appears as large as the starring cast, especially if it is the only relevant name on the poster (in cases where the actors and directors are unknown to the public). This is due to decades of marketing experience and lessons learned from the advertising world.

Years ago, the producer being known within the industry was enough. But nowadays, it is assumed that the names of certain producers can arouse the public's interest because of a simple association of ideas. The reasoning is: If the person responsible for a previous success has enough self-confidence to believe that they are worthy of the public's trust, people will expect the new product to be of the same quality as the previous successful film. Most people assume that the producer has the commercial eye to detect a good film project and will maintain the same level of quality.

That is the initial reasoning, but in big-budget blockbusters, this claim effect is a little diluted. Large productions have many relevant attractions, so nobody cares who is producing it (even less than usual). There are many names of producers that people do not know, even if they have great successes on their credits. For this reason a tagline was created: "From the producers of..." along with the title of their most significant films (both recent or classic that can be remembered).

Egos aside, we previously mentioned qualities that every producer should have and how easy it is to fake them. You might be wondering if learning a bunch of stock phrases, memorizing them, and repeating them over the years is what makes someone a good producer. Although, before that, you could wonder: What does "being a good producer" mean? If we solely look at business and financial results, practically all producers are really good. Is it about business people being more or less sincere? Honest? Empathetic? Nice? Polite? Charismatic?

As we have said, anything related to appearances and public image, requires consideration of personal values and principles, such as the conception of truth and falsehood. Once you understand and normalize something so basic in this business, the change of mindset becomes easier and less harmful. And that is one of the big reasons why so many people end up losing their connection with reality. As we have seen, if everything is said because of customs, words end up losing their meaning.

As far as conventions are concerned, one of the most obvious clichés is having everyone state how super excited they are about working on the project. Producers, directors, actors, technicians, or whoever (literally everyone). You cannot distinguish who means it and who is saying it routinely. After all, it costs nothing to smile and proclaim overwhelming passion and illusion, right? And this "everything is awesome" philosophy is the least one can expect from people who have been given the privilege of working in such an elitist industry. The problem is that having compliments and flattery as a standard, flawed routine, means that many do not bother making the effort to look convincing.

THE FILM AND AUDIOVISUAL INDUSTRY

Of course, this falsehood is not exclusive to the entertainment industry. Anyone who has ever looked for a job knows that showing enthusiasm and interest in the position (whether real or pretend) is received positively in the interview process. As much as not showing enthusiasm and passion is perceived as negative.

The ability to deal with ambiguity is absolutely fundamental for business management. This is why producers might seem to have an apparent superiority in conversation. On the other hand, directors and actors (at least the good ones) can naturally manage nuances and techniques to fake emotions. This often causes awkward moments, when everyone in the room knows who is lying to whom and in regard to what. Undoubtedly, everyone will keep calm and smile, no matter what is said in that room, knowing perfectly well that a few minutes later, the tense formality and politeness is going to explode in private, in the forms of stress, concern, frustration, anxiety, rage, sadness, etc.

Many people say that the attitude inside is the important one, and not the attitude seen outside. It is forgotten that attitude is precisely the way you are willing to behave, independent from what is happening inside of you. There are not different kinds of attitudes, it can only be what it is: The way you decide to reason, speak, and behave beyond what you may be feeling. It is no coincidence that, in any job descriptions, a positive attitude is always required. What is actually being asked is to "pretend" to be positive, which is the only thing needed to maintain a pleasant working environment, absent from conflict without negativity. Nobody cares about what you really feel. The important thing is that you do not externally show a negative attitude that affects the environment, even if you could have reasons. No one can force other people to feel positive, as it cannot be demanded to feel happiness or personal fulfillment. If someone's attitude is their response to true of false feelings, it cannot be demonstrated empirically unless they express them outwardly. That is, an attitude change. But again, one could question the genuineness, whether it is true or false. (And this would be a meaningless loop, yes, so let us not move away from the subject).

THE FILM AND AUDIOVISUAL INDUSTRY

Before we focus on the omnipotent billionaire producer and the inherent complications of Hollywood, let us talk about a more modest kind of producer. Despite having enough resources, a decent amount of money, and even a good company producing quality films, the producer needs to draw the attention of the gods of filmic Olympus once and again. Previous experience brings strength and credibility to their profile, increasing their chances of success during negotiations. But apart from that, the process to sell your new project is difficult every time.

Those famous presentation meetings (called pitch meetings) are crucial to the selection process. The art of pitching is hard to do and learn, given there are few possibilities to be successful and not exactly because of the quality of your project or idea. You could have a couple of meetings or dozens of them, and they could all be very positive, but that will not actually mean anything conclusive. (Do not believe anyone that is telling you the opposite, unless you are one of the lucky ones, receiving the unlikely green light). Many great, successful movies were stuck for decades before getting the final support of someone, receiving nothing but frustrating rejections everywhere.

These pitch sessions are offered to producers or executives, by scriptwriters or directors; but also by other producers looking for funding, association, coproduction, or just a good sale.

Actually, every moment can be good, or bad, for presenting your project. As casual and brief as the conversation may be, in a couple of minutes you can catch someone's attention and get their enthusiasm. Just as you could ruin any possibility in the same lapse of time, after an unfortunate start. It is just the abyss of subjectivity. At first, it is hard to accept the power of decision that lies in these very few people, especially when they do not seem to have the faintest idea what they are talking about. A priori, an idea can be presented practically at any time and place but common sense must be the norm. We saw in Chapter 6: "Screenwriters' Reality," that no one should ever try to corner a producer directly. The only way these elitist personalities are accessible is when they themselves show interest.

In any other case, many producers with some experience make the mistake of considering themselves equals when, by chance, they coincide with a fat cat. This can happen in work-related events such as festivals, awards ceremonies, charitable acts, and the like; but also in many other situations of everyday life, such as in a restaurant or on the street. These are particularly delicate situations though, because cordiality and good manners should prevail when surrounded by other people. But it might not be like that. Everything may seem to have worked well, but you might actually have been added to someone's blacklist, as an inconvenient, annoying pain in the ass.

There is always talk of this typical moment in which someone is cornered in a restaurant, but sometimes there are also more distended and less risky circumstances. Situations where a polite presentation among gentlemen could occasionally make sense, naturally inviting a casual conversation about work, which could lead to organizing an official meeting, if the other party is interested. It is all a matter of opportunity and luck.

In some countries, there are also specific committees that, in order to grant public aids, act as a tribunal before producers' oral presentations. While in other places, for example, they only revise and evaluate written documentation, omitting the pitch sessions. These presentations may seem simple but, even having a good project in hand, not everyone is good at public speaking, explaining themselves, or synthesizing their speech. By adding personal charisma (or lack thereof) and a well-known subjectivity at the other side of the table, it all gets even more complicated: Nerves, blocks, fears, and frustrations. Fortunately, there are also many ways of overcoming these types of problems. There are courses, workshops, therapies, good preparation, or just practice.

Falling short (not getting enough interest or not mentioning key parts that would sell the project better) may be as bad as talking too much (being boring or giving overwhelming, unnecessary information). This communication game is fundamental.

Even if you potentially have the best film in the world, what you are trying to sell now is something intangible, it is just selling castles in the air. And no one can get into each other's head to visualize the same images or feel the same emotions as the person pitching the personal project.

Beginners usually make two mistakes. They give excessive details that they themselves consider quite exciting, but that are not interesting for the listener. (This is a typical mistake that directors make.) As well as they forget to highlight certain concepts or viewpoints about the project, and these might make a difference. Moreover, the one aspect that beginners never fail at is enthusiasm. Sadly, that is not enough to succeed. All newcomers are full of passion. But it is not a good sign if after business meetings, the only thing people highlight about you is your passion. "We love your passion." If that is the only conclusion they get from your conversations, it basically means that you still have a lot to learn.

There is no special standard that defines the science of pitching, but you can find a lot of conventional good practices about it and public speaking in general, which ultimately have the same basics, like having good communication skills focused on selling a film project.

The first thing you have to do when pitching, is to briefly greet and introduce yourself. It is very possible that the person you are pitching to barely knows who you are, or even what the meeting is about. They are people with very busy schedules and, for sure, little interest in what you have to say, especially when you are still a nobody. These people find it difficult to distinguish some projects from others or remember who you are, even if they have received prior information about you. (There is an exception if they are the ones who made said introduction. In this case, they may praise your work, which would be a good sign.) In any case, for one reason or another, they are there at that very moment, sitting before you (or on the telephone), and maybe it is the only chance you will ever have to get their attention. As a beginner, your perception of these processes will be pretty exciting in general, so you must always try to keep calm and make a good first impression.

THE FILM AND AUDIOVISUAL INDUSTRY

The most important thing would be to make a good global, synthetic, and coherent summary of the strengths of the project. There is no fixed scheme here, because the relevance of each point will be directly related to the content. Some may think that starting out by saying their project needs a big budget of 100 million dollars goes straight to the point and is useful for quickly perceiving if listeners are open to the possibility (so no one wastes further time and effort). Moreover, leaving something so relevant for the end might give the impression that you are trying to hide something. As if you are afraid to talk about it, among other insecurities about your project. On the contrary, others might think that the project has so many attractive elements, that the cost should not be particularly relevant when starting talking about it. Whatever you decide to do, just be consistent in your speech. Considering that every word you say is going to be judged, it is crucial that you speak with confidence and security. So, just highlight the strengths of your project and disguise its weaknesses a bit, but never try to deny them.

Apart from the strength and quality of your idea or project, the major keys regarding your selling skills are, in short: To be calm and organized, to summarize what you have and what you need, and to know the profile of your audience well. Because one thing is clear, no executive will approve of a big-budget production that comes from a novice producer or artist. That is just not going to happen. So, every strategy should start by selecting the right project for the type of people you are going to meet.

FRIEND OR ENEMY?

We have seen that the role of the producer is more than necessary (it is mandatory, essential). Productions would not exist without someone starting the engine; someone putting the pieces on the board and giving the order to start playing. We also mentioned that everyone has a boss, everyone works for someone.

And although producers may need to count on others (studio executives, co-producers, private investors, distributors to negotiate with, etc.), everyone in the production line are actually working for them, and that is what defines their unquestionable position of power. This is also what justifies the excessive egos and the most capricious decisions among the many follies that can be seen throughout the development of any project.

As it could not be otherwise, one of the main victims of these deified personalities are the directors. They are next in the hierarchy of authority, as well as in caprice and self-importance. Directors are the first ones that producers must start looking for when they are thinking of producing a new script. Ideally, both should work together and agree on all decisions throughout the entire development of the film. They must confirm that they are on the same page, that they understand each other, and that they coincide in the result they would like to see at the end of the road. This is not easy, because when it comes down to it, these two profiles have very different interests and, as we are saying, none of them usually stand out for their humility and patience.

On the one hand, producers start from a more comfortable situation (they are set up for life, we can say), but it is also true that with every production, for every producer, there comes a stressful trial in which time is money. As people in charge, they are the ones who must ensure that the cost, schedule, and objective quality of the product meet the expectations. However, for directors, quality is much more subjective, responding to a series of artistic factors that are fundamental to them. Like audiovisual beauty, underlying meaning, emotional impact, and narrative correction. Things that the audience only perceives in a tangential way, and only in the few cases when someone is actually perceiving anything (as the producer would think).

Directors are also worried about technical quality, of course, but both parties (producers and directors) can assume on counting on the necessary means in every professional production of a certain weight (since it is just a matter of budget).

THE FILM AND AUDIOVISUAL INDUSTRY

With the appropriate amount of money, you can pay top-class technicians and artists to design, create, and take care of every detail regarding decorations, costumes, props, or special effects. As well as having access to the best technological equipment in order to capture everything in the most spectacular way possible (even for the simplest production, the best photography quality will mean more time to shoot).

Although these artistic factors contribute to some degree in enjoying movies more, the producer has an obligation to monitor and ensure that certain limits of proportion are never exceeded. That is to say that the amount of effort and money allocated in these details do not exceed the level of impact they will have on the public's enjoyment. In other words, never waste time and money on details that nobody is going to appreciate later (since it will not return in any benefit). For example, stereoscopic 3D continues to be used because the extra cost of its creation still compensates well in the box office (it is not because S3D is the greatest invention in the world). And in case it is no longer profitable, it will be no longer used. It is that simple.

This is why art house films and experimental languages are avoided. Studios have nothing against art in particular, and if the majority of the public actually had artistic sensibility, studios would sell art only. Majors will produce what people are willing to pay for (which up to today, is fun and entertainment). Nobody wants to pay to see weird things that they are not going to understand. For example, contemplative introspection that remains in simple, soporific pace; unusual temporal structure that provokes chaos and disorder in the story; cryptic symbolism or surrealism, which is confusing more than it is intriguing; too personal of stories about the author's life or deep mind, which is not interesting to anyone. In short, all these iconic traits of modern and contemporary art: Provocation, rupture with conventions, abstraction against figuration, and conceptualism above formalism. All of these ideas come from that "avant-garde" postmodernism.

It is so outdated now but the art market is still bragging about it, and it loses all sense when applied to narrative art (even if you can obtain some interesting details from time to time, in terms of aesthetics). That happens mainly because, in order to exist, the products of the audiovisual sector must have a commercial output of mass consumption. (Unlike contemporary art products, for example.)

Apart from the most obvious artistic contributions, producing one single film requires an immense amount of technical processes (that have nothing to do with creativity). They are simply to obtain intelligible work. Actually, this happens in any other artistic processes like paintings, novels, or songs. They have certain basic technical processes that must be executed correctly, or the final work might not be good or professional enough. How it is possible that an awful piece of art, executed with shameful quality and/or no real value at all, is worth millions in the contemporary art market? It is just a particular abnormality of said market, due to different speculative interests unrelated to the topic of this book.

On the contrary, the film and audiovisual market works in a more empirical way. Profit is obtained by accumulating the cost of individual tickets. Asset values are then calculated from those empirical results or from valuations based on such data. That is why producers only want to produce safe, reliable, and empirically successful things. Any new, groundbreaking, or experimental ideas suggested to a producer must be included in a minimized proportion, or the only thing the producer will hear is the word "risk."

Actually, the dilemma arises when producers must choose between the certainty of the known, (where the risk remains boring and "more of the same") or the painful business truth of "no risk, no glory." Today, more than ever, we live surrounded by hundreds and hundreds of motivational phrases about the typical philosophy of taking risks to succeed in life, and indeed everyone who is successful in business knows that is a great truth (which does not mean that you do not have the same chances of failing).

Apart from this difficult decision, if there is one characteristic producers and directors have in common, it is the absolute certainty that they always know what the audience wants. This can be a serious problem because, the more successes they have, the more legitimacy they give themselves. And when two successful figures face each other, whose opinions are more valid?

We also have this "creative producer" position, who compared to the executive type, has a greater right to provide creative and artistic solutions to the film. It is not that this credit is necessary, since no producer has to give explanations to anyone, but this profile can appear in two ways: A posteriori (for having contributed to the production's creativity in a relevant way) or required by contract (hand-picked by the studio or the main investors). Directors on the other hand, are forced to fight tooth and nail to defend their ideas in every moment. And, in the case of disagreements, the only thing they can do is try to convince producers to change their minds (which is no easy task, by the way). That is, in fact, one of the greatest frustrations for directors.

In general, even those with a commercial vocation (without strange artistic ambitions) will always have a greater talent and capacity to perceive the tastes of the public. They usually come from a humble environment and have been in more contact with "regular people." They have better emotional empathy, more knowledge about the craft of filmmaking, and a better understanding of movie details that achieve success. So, it is frustrating to know that your movie would be even more commercial by doing something specific that you are trying to propose, but the producers deny it because they are not able to see it.

It is a difficult issue to address because, as we have repeatedly said, the only parameters that producers use to measure success are economic outcomes. This causes, over time, deviations from logic and "good judgment," and refers only to what works better or worse in the box office. This is how so many illogical things become fashionable, no matter how silly they are, until another new success or failure changes the trend again.

For instance, let us say that a film stars the most popular actor and actress of the time. It is taking place in the 17th century, telling an absurd story about pirates and aliens. The script includes some kind of unorthodox narrative, like starting with the end and finishing with the childhood of the characters, going backwards throughout the whole film. By just reading these three points, you will begin to build a series of reasonings in your mind, according to your own intuition and experience. For example: "Just thanks to the actors, it will be a million-dollar success." Or on the contrary: "The mixture of pirates and aliens is so stupid that it will be a disaster." And regarding the last premise, let us assume that it feels less relevant: "I do not think such detail is going to affect the box office," one could think.

Well, this just tries to reflect the huge risk in evaluating a project's content according to their economic success. In the case of breaking the box office, you can never be totally sure which elements of the formula have been crucial for that. Any of the arguments mentioned above may be true or false. But you can be sure that the industry will be open to considering ideas like "aliens and pirates" for a while. As much as, in the case of being a fiasco, you might wonder how it has been possible with such an impressive spectacle of visual effects and massive distribution. But the thing is, the mix of "aliens with something" will be cursed for many, many years. At least, until someone decides to take the risk and try it again, defying the market (because if it were successful, there would be no competition).

Finally, despite not being a very significant element, the unorthodox narrative trick would also be connected with disasters from that day and labeled as "dangerous" by everyone. So, any screenwriter or director trying to propose something like that, in the next few years, would get an automatic rejection. Only until another movie is able to win an Academy Award by using this trick again. In which case, everyone would be surprised by the brave one who decided to approve something so risky, betting against the curse.

THE FILM AND AUDIOVISUAL INDUSTRY

Producers do not have the need to look for something novel or innovative. No matter how many times you hear: "We are looking for something new and original that has not been done before." It is important that this is totally clear, not to confuse anyone. That statement is just a lie. Everyone loves to say it because it makes you look cool. It saves the appearances and perpetuates the cliché, but there is nothing further from reality. The most basic syllogisms are the law in this industry: "If it worked this way, it will work again." We already saw it: By making a few anecdotal and superficial changes, you can have the same thing over and over again, but make it look like you are selling something different. The only areas where a little freedom or experimentation are allowed are precisely in the most superficial areas: The theme, the plot, the premise, and, at most, a few small stylistic resources that do not hinder what is already a proven guarantee of success (which is mandatory to be included).

As said before, directors usually come from less affluent scenarios, in contrast with producers. Although, there are some of them who come from wealthy families or are well-known within the industry. Filmmakers often have more humble origins. There are many other creative and leadership jobs that people with these skills can exert. Filmmaking is usually a whim they aspire to, beyond other realistic, but less interesting jobs. That is why they tend to devote so much time, effort, and money from their own pocket, because they are convinced the sacrifice is worth it.

Directors have always had a deep interest in getting and keeping their job as a director throughout their whole lives. Therefore, they will be the ones forced to learn how to handle and withstand their creative differences with producers, much more than the opposite. Only directors with the highest prestige (those who really guarantee million-dollar success) could handle a clash of egos with a producer, which eventually might put the production in danger. For example, a producer could also be under external pressure (by the studio or other investors), so that they could not even fire the director.

THE FILM AND AUDIOVISUAL INDUSTRY

These top-class directors know that they have an advantage over others. With many years of experience behind them, they usually want to participate as producers and still keep some tricks under their sleeves. For example, there are a few privileged ones who demand several millions just to sign the contract, no matter if the film is eventually produced or not. As you can imagine, in these cases, there is a greater chance that an authentic executive war may be fought for artistic, economic, technical, or managerial reasons (any excuse is good to fight in a good power struggle). All of this is just underlining the obvious lack of power that young directors have. There are very skilled and promising talents out there with good faith and manners, doing the unspeakable to obtain one simple meeting.

In these meetings, they will be mercilessly crushed by the classic conceited businessman/executive, who is cocky and even impolite, and who does not seem to have a philosophy other than: "There are already too many of us in this business, you better do something else." However, seeing it from the opposite side, it is also true that there are a lot of arrogant beginners, showing off their short films as if they were Academy Award winners, convinced of their moral obligation to revolutionize the world with their art. They firmly believe that they are morally superior to the corrupt executive scum and many of them are ready to spit in the face of producers. And these producers are just human beings with their own lives and problems (perhaps wonderful people), who might be dedicating some of their valuable time to see if a promising talent has something special to contribute to their future plans, either short or long term.

So, this is a classic David versus Goliath showdown. For those who cannot understand the big picture, it is quite understandable that the guy who can change your life forever and decides not to do it, by definition is a deeply-hated enemy. Apart from the proven fact that envying the rich and powerful is in our nature.

THE FILM AND AUDIOVISUAL INDUSTRY

In many cases, this tortuous relationship is maintained over the years, since the struggle to get the green light never ends. There are people who understand each other well and are capable of working comfortably and trusting each other. Although, there are very few people that you can call "real friends" in this industry.

In particular, between these two figures there is already a centenary suspicion. Not only because of personal resentment, but more generically, as an innate aversion to hierarchy. Actually, the most frustrating thing for both sides is the obligation to work together. It is still their job. As in any other profession, there will be things you like to do and others that you do not. But if you want to be paid, you will have to do them.

THE FILM AND AUDIOVISUAL INDUSTRY

THE FILM AND AUDIOVISUAL INDUSTRY

THE WORLD OF ACTING

Acting is much more difficult than people would think. Not only is it hard to become a good actor, it is really hard to become a professional actor. Everyone has the impression that it is one of the best paid jobs in the world, because we all know the astronomical salaries at the highest levels of stardom. In fact, a huge part of all that money must be used to have an "enforced" life in the elite. A life that will always be, by default, far away from the lives of regular people; both physically and conceptually. We all know that it is impossible to lead the same life that one had before they became rich and famous, but the issue is more complicated than that. Because not all actors can become stars. There is a modest level of success where little fortunes can provide enough to live comfortably and in good condition for the rest of your life. But nothing close to that of the million-dollar life that people will assume you have—simply for the fact that you are well known. And it is even worse for most anonymous actors. They are the people who must work really hard in low-cost movies, ads, TV, theater, or wherever they find their next opportunity, just to have something barely close to what can be considered a regular job.

THE FILM AND AUDIOVISUAL INDUSTRY

The classic question is: Can you earn a living as an actor? In theory, the industry union agreements of each country should be able to guarantee minimum salaries, making it able to earn anywhere between nothing (voluntarily accepted) and about $1,000 for a single day. In movies for example, all schedule calculations are based in weeks, so actors are able to make up to $3,000 or $4,000 depending on the importance of their role. Taking into account that it is very likely that they are not working every week and month of the year. If they are lucky, actors can end up making an annual salary like any other person (some years more, some years less).

Like most professions in entertainment, actors do not have a permanent job, but they have to rely on third parties who want to hire them for a specific project. So, if nobody calls them, well, they will not have any jobs. This is one of the reasons why many actors intelligently take advantage of the lucky periods, and try to have a higher position in the filming hierarchy, like producing or directing their own movies. As well as investing their money into other types of assets and industrial sectors. Why not? Depending on the capital, we are talking about the stock market, real estate, or even starting their own business. Like hotels, restaurants, clothing, luxury, and maybe a whole franchise (what is never missing is opportunistic people telling you what to do with your money).

Although they are not exempt from risk, these operations allow actors to have another type of income more stable for the future, in case of lower economic prosperity in the future. Being cautious never hurts, especially for young people who are immature, impulsive, capricious and easily seduced. We all know that they immediately succumb to luxury and ostentation; but also, to something much more dangerous: arrogance.

As if being successful in such a complicated profession were not reward enough, many actors (and not only young people, but especially them) feel it imperatively necessary to reflect their success at every moment, in every facet of their lives.

THE FILM AND AUDIOVISUAL INDUSTRY

It is absolutely true that fame and money boost the most basic and hidden instincts of each person, so narcissistic people could perfectly project their personality in a compulsive way, to seek other people's envy. But beyond that vanity, what they are usually looking for is closer to a certain self-affirmation through the public confirmation of their success. Something you give to society so that, in turn, it may be returned to you as "objective" information. In other words, you are rich and famous as long as everyone says you are.

It is no coincidence that as time goes by, many of these people cannot maintain the crazy lifestyle they are forced to lead. It is too easy to fall into one of these vicious circles and no matter how many times someone hears about them or is warned, there will always be people misusing their money and causing them to file for bankruptcy. However, we must also recognize that it is very easy to talk about fame and money, and their consequences, without actually having such problems in our day-to-day.

The hard road that most actors go down before gaining success is widely known. And despite that, many of them still dream of being world famous overnight, just as it happens to younger stars. Indeed, all kinds of stories are being told, so people of all ages are needed to play characters of all ages: children, teenagers, and young people too. And that is the first great difficulty aspiring professional actors face. At no point should age be in favor of or against your possibilities. But in regard to the competitive factor, will not younger actors have more options simply because they started earlier? The more professional experience you have, the sooner the public will like you. Therefore, every professional experience contributes to strengthening your fame, technique, and contacts. No matter how small it is or how early it happens.

Similarly, beginners cannot opt for a lead role that is conceived to be played by a famous star. This is not a disadvantage or injustice. In movies, it is the most basic sales strategy at the highest level of executive decision. The only doubt is which famous actor will end up getting the role, but that particular film cannot be done without A-list stars.

Fortunately, there are films designed to create new stars and introduce them to the public. Films and series telling stories focused on children and teenagers, serve as a perfect launching platform for new talents, to draw attention.

Independent of their age, we could say that newcomers all have the same possibility of getting a role (protagonist or not, depending on the film). But as we will see throughout this chapter, there are many conditions that must be fulfilled. Not only to get the part amongst many others applicants, but also to continue being an actor or keep trying if they are not one yet.

Everyone has factors that can increase their chances of success, just like there are many others that can reduce them. The sum of all said personal factors, combined with luck, randomness and coincidence, determine how many jobs actors are going to get throughout their careers. But first of all, let us start by distinguishing the different levels of this profession.

The first level of acting, which everyone knows, would be playing in theater plays at a local level. For example, kids who begin at school, teens who learn in courses or workshops, and amateurs of all ages who act in civic centers or small amateur companies. In short, novice actors who are gaining experience, confidence, technique, and, in a sense, commitment to the profession. In the beginning, everything is new and illusional. There are exciting feelings, but when there is a genuine professional interest in the matter, sooner or later the daunting reality of this sector makes an impact.

The vast majority of these dreamers will not be able to make a professional career in the industry, and almost surely, in the end they will dedicate their lives to something more fruitful and profitable than professional acting (good for them). But it is also true that there are two important elements that are always there, deep down inside, in the heart of professional actors: Vocation and natural talent. You can be a successful or totally unknown actor, but no one can fight these furious elements.

THE FILM AND AUDIOVISUAL INDUSTRY

Unfortunately, vocation does not serve to guarantee any work for the future, but it gives any natural born actor something much more important: an identity. Not necessarily happiness, fair enough, but a genuine reason for being. True actors are born with the vital need for this, so it does not matter if professional remuneration becomes a reality or not, or if they become a great success or failure, because they cannot renounce the identity anyway.

And as far as talent is concerned, it is usually detected at first sight, or how fast someone can develop remarkable skills and abilities over others. That is why any aspiring actor who wants to go pro must work very hard to stand out. That must be the first goal, even if he or she already demonstrates some good skills.

What we call natural talent is found in those who do not struggle to look credible, realistic, or totally natural when they are acting. People who, with little or no theoretical knowledge at all, seem to be transformed into other people, living a fictitious situation in a way that feels totally real. Therefore, the lucky ones who have that gift will also be able to learn advanced tricks and techniques much easier, with proper training. Hence, the interest in finding promising talent as soon as possible.

At the next level, we have professional theater actors (usually grouped into one or several companies), and the actors that appear on local and national television. In the case of theater or advertisements, it is more difficult to be remembered by the general public, (to stand out in both things: quality and visibility) due to those platforms' limitations. But, if there is something that gives you visibility, it is television. Not all profiles working in front of the cameras require acting skills (albeit always preferable). In fact, it is relatively easy (and quite common) to start working on TV by being directly handpicked by influential people, even if the chosen person is not ready or good enough (which usually affects the final result, of course).

In the case of advertising, the norm is just to look for attractive models, or exactly the opposite, as close to regular people as possible (depending on the campaign's target and goal). And again, acting knowledge or skills are desirable but not required, since decision making is based on physical aspects only: facial features, skin color, or a specific segment of the population. And it is nothing superficial, sexist, racist, or discriminatory in any way, it is just the direct consequence of having market research dictate the rules for everything. Its impact on advertising is direct, absolute, and immediate. Putting aside the current canons of beauty, in television there are things that can make you a celebrity much faster than performing complex Shakespearean plays. To mention a few random examples: Having a lot of freckles, tattoos, piercings, a shaved head, a big mouth, separated eyes, being albino, or redhead, etc. (You get the idea, right?) Everything depends on how you look and how special your ad is. (Because the more people remember the ad, the more people will remember you.)

And finally, the most demanding level in terms of performance requirements: Film, television, series, and prestigious theater. (If anyone is wondering what type of prestige is comparable to film and TV, just look at the street that the theater is on, the cost of tickets, and if the play's actors are famous or just unknown). For certain types of work, such as a feature film, previous professional experience tends to be mandatory so that no one has to explain to the beginner how the mechanics work, or how to behave on set. However, there are cases where it is impossible to avoid some training. For example, when there are reasons with greater importance than academic or artistic background, in order to choose a certain actor or actress. On the contrary, in the case of professional theater, the situation is quite different. Proper training is a must, since we are talking about a form of live performance that works in a very particular way. The more experience an actor has, the more comfortable everyone will feel (the audience, the producer, the rest of the cast, and themselves). But by having a good memory, an agile mind with a capacity for improvisation, and a solid presence on stage, any debut actor can achieve a fantastic performance, if properly prepared.

THE FILM AND AUDIOVISUAL INDUSTRY

During a theatrical performance, everything has to be played in front of the audience, with unavoidable continuity, and with no possibility of making a mistake on stage. Theater is truth. You cannot pretend, while in films, virtually everything is fake. But none of this has the same importance in filmmaking, where you can shoot scenes in small, non-consecutive fragments.

Along with numerous interludes for technical preparation, this favors the possibility of rehearsing the next scene in a hundred different ways, and then forgetting it completely just after filming it. On the other hand, one of the hardest things for actors is the number of times you have to repeat the same thing over and over again.

In theater, it is because of daily performances (maybe even several in the same day) and, in movies, it is because the director (or themselves, or any other department head, or due to technical reasons) does not consider the take to be valid or good enough. But also, for many other reasons. For example, to capture the same shot from different camera angles, to get different creative proposals, to try different intensities, to focus on the details of each character, or the details of each action. And all this is done with boring pauses between takes, due to the multiple checks and technical adjustments that must be made before starting a new attempt.

Undoubtedly, one of the greatest myths about filming is that it is fascinating and fun. It may seem that way, but it looks very different inside. Never lose perspective, it is a job. And as such, it is something that must be taken very seriously. When filming a production with beautiful costumes, sets, locations, and props like weapon replicas with which you can play... imagine on top of that that you are being paid to be there.

Even the most professional veterans can wake up the child within and enjoy the privileged pleasure they have been granted with. But above all, you have to know how to be professional, and some people forget that sometimes.

THE FILM AND AUDIOVISUAL INDUSTRY

TALENT AND SKILLS

This book will never try to be an actor's guide. Anyone is free to interpret and assimilate the content of this book as they prefer. But unlike most "official" training actors receive in courses, workshops, and academies, we are going to share some interesting conclusions that industry professionals end up realizing sooner or later, but not one usually states them aloud, or much less writes them down anywhere. Some people may consider that sharing these reflections does not help beginners and that they might even be counterproductive, but that is precisely one of the most important objectives of this book: To wake up the minds of those people interested in these topics, satisfy their curiosity, and challenge their critical thinking in the reality of the profession. If some aspiring artists are affected by this content, they will have to gain greater strength and security to face their careers. As much as some people could decide to quit even before trying. In any case, it is not possible to make such a radical decision so easily, just because of a few lines. And most likely, even in such cases it would be the confirmation of something that, ultimately, people knew perfectly well within themselves. In a society like ours, where people are always promoting the culture of winner and loser, it would be nice to introduce a new approach. "Avoiding failure" as a way to success. On the one hand, everyone has the right to have dreams, illusions, and hobbies, and everyone is totally free to spend their time and lives in the way they consider more appropriate. But on the other hand, it should be welcomed if someone saves you a significant amount of time, money, and effort. Effort that you could have dedicated to something much more productive other than chasing that classic, unattainable dream of being an actor, director, singer, or musician. Actually, if you think about it twice, people usually just want to be "a celebrity." That mythological creature that is admired and desired by everyone. Because all of this is about fame. Fame and love. So in one word, vanity. (And money, of course).

THE FILM AND AUDIOVISUAL INDUSTRY

Let us start by talking about the most obvious requirement for being an actor: the acting skill. One of the most common beliefs is that acting is not that complicated. "I like to disguise myself," "I am a very good liar," or "I can make myself cry on demand" are phrases usually accompanied by the classic "I want to be an actor/actress." Well, all these things could indicate an innate ability, but not necessarily. The first thing to keep in mind is that acting skills and talent are not the same. A person's ability can be good or bad, but talent implies a natural flair, which easily surpasses ability. Not everyone has this and it is difficult to acquire although, it is certainly not impossible. With a lot of practice and self-knowledge, less talented people can improve their acting skills to a reasonably high level of quality. They might have to work harder than people with a natural gift. And they may get satisfactory results at a slower pace, but that is life. There is nothing wrong with that.

Most acting lessons in schools and books are focused on true feelings, on the real load of emotions the actor must feel on stage. The logic seems to make sense, more or less. If you feel something for real, the audience will see specific reactions in your body, from the outside. Some of which will be totally realistic, right? Well, not exactly. Yes, but no. Because it is very easy to talk about tears and screams, but what happens to the other everyday moments of life? Anyone who has ever been on stage or in front of a camera knows how hard it is to make a simple conversation or the most basic interaction with objects credible.

Before we get into the emotional guts of the actor, it must be clear that the only thing that matters, both on the screen and live on stage, is what the audience or the camera can see and hear on the outside. So, does it matter if actors are actually feeling what we see? At certain intensities, it is very difficult to not get inside the character so that the reactions of the real person are not affected. We are talking about a masterful use of empathy after all. It is not too different from what the audience feels in their seats. In both cases, there is a communion with the fictitious people who are supposedly "living " those situations.

Ultimately, it is a way of empathizing with the small portion of humankind that the story is representing. We are touched when we see ourselves represented. The characterization is closer to the physical resemblance of the character (through costume and makeup), but transformation is the moment when the actor gets carried away with the attitude and feelings of the character and for a moment, the character takes control.

There is a point where we can hardly pretend what our faces or body reflect when we feel certain things, and you have to decide what boundary you are willing to cross to capture that realism. Actors control their facial and bodily muscles; and also their ability to transform themselves into other fictitious people. The real challenge is connecting the emotions of both sides, the person and the character.

It is very common for beginners to believe that they are giving a great performance (because of what they are feeling), while the other people around only see an immutable, boring face. Rookies do not understand that what matters is not what you feel inside, but what others see on the outside. Not for nothing, the famous Stanislavski's method was initially called "The Method of Physical Action" (so essentially, what is seen on the outside).

Konstantin Stanislavski was a Russian actor and theater director from the late 19th century who consecrated his life to the art of acting like no one else in history. The frustration he felt when realizing his handbook was not understood well or applied by his contemporaries, led him to perfect the system throughout his lifetime. This man was determined to document and standardize all the techniques that actors can use to control their bodies and minds, starting from the singularity of each person. We all are different and capable of transmitting the same thing in very different ways. And that is one of the first essential learnings. Different does not mean better or worse. Hence the importance of knowing yourself and your own limits and understanding your strengths and weaknesses well, so you can choose the best roles for you.

THE FILM AND AUDIOVISUAL INDUSTRY

"The method" is often summarized with the premise that you must be the character, so that your character can be (can exist). So you must suffer for real, so that your character suffers; you must feel pain, so that your character feels pain, and so on. Some actors become obsessed with this and it can become a serious problem with an erroneous or radical interpretation. Above all, Stanislavski defended the naturalness of actions, i.e. intonation, gestures, movements, and reactions. He mentioned that the inner experimentation is a practical exercise, because it can be really useful, but he was mainly talking about learning to "think like the character," so you can "behave like the character."

He was looking for truthfulness, yes, but he was the first to say that each one has to cope as best as they can to obtain that truth. He worked several techniques for that, and his favorite choice was always free experimentation. But the only thing he considered essential was to never violate the basis of a credible action. One of Stanislavski's most important principles was, precisely, the need for peace of mind and muscular relaxation when performing. (You have probably seen a lot of actors doing relaxation exercises with their faces, necks, arms, and perhaps their whole bodies, almost like warming up for sports.) With regard to real suffering in particular, if it is the only way an actor can achieve truthfulness, the method can accept it as a personal commitment, but there is no reason to take the art of acting as a masochistic thing. The best weapon actors have, has always been and will be self-control (yes, even when they go crazy).

After his death, the greatest precursor of his teachings in Hollywood was the Ukrainian theater director, producer, and actor Lee Strasberg. He used his own theater company called "The Group Theater," that 20 years later would serve as an inspiration to the legendary Actors Studio, which was directed by Strasberg himself, since the year 1952. He led it to its current world fame. He was considered a radical experimenter, which inevitably took actors (too often) to excessively extreme places.

Although, as previously said, this was perfectly justified by the rules Stanislavski defined. Besides, we must also recognize that it has been proven that any excessive intensity will always toughen the artist, in one sense or another. So, it cannot be said that it is an unnecessary or excessive method, if it fulfils its mission which is to contribute to the vital experience and self-knowledge of the actor.

Hands down, acting is no more (or no less) than controlling all the muscles in your body to do whatever you want with them. That is the connection. In real life, any human reaction is seen in a specific way from the outside. The challenge of any actor is to know how to reproduce it to perfection, so that another person who sees it from the outside cannot distinguish whether it is real or false. That is the quintessence of acting. And no one says that it is something easy to do. We mentioned before that the ability to control our body can be improved with technique and practice so to a large extent, the natural ability to exercise such control will affect the possibilities of becoming a professional.

Unfortunately for them, there are people who have an innate shyness that prevents them from facing certain situations in public, like modulating their voices appropriately, showing confidence, or moving securely. There are even those who feel ashamed just attracting everyone's looks (a bad sign). These types of people will have, in principle, an important handicap for being an actor. Yet, acting is recommended as a therapeutic activity, perfect for overcoming these types of psychological barriers (as a sort of shock treatment). Additionally, on the other end of the spectrum, you can find those who can control their body and facial expressions with ease, demonstrating natural talent for veracity. (Which should not be confused with the ability to do impersonations, which could imply a talent for comedy, but not so much for drama.) Naturalness is a very interesting thing. Ordinary people with no special ability for controlling their bodies or faces could actually give decent performances before the camera, provided they play "themselves." As a primary example, we have some background actors with 0% acting knowledge, who are selected to provide 100% realism in a specific context. This is usually more of a creative decision than a practical one, on the whim of a director and/or producer (or simply to optimize resources). These cases used to be random participants only, and usually required detailed, intensive direction (every movement needed to be explained, tested and repeated, just to look decent). Good examples can be: Very old elders, indigenous people from remote regions (using even their own clothes and authentic appearances), people with some disability or deformity, professional athletes, or stunt performers. In the case that someone shows a natural ability for acting, perhaps in a previous audition or during the shoot itself, they might be asked to say one or several lines, for various reasons. But without a doubt, it is more common for the opposite to happen, for the simple fact that having a camera in front of you provokes the typical stiffness in rookies' bodies and movements, along with the classic trembling voice and blankness of the mind from nerves.

At a similar level, we also have those who have no acting skills at all, but must participate for some reason like models who are chosen only for their physical appearance (literally from a catalogue), or celebrities who are hired for publicity purposes. Trying to film anything with them, just to obtain a minimally decent result, turns into a nightmare. This is understandable in the case of elite athletes, for instance, but there are professions in show business where one would expect higher aptitudes for acting in front of cameras, like singers for example. Obviously, they do not suffer from stage fright, and they even have an advanced understanding of voice modulation, but that does not mean that they have to have a natural gift to look credible when trying to be a different person, or even themselves, reacting in a fictitious situation. In that sense, they could be at the same level as beginners, not only the young, but anyone in the previous category who starts to consider acting as an option.

THE FILM AND AUDIOVISUAL INDUSTRY

This profession tends to be vocational from childhood or adolescence, but there is no reason why people of any age cannot start learning at any time in their lives. During the beginning of their careers, rookies start to understand the function of their bodies; to manipulate the muscles and minds to obey their brain, immersed in brief, false realities. And some will learn faster than others, depending on the ease they have, the theoretical knowledge they absorb, the practice and effort they devote, the method of learning they follow, and the more or less professional environment they surround themselves with. Sooner or later, to a greater or lesser extent, they will reap what they have sown. Which can be a lot or a little. Depending on this, after a while there are beginners who decide to quit forever, while others keep it as a hobby, and only a few begin to receive their first professional opportunities. That is how your career starts: By gaining experience with theatrical performances, short films, commercials, and auditions. And from the very moment you start to get paid, you can call yourself a professional.

At this point, one can have better or worse moments, more or less visibility in the scene, and even sign a representation agreement with an agent or agency. But we have already said that there is only one way to enter the industry, and that is to gain the attention of someone on the other side. That is not an easy task.

Although it may seem like the talents they are looking for are always more of the same, they actually have the most varied needs. You have to know how to sell yourself. There are a lot of good ways to showcase yourself: Pictures, videos, websites, previous works, or an audition that you nailed and someone remembers. But there is always that "special something" that people speak about, but no one can explain. That "thing" is what people on the other side, expect to see in the actor or actress that they are looking for. Young people always think that they are the most special person in the world and utter the classic: "I am going to surprise you," but when it comes time to prove themselves, you usually never see any talent (which is usually followed by: "Give me another chance").

The ultimate goal of an audiovisual work is to narrate a complete story; while the only goal of acting is to be believable. Although the visual ensemble of a scene may be poor, we have mentioned that human beings are capable of transmitting complex emotions through simple empathy (hence the force of live theater, which can even dispense with figurative visual context).

In movies, it is quite to the contrary. Directors use the overload of audiovisual elements to manipulate the viewer's feelings (leveraging the emotions they want to transmit). That is the best way to make sure that no one is indifferent, even if just by saturation. But the most important thing (and everyone agrees on this) is that an actor's performance is credible. Any other artifice may be expendable or low-quality, but never the actors' work. Bad acting will always be noticeable and exposed clearly, no matter how many fireworks and ornamental distractions you can create around it.

Actually, there is a certain subjectivity on this. Each viewer's sensitivity (in terms of their ability to empathize with others) is what determines which kind of actions are perceived as credible and which are not. Things like knots in the throat, hairs standing on end, goosebumps, tense muscles, trembling legs, smiles and laughter, chills, sudden frights, watery eyes, and crocodile tears. They all are irrefutable signs that the actors are doing their job well. Within a bad story (or good but poorly told one), human beings are able to release emotions in such a way that, in a matter of seconds and without any context, they can make others feel it as well, with the same intensity. That is the real connection Stanislavski was talking about.

For actors, the biggest challenge is real tears. Crying is one of those sensitive extremes for human beings. No one likes to see another person crying. It makes us feel uncomfortable. The use of artificial tears (that perfect drop always falling from everywhere except the lacrimal) is beginning to be a bit abusive. But, it is also true that no matter how sweetened and manufactured crying looks in movies, it still works (and that is why everyone is abusing the same tricks, once and again).

Additionally, thanks to that simulated artifice, so aesthetic and measured, when we see a really heartbreaking performance with true intensity and real expressiveness, it generates a much greater emotional impact.

So, we conclude that there are great actors capable of transmitting feelings that are 100% realistic, regardless of the method they use to achieve it. But in real life, not everything is made of intense emotions. What happens to all the regular day-to-day actions and conversations?

Once again, the perfect reference is teenagers. They are learning to be actors, while still learning to be human beings, to be "adults." They do not know how to express or hide those complex feelings that, in real life, are still new to them. Before knowing how to fake certain human reactions, you will first have to know them and understand them. Having professional experience as a child could help but would not guarantee continuity anyway.

Young people are always a risk for many reasons. For instance in television series, the evolution of a performance quality is unpredictable (both for the physical and personality). We will talk later about the issues with age, but for now we will just mention a convenient truism: Only a real teenager can play a teenage character (unless you want to have one of those hilarious high schools with actors in their 20s).

The positive part is that when teenagers play themselves, they at least have the opportunity to be natural and there is a better chance that their performances will be credible. In fact, in most films and series with younger actors, you can find both good and bad results, sometimes even within the same production.

Generally, films that are targeted toward adults will always look for the best talent and are really demanding with quality and preparation. However, films that are targeted towards teens are sufficient in finding a few superficial connections, even if there is a mix of good and bad actors in the cast. Due to their inexperience in life and human relationships, a teenage viewer needs a much less demanding quality level to perceive a performance, while adult audiences (not to mention professionals from the industry) are just watching insipid or overacted performances. This is why decision makers in the industry usually ask for advice and opinions from family members or friends with children that age.

As we always say, exceptions are given and there are talented youngsters that demonstrate appropriate control of their bodies, faces, and voices both when acting and behaving on set during shooting hours. And it is not a coincidence that you will start to hear good things about the talent of those boys and girls who demonstrate how mature they are during a shoot.

We have made it clear that every actor must be natural, that is the main goal. This is something that becomes more difficult when the actor must incorporate more and more concepts simultaneously, in addition to knowing basic know-how. The value of aesthetics in acting is essential. An inappropriate gait, a misplaced step, a confusing or out-of-context gesture, moving a hand when you should not, or the fingers' simple posture. The whole body's movement has to be natural but also beautiful and aesthetic. The tempo and the speed of each gesture should be appropriate and necessary to be realistic and, at the same time, understandable to the viewer's eye. Movements must be accurate and happen at the right time, not before or after they should. And, by the way, what about the voice?

Well, the voice is a whole world apart. Just like with any physical part of the body, the voice must also be controlled and directed towards a specific purpose. Intonation, rhythm, and volume define what we say, or rather, what we convey when we say it. In theater, there is much talk of voice projection, so that the audience can hear the dialogue from their seats. But the fact that movies use microphones to record sound and huge amplification systems in screening rooms, does not make voice projection any less important for an actor. It is not about the volume, it is about the appropriate sonority that we use in our real lives (just unconsciously) and therefore, it will be define how realistic the scene is. For example, rookies always tend to declaim with poor "theatrical" intonation that is so standard and naive.

They do not understand or control intonation and projection, or even separate the two; therefore, you always get that pompous, unnatural recitation, like old classical theater that is out of context. This is quite noticeable and annoying on television, but it is completely unacceptable in film (or at least in decent productions).

Concerning foreign or regional accents, there is no reason that it should be a problem for actors. The only cases where it would be a problem is if the actor is incapable of changing their natural accent to that which would illustrate their character's origins. (It is true that it could actually be perceived as a lack of versatility.) Quite the contrary, controlling different accents is, in fact, considered an added value, not to mention the domain or knowledge of other international languages. Having a strong accent may restrict the type of roles you will be offered but at the same time, it also guarantees you a certain amount of possible work. Perhaps it may always be the same thing, but is it not better than not having a job? Besides, there are always tons of undefined roles out there, suitable for all kinds of people. There are characters who have no special feature of origin or race, to which adding a specific appearance or accent could enrich the character and their background.

Something similar happens with the type of voice that actors have. It is mostly a subjective thing. High or low pitches with soft, hoarse, or raspy textures. The exercise of visualizing a character before he or she exists is something that directors have to do all the time. From the time you start reading a new script, you inevitably build a first impression of how the characters could be. What they themselves inspire and project, as variable creations that still admit changes. The same happens in theater too, but directors and actors must build the characters in a more intimate way. And in television, this is more extreme, since the audience dictates everything. So characters can drastically change overnight, as much as the overall tone of the whole series. On the idiot box, the goal is always to draw attention, so all rarities are welcome as a differentiating element of interest.

THE FILM AND AUDIOVISUAL INDUSTRY

When speaking about movies, the decline that silent film actors suffered during the arrival of talking films is well known. The old theatricality of body and facial expressionism had no place in the new realism that cinema was looking for. The possibility of listening to the voices of the actors, along with the sound of what was happening around them, removed a lot of that dreamlike atmosphere that films had. Since the release of *The Jazz Singer* in 1927, there was a series of events that led to a radical change in the industry, in just five years: Warner Bros. saved themselves from bankruptcy, thanks to the success of this movie and the next ones. The new standard for film cameras and projectors would be 24 frames per second, since this was much better adjusted to the calculation metric of sound waves (obtaining, therefore, a better visual fluency). Movie theaters from all over the country started installing speakers on the walls and behind the screens. Creators began to experiment with the dramatic impact of noises, environments, musical language, and even silence as a deliberate pause (now more dramatic, because of the contrast). And definitely, the most interesting of all advances was that, as dialogues became indispensable, a great number of writers found the opportunity to tell their stories without the limitations of a theater play, but with excellent new narrative possibilities (as it was proved very soon after). Unfortunately, not everything was positive and many actors of that time did not manage to stay active after said changes: Harold Lloyd, John Gilbert, Emil Jannings, John Bowers, Norma Talmadge, Mae Murray, Pola Negri, Clara Bow, and Lillian Hall Davis, just to name a few. Despite being great stars, many had foreign origins and strong accents and, in many cases, they barely understood English. So, some returned to their native countries or voluntarily resigned (or lost their interest in making movies); others suffered severe depression and even committed suicide. Some were never that extremist, but suffered the shame of the public not liking their voice or the simple fact of not meeting expectations (in comparison with the fame of their face). This relegated them to a gradual oblivion until they disappeared without much fuss.

THE FILM AND AUDIOVISUAL INDUSTRY

An actor's voice may be one way or another, but that does not necessarily make them better or worse. One day, that trait that makes your voice special can be just what someone is looking for. Special features can have the most diverse utilities. Without going any further, versatility together with diction are the most important features for being a voice actor. It is essential to have textures that are as varied as possible, since you need the voices of the characters to differ from each other as much as possible (otherwise, all men and women would seem the same, even if they look different on screen). For this reason, when dubbing for animation, there are always all kinds of voices. The added incentive is that you can get very attractive characters that you could never get in live action, due to your appearance or physical condition (like being the muscular hero who saves the world, without needing several months in the gym).

SELF-KNOWLEDGE

Before talking about all the circumstances that are beyond the actor's control, let us first see which ones they can control. Those elements that depend on the performer's skills and can be developed and improved upon with time and effort (by definition, the things that depend on you can always be improved). We live surrounded by examples, proving that with hard work and desire, you can always overcome and be better in your field. Whatever discipline and context, this is always true, as long as we depend on ourselves. (It is a different thing if you expect to receive recognition from others.) Based on this, actors are no exception; as well as musicians, writers, or cooks. The more you practice, the better results you will get.

There are a number of exercises that beginners can do to gain practical experience, although, professionals must also practice and improve (without going any further, many stars get used to the workflow in movies, so much so, that coming back to work in theater can provide a frightening challenge).

Practice is based on subjecting your body to different situations and reactions in order to exercise certain habits: Mental and muscular agility, attention and concentration, body coordination, dynamism of movements, energy channeling, and breathing control. This is why in the earliest stages of learning, both children and adults play games of imagination, creativity, and trust. Some people think that these games are naive and childish, but they are actually considered quite useful to establish a first approach between body and mind. Not surprisingly, theater courses and workshops are usually recommended for health and psychology therapy for people with different degrees of shyness, autism, and many other problems related to social interaction.

But the hardest exercise is always self-criticism. When there is something that we do wrong (or someone thinks we do wrong) it does not matter if you are a novice or a veteran, everyone has limitations and you can do four things with them: Ignore them, deny them, simply accept them, or try to overcome them.

Ignorance is the worst problem for beginners and the cause-effect relationship may have no end. Perhaps their acting is bad, what is worse is not knowing it or being incapable of detecting exactly what is wrong. These people can see impressive performances in a movie and then see home recordings of themselves, without detecting or understanding where the most basic differences lie between the two performances. It is not about being a famous actor or working in a million-dollar budget movie, these are not excuses for poor quality in an actor's performance. Any reputable actor should make every scene look natural (in a professional way, we could say). Even in the case of a scene that is not well written, good actors do their best to change that into something decent (at least in regard to their characters). However, even if a beginner chooses a great scene from any masterpiece film and tries to repeat it, what you get is an impersonation in a greater or lesser degree of parody, at best.

In fact, it is a very good idea for an exercise. Reenacting movie scenes is quite useful for rookies, in order to understand (even if not very naturally) the sense of pace, importance of movements, subtle details, and professional diction. This also guarantees that good material is used, so that you can be sure if something goes wrong, it will be because of you and not the material. (Additionally, using your own unprofessional material might make the quality of your performance even worse.) But this is just an interesting exercise, and it does not mean that you must learn to mimic famous actors or always use the same artist as a reference. Apart from the fake "impersonation" feeling that we already mentioned, you could add quirks, tics, flows, and charismatic features from recognizable actors who might not be compatible with your own style. (It does not make much sense for a teenager to pretend to act like Anthony Hopkins or Robert De Niro.) Apart from being fun, these exercises add a lot of value, especially if they are shared with other people pursuing similar goals for learning. Pressed by impatience, rookies always want to film ambitious short films with the logical complication that telling a complete story involves (which has many other favorable, good things, for sure). And, considering the amount of time, effort, and probably money that they are spending on filming, it makes sense that they want to show their work proudly. But this is a different type of exercise. Without the additional pressure of having to show anything to other people, you are free to experiment and focus on the most important thing, which is learning. Camera operators, cinematographers, lighting technicians, directors, and actors. A small team of beginners wanting to practice can get the most surprising results with the right dedication. It all depends on how many challenges you are willing to accept (and getting professional results without the proper means is already a huge challenge in itself).

Whether you shoot with decent professional equipment or just with a smartphone at home, focus on simple exercises where you do not have to worry about the camera angle, the location, or the clothes you are wearing. Nobody is going to see that, the only thing that matters is what you do with your body and your voice. It is about practicing and analyzing yourself. Being aware of your own limitations is very important for an actor's maturity.

Moreover, no one says that limitations cannot be reduced over time, so you do not have to be afraid to find them and confront them. With practice, it is very likely that your technique will improve and your limitations could disappear completely (even those which might be, a priori, preventing you from being a professional actor).

Coming back to what we mentioned earlier, you may also react to criticism by denying your own shortcomings or limitations. This is something that you should be really careful about. Concerning our inner demons, ego and pride will always be human beings' worst enemies. (So you can imagine how detrimental they are for artists, and within artists, actors.) It is ridiculous when beginners consider themselves to be great talents, especially due to the lack of experience. Attitude is as equally important as having good skills. And the most important one, above any other in this business, is always humility.

If you do not want things to get complicated for you, as an actor you must try to keep yourself humble throughout your entire career. It is really difficult to find an actor or actress who is not aware of their strengths and weaknesses. By all means, there are issues that come along with ego, envy, and pride at all levels, but this does not mean that even the most arrogant stars do not know their limitations. What happens is that, precisely because they know them well, actors try to hide any weakness and avoid exposing themselves by all means. Hence, the importance of knowing how this industry works. This knowledge helps great actors to only select and accept parts that make them feel comfortable. Thus, although an actor's insecurity is always present, only a very extreme misalignment between the actor and director could reveal these insecurities as real limitations in the final result of a film. Mediocre performances will not favor anyone, neither the actor, nor the director, nor the producer.

They are all forced to cooperate and support each other, for their own good. The whole crew contributes to making the actors look as good on screen as possible. This favors Hollywood actors, but goes against unknown actors in more modest productions.

Without the proper time, budget, and resources, it is impossible to focus on dignifying and beautifying actors with the same effort. It is also important that costumes and scenes look as good on camera as possible (or at least, credible enough). The problem is, characters will always be the most important part of any story because the audience is looking at the actors the entire time.

Not being aware of your own limitations (both technical or artistic) is most dangerous at amateur or semi-professional levels. It is equally important to know your greatest skills well and to use them in your favor, as much as knowing the things that you do not do well or have less talent for. They can be anecdotal, solvable trifles, such as not knowing how to swim, or ride a bike, but it is also worth mentioning more personal disabilities. Some personal characteristics that are impossible to overcome, for whatever reason, but that you must accept. For example, people who have always been clumsy with their hands, or those who have never been able to sing and dance, or people who have no talent for comedy, as much as they try. We are referring to the inexplicable ability that some people have for making others laugh, without any special effort. It is not even necessary to look funny or tell any jokes, there are great examples of actors with serious countenance who have played great comedic characters, as well as comedians who have succeeded in dramatic films. (It must also be said that in both cases there have been different fiascos).

PHYSICAL APPEARANCE

Beyond the script content, which just defines the events happening in the story, we can say that someone is a good actor or, at least, professionally qualified, when all movements, behaviors, and dialogues look natural. As we have already said, we are talking about the imitation of reality, in the sense of credibility. So, assuming that we have a huge list of thousands of professional actors, all of them with really good and amazing experience, why should we choose one over another?

THE FILM AND AUDIOVISUAL INDUSTRY

Think of any other type of job offer, in which thousands of applicants fit the position. There were many objective factors that helped to reduce the list. Resume, experience, and education for example. Now let us imagine that in addition to the basic knowledge expected from all of them, you need something even more special that only a few candidates are going to have. No matter how many degrees, masters, years of experience, and objective quality they may have, those without that special "something" would no longer be eligible.

Likewise, having a very few final candidates, you will have to end up picking one of them. And it is inevitable that in any selection process, there is a subjective side. It is that simple. There is always someone who decides the fate of others according to their personal criteria. Even with the best resume and the best references, personal interviews are made for a reason: To assess the candidates in a more subjective way, carried out by personal intuition. It is always the decisive final step that must be taken before hiring a person. Maybe you will get the most prepared candidate or not, the most appropriate or not, but once someone is chosen, for whatever reason, the decision has finally been made. For good or bad but, in any case, the game is over for the other candidates. This subjectivity can respond to very different causes and motivations, not to mention the many influences, bribes, favors, extortions, and personal compromises that can be used in this industry, throughout someone's professional career. But no one will be surprised that, in this particular area, physical appearance is especially significant in the selection process (in fact, it is the first factor of elimination, but not exactly in the sense that you might think).

From the very moment a story is conceived, the creators and key decision-makers (screenwriters, directors, and producers) already have a rough idea of what they want and therefore, a mental image of what they need. This can change and evolve over time. But there are many decisions that are pre-established in each one's imagination, along with other obvious things that are forced by the story itself. For example, only a very tall actor can be a basketball player, a very thin actress can be an anorexic girl, or a black actor can be an African American character. And there is nothing superficial, racist, or xenophobic about any of this, it is just common sense.

When beginners express their desire to become professional actors, one of the most offensive prejudices they can face is that they are not "handsome enough." This is very important to point out because the industry needs people with all kinds of physical appearances and who have good acting skills. After all, every single real-life stereotype has a very obvious physical appearance that easily helps to identify them. Either the muscular athlete, the funny chubby one, the clumsy nerd, the superficial sexy cheerleader, or the ugly friend with a good heart. Never forget that characters are fictitious but based on reality, and the public's identification with the characters is decisive. Everything must be credible or the lies of the filmic art will not work.

The story varieties and possible situations lead us to a relative abundance of roles, protagonists or not, for all kinds of people (at least, in theory). At some point, apart from looking for jobs and paying the rent, every beginner actor must also think of how he or she is going to face auditions. They need a strategy, even if it is pretty basic. They must ask themselves: "Am I interested in drama lessons?" "Am I going to attend every audition in the city?" "Maybe in the country?" "How selective am I planning to be with possible offers?" "What will my personal limits be?" "Should I focus on a certain type of character or product?"

For example, someone interested in starring in action movies would always have to be muscular and in perfect shape; because it would make more sense to hire an actor who is already fit on their own, rather than hiring someone obese who would have to lose weight and train a lot to fit the role—no matter how good of an actor they are. On the other hand, it is also very normal for actors to undergo radical physical changes for certain roles. They can do it with simple styling, which means being seen with different looks (dress, hairstyles, haircuts, beards, etc.) or by extreme commitment and personal sacrifices; such as weight changes or aesthetic surgeries (for example, changing your personal appearance on screen or to compensating for age, to remain eligible for roles of a younger age).

While it seems that we are changing the subject, let us talk about the famous mandatory convention that every film should contain a love story. No matter how subtle or forced it is, there must always be at least one of them, and unless the story says otherwise, the actors must be chosen according to the canons of the beauty of the moment (for all the reasons which we explain below). More specifically, in accordance to the trending stereotypes among the potential audience that the product is targeted toward. Logically, adults' opinions about what handsome men or beautiful women look like, does not have to coincide with teenagers and young people's opinions.

Although the established canons are always changing and we assume beauty as something relatively subjective (symmetry and softness of forms are pleasing to humans, that is science), in this industry we always seek attraction at a more generic level, more "animalistic," so to speak. It is important for viewers to be attracted to the people who appear on the screen. The audience must like them. It is a faster and more effective way to get people to care more about the characters. This is noteworthy because it is scientifically proven. It is not a superficial attitude.

In real life, we behave better and we are more pleasant and helpful with people who we find attractive. We empathize instantly and are more complacent with people we like. In other words, if we are attracted to the actors, we will like the characters more and immediately care about what happens to them, which means then that we will be more invested in the film.

This is also one of the bases for the famous "fan phenomenon." Teenagers' most basic behavior is to be infatuated with idols. To varying degrees, romantic and sexual awakenings tend to be more forceful for distant figures that are unattainable by the very concept of idealization. Even if we can also be infatuated by people in our close circles the constant, regular contact demystifies the effect and even the real possibilities of correspondence. However, celebrities are unattainable and impossible to know. And everything we see of them is always idealized, calculated, manipulated, and shaded to simulate perfection (or at least, a perfect perception of desire).

But this does not mean that actors must always meet the most demanding beauty canons of the audience—not even the protagonists. Basically, stories must have a minimum conceptual consistency, that is all. In real life, we see all types of couples: Handsome with ugly, handsome with handsome, ugly with ugly, etc. Therefore, movies must reflect the same: Tall with short, fat with slim, and any other possible combination you can make, among people of all shapes and conditions.

Romantic relationships (or emotional, sentimental, or however you want to call them... love stories, in short) are the relationships that humankind has tried to analyze and understand since their remote origins. We have not reached any clear conclusions. For this reason, no matter which story you want to tell, you must tell it in a credible way. It is important to use actors that match the prototypical archetypes that you would find in real life. Those that would live that love story as realistically as possible. The viewer has to consider it minimally feasible. Hence why not only must the physical appearances of actors be relevant, but also the chemistry between them, as well as how the relationship evolves in the script. If you look at the content of most stories, the way characters get certain things is usually based on controlled relationships; their control and power over others. This is a given in our everyday lives, precisely because of the superficiality we were talking about. A seductive gentleman will only be credible if the women in the audience consider the actor handsome. A manipulative femme fatale will only be able to carry out her plans if the actress is beautiful. And the same goes for many more characters that inevitably need to be physically attractive for their stories to be convincing, like trophy wives, "perfect" husbands, handsome playboys, sexy top models, etc.

THE FILM AND AUDIOVISUAL INDUSTRY

This preconceived image of the perfect man and the perfect woman, which is projected onto the actor's physique, is extrapolated, in a subconscious way, to all film characters. The irony is that the audience may love or hate the characters as much as the film's screenwriters want them to (or are able to get). But also, beyond the fictional characters, our opinion of a movie may be predetermined by how attracted we are to the actors—by just seeing them on the screen. (We enjoy activities more in our daily lives, if we are in the company of someone we are attracted to.)

THE STAR SYSTEM

Attraction is also one of the fundamental pillars of what we call "the star system," which is the main source of influence not only in movies, but in all of show business. The star system was devised at the very beginning of the industry, when the first film studios were created. It reached its maximum expression during classic Hollywood's golden age, around the 40s. It basically consists of the idealization and mythification of the most well-known faces (celebrities), under the premise that the more famous your actors become, the more famous your films will be. If people are devoted to a series of famous icons, they will look forward to their new and upcoming work (movie, song, or whatever they do). Anything for the momentary illusion of feeling like them or being closer to them.

Its origins lie halfway between skillful strategy and sheer chance. In the early 20th century, newspapers knew that sensationalist news headlines meant higher sales. And on another note, the first silent films had a decent number of followers, having noted that the audience idealized the characters that appeared in those movies (the characters, not the actors). Interestingly enough, people were capable of recognizing actors by their faces, but not by their names. Back in the year 1910, the monopoly of Thomas Edison (which we already mentioned in Chapter 4: "The Studio System") prevailed in all its splendor.

THE FILM AND AUDIOVISUAL INDUSTRY

Among other things, one of its rigid prohibitions was that the actors' names did not deserve to be credited, neither in the film itself, nor in the promotional posters. However, producer Carl Laemmle (just a couple of years before founding Universal Studios) knew that using popularity to attract audiences would work exactly the same as in theater or music recitals.

He elaborated an ingenious promotion experiment to advertise his next film shoot. In order to draw attention for hiring the young actress Florence Lawrence, he anonymously published in a newspaper that she had died in a horrible traffic accident. Later, an official statement from the production company was published which denied those rumors. This seized the opportunity to mention that she was, in fact, shooting the film *The Broken Oath*.

As Laemmle had anticipated, when the movie was released, it generated such an expectation that it became a resounding success. So, he did not hesitate to promote Lawrence's name and image in the future, just as many other producers began to do the same with their respective actors. This was part of the numerous acts of rebellion against the established industrial regime that occurred at that time.

The idea of massive exploitation would gradually emerge, developing in parallel with gossip magazines. That was the legacy of the so-called "society chronicles." Magazines dedicated to aristocracy and high society gossip. Actors not only ended up hobnobbing with such people, but would come to be positioned much higher (supposedly in the skies, shining with their own light). Loves, hatreds, fights, break-ups, weddings, divorces, pregnancies, births, deaths, etc. Curiosity and morbidity generated a never-before-seen dependency on celebrities. While movie theaters were crowded with public-persona worshipers, with total independence from any cinematographic interest. This was establishing the bases of the collective hysteria that stardom would become years later, with the arrival of Elvis, The Beatles, and all that had yet to come.

THE FILM AND AUDIOVISUAL INDUSTRY

With the evolution of the press came emerging interviews, exclusives, product advertising, fan clubs, charitable events, selective private parties, and more. The film industry reached its peak during that time, only to suffer a slow decline until this new century, where media stars shine more and higher than ever (it makes sense, now that public exposure is, apart from inevitable, mainly voluntary).

The most important thing about the system is that, like the ancient Greek gods, celebrities can seem far away (as bright and unattainable as the stars in the sky) while at the same time, seem as close as the rest of the mortals. Without losing the divine and glamorous perception of their lives (like luxuries, whims, and eccentricities), having vices, defects, and problems humanizes them. It makes them more "real." To be fair though, not everyone dreams of living the life of a star. Actors, singers, and elite athletes' successes are as public as their failures. We see their joys and their sorrows, and that is not an easy life to live. The psychological pressure is very, very high.

It is no coincidence that celebrities can only relate to other celebrities or people with similar purchasing power. Mainly for natural reasons, like the residential area that they live in, but also for the most basic compatibility between the ways they perceive and understand life. People who have a lot of money also have a lot of problems, but very different ones from those who can barely save money or even live decently on their wages.

And the same goes for family or romantic issues. It is not that couple issues are different for the rich than for the poor, but there are nuances that differentiate situations from what regular people have to deal with. People of the same status will always be able to understand each other better. And in the case of professions like this one, where public relations are so important, the most logical thing is that friendships, couples, and families tend to have some kind of relationship with show business. Otherwise, estrangement will be inevitable.

As far as romantic relationships are concerned, celebrities immediately understand the type of partner they can and cannot have, and they always have to start by analyzing which terms are valid for each side. Obviously, they would understand better than anyone what this profession entails. And at the same time, both parties are perfectly aware of the benefits the star system awards you for simply being in a romantic relationship. Beyond the obvious personal satisfaction, there is nothing wrong with taking advantage of the situation to earn some extra money. Even if it means having to plan an entire professional strategy on that basis, without having to be in a real relationship. Why not? As it is often said, it is a crime without victims. Everything is okay as long as nobody gets hurt. So in addition to authentic couples (of course some of them are real), there are a lot of public charades that have been orchestrated between good friends, gay people who prefer to keep their homosexuality a secret (nowadays, probably more because of commercial interests than fear or shame), as well as great opportunistic stars whose popularity would soar like a rocket, if they had a relationship at the right moment.

Moreover, all of this has a lot to do with public propaganda in favor of the traditional family system, as a social value, i.e. being married and having children as the natural order of things. (Especially having children, because the current tendency to divorce as part of the game demonstrates the futility of the previous step). In these days anyway, everything previously stated is much easier to do now than before. Couples are no longer judged for living together without being married or for signing prenuptial agreements. And long-distance relationships are more credible and bearable than ever, thanks to the hundreds of communication forms we have today. Open relationships have become accepted as a way of life and as valid as traditional monogamous exclusivity. Women enjoy such a level of independence and self-sufficiency that they decide to have children without needing a man in their lives. (Beyond the favor of contributing the genetic material or pretending to be a happy couple, in order to adopt in an easier and faster way.)

THE FILM AND AUDIOVISUAL INDUSTRY

Although we have gotten used to these things today, and it seems hard to believe, the star system was much more invasive by origin, ethically speaking. Taking this philosophy to the extreme, studios created totally fictitious figures from scratch, looking for anyone who was just interested in money. It was irrelevant if wannabe stars had any skills or if they even liked acting or not. False identities and lives were completely invented, which had to be played, sometimes with more dedication than the films (yes, in everyday life). It was intentionally incited and even imposed by contract, to engender a symbiosis between the real person in daily life and the working project.

This may sound familiar, since many celebrities today are working on their public image at all times, making the limit between private and public practically nonexistent. In addition, more and more people every day are willing to simulate anything in exchange for fame and money (perhaps the "reality television" format is the most direct heir of all this). Many of those starlets even had to learn something about the performing arts and even developed not only certain interests, but great aptitudes. Like what happened in the beautiful Marilyn Monroe's case.

Her stay in the Actors Studio was a before and after for her artistic career. This popular icon is still, to this day, a perfect reflection of the accomplishments and failures that these kinds of strategies assume in celebrities' lives. The contractual obligation, along with work pressure, led many actors to live a life of suffering and personal horrors. Victims of the times, most of them lived succumbed to alcohol and drugs too. This was not surprising, taking into account that drinking at parties or taking drugs to increase their productivity during abusive shooting hours was part of their contract.

These fictitious relationships are usually focused on actors, since they are the most visible side of the movies (wherever they go, they are ambassadors for their latest production). Although, during the classic Hollywood years, directors who proved to be equally powerful in the media were often incorporated in this system.

THE FILM AND AUDIOVISUAL INDUSTRY

It may seem like something that is a bit extreme, but this is still something that is used today, however, in more of a natural and voluntary way though, as we stated before. The thing is, you can no longer differentiate celebrities that are creating a shameful scene that has been meticulously studied as a self-promotion strategy, (Good or bad, it is free publicity after all.) from those who are actually going through rough times in their lives and are publicly exposed in a pitiful way. Is it real? Is it fake? And going even further, does it matter?

These are delicate subjects. Taking advantage of the media or being a victim of it. Even farces have their limits and there are some things that cannot (or should not) be pretended. There are some tricks that you can discern with a certain margin of accuracy, as if something is a self-promotional maneuver or real. On the one hand, you can see the consequences of the scandal, after a while. The impact it has on the next projects, professional cachet, and their personal life for example. But on the other hand, you just have to pay attention to details. Despite what many people think, press releases are not contrasted in any way. They are solely based on the source's reliability (that is the power of big news agencies). So, in this business where everything is entertainment and spectacles, it is even less relevant if news is real or false. The important thing is that the news can be part of the show. Just to emphasize the concept: This is not to say that everything is a lie, but rather, that it is not especially relevant if things are real or not. That is not the purpose of news or media, if you think about it.

So, the options are there for anyone to choose them. This industry wants people who are willing to become media titans and those looking forward to generating constant content to feed the monster. Whatever it takes, by hook or by crook. And as it is often said: everyone has a price.

As we saw in Chapter 5: "Getting into the Industry," stars are advised by their management team in various aspects of life. But as we have repeated several times, there is an important detail that changes everything: personal will. Nobody says that it is easy or that there will be no consequences but, at least, every artist has the possibility of freely choosing their way and defining their personal and professional path. The majors have brilliantly learned to wash their hands of these matters. They got away with prudence, but not without making sure that the most basic mechanics of that old system were still effective in some way. It is an undeclared cause-effect game that, while still being very dangerous for the artist, is also outrageously tempting. Even if there are victims sometimes (in a metaphoric sense or not), let us say there is no killer (at most, what happens to you in this regard is probably your own fault, as a responsible adult).

But not everything has to have extreme public exposure or big changes in one's personal life. We must also take into account that it is relatively normal to have "access" to celebrities. Once the audience is charmed by a celebrity (because of the movies or songs or whatever), there is a parallel contact with the real person (supposedly real, but not at all) through public appearances at promotional events, interviews, casual mentions in the media, photographs, etc.

To see them and "know them" through the media is more likely than the remote possibility of doing it in person besides, it is much simpler, due to the continual exposure we are subject to in the midst of the digital age.

Public relations are the best weapons that celebrities have to either make or break their personal life and their career. Public relations with the audience, with their professional colleagues and, it should not be forgotten, with all the people in a higher hierarchy inside the industry. As it has been said several times, kind and affable treatment is the best bargaining chip in show business. It is not a guarantee of success, for sure, but you can be sure that anything contrary to that will guarantee failure. You are never going to get anything being impolite and rude but, at the same time, you have no guarantee of getting anything just with smiles and compliments. Fortunately, it is not relevant if such kindness is even sincere or not. Remember, everything will be alright as long as appearances are kept.

THE FILM AND AUDIOVISUAL INDUSTRY

The logic is overwhelming: If everyone focuses on being nice, smiling, and pretending to please, no one will have time to be annoying. So crying, cursing, yelling, throwing, and breaking things should all be done where everyone does it ... in the warmth of their home.

Surely, it is the most sacred golden rule. As stated previously: Never offend anyone. Do not criticize anyone. Never. Ever. No matter how creepy, vile, or despicable some individuals are being. No matter how much evil someone did to you or others you know. Because you do not know who you are talking to, or talking about, or how that person is connected. You never know how far someone can go, or the advantage that the person who is listening can draw from that conversation with you, now or in the future, sooner or later. This is a world where you do not want to have any kind of enemy (the journey is already cumbersome and insidious enough, only having friends). And, if there is something that must be made clear from the beginning, it is that the word "friend" has a very different meaning for industry workers. And yes, everything that was just previously said explains many of the polemics that have made headlines in the last few years (as well as why so many people have decided to quit). It may sound kind of intimidating, and it is certainly quite stressful, to have to measure your words constantly. It is part of the job, always being aware of what is said and heard, for so many different reasons. But in the end, it is all a matter of will and practice.

For example, one of the most useful tips given to young actors (they can realize this by themselves, but it is usually veterans that give this advice to beginners) is that they should always say publicly that they are shy people. Surely you have heard that more than once, from a lot of celebrities.

It is a good defense because it is credible and contributes to relieving the stress of public exposure. By using this technique, you are able to separate your own person from the celebrity, with whom you can treat as one more character. At any given moment, this false shyness can be of great help. It allows you to speak less in public and/or slower.

THE FILM AND AUDIOVISUAL INDUSTRY

It also gives you time to make better word choices before speaking (therefore, reducing the chances of blundering), have better volume control, and use a more pleasant tone of voice. In conclusion, you can behave as a quieter, more thoughtful and sensible person. No one actually knows you, so no one will question the personality you decide to show in public. The image that everyone sees will be the new you.

The most interesting thing is that, in reality, it is unlikely that a shy person can be a good professional actor. And as soon as you think about it, you can easily understand why.

People that are truly shy are victims of a series of physical and internal processes that react to certain public situations. They suffer some of the following symptoms (if not all) that are impossible to avoid: Blockage, hesitation, trembling, stuttering, losing their voice, volume control, and the appropriate tone, and deep blushing in their cheeks, face, and body. In extreme cases, they develop nervous tics such as continuous blinks, nausea and diarrhea, or panic attacks.

Needless to say, one of these symptoms can incapacitate a person from working in front of the cameras or on the stage. What is more, fear of ridicule is what generates body rigidity that is so typical of people without acting skills (which is most people). As previously said, it is not that one cannot overcome these problems, like many other phobias, but the reality is that if you had to add learning and refining acting skills to the personal triumph of all these personal complications, the challenge would be more difficult for that poor aspirant.

The most interesting thing about a shy personality is that it arouses automatic empathy and appreciation from others. The public responds with greater kindness to calm, docile, pleasant and, in a certain way, vulnerable appearances. Human warmth is generated between both sides.

It is also very useful to avoid uncomfortable or compromising questions. Speaking less or very slowly is a great way to avoid them, especially since interviews (on television, and at press conferences or premieres) always have limited time.

THE FILM AND AUDIOVISUAL INDUSTRY

During interviews, the interviewers are the ones who have to worry about the content being interesting, engaging, and agile—not the person being interviewed. When an interviewer notices that a question or specific topic is getting bogged down or boring, even the most persistent ones will cease in their efforts, due to the serious lack of generated interest. So yes, it is a smart and prudent choice.

On the contrary, those who are always trying to put on a show, spread their awesome wisdom at every moment, and dogmatize the rest of the world with their own ideologies (when someone puts a mic in front of you, it is not easy to resist temptation) will probably end up being victims of a merciless hurricane of their own making. Even if someone starts to successfully do this (there will always be people who hate what you do and say, although many others may adore you), people will always ask for more and better. So, you must always try not to put your foot in your mouth. Being a loudmouth will probably turn against you in these times of constant public exposure.

It is well known that these people have to deal with hypocrisy every day of their personal and professional life. A routine falsehood that ensures a good career in this sector, but forces you to sweep all the dirt under the rug. The interesting thing about all this falsehood, is that when it is positive, it connects well with ordinary people. We all like to hear about happiness, love, friendship, sincerity, honesty, and integrity rather than all those dark, negative things about this industry that some people insist on highlighting (as could be said of this book, for instance).

Let us not kid ourselves, the world of show business has always had that dubious celebrity that we all know. And as every insider knows perfectly well, it is part of your professional duty to keep the rubbish well hidden under the rug, for your own good. The problem is disguising those annoying lumps that form when garbage accumulates in certain places. You can try to cover the smell with air fresheners and smooth the lumps as best as you can, but at best, the only solution is to move the lumps to another part (Sometimes it is enough if the problem goes to others, right?), or tear the rug up, or have the trash overflow to the edges. Luckily for the majority of us simple viewers, the red carpet is there to see celebrities parade around before our eyes, from the comfort of our own homes. So, who cares how it smells?

The two faces of fame are really annoying. Everyone knows that "someone's" face, but that "someone" cannot know everyone. It is a totally unfair situation of automatic helplessness, especially in the case of television. The halo generated by movie stars or music celebrities, for example, is much more distant. They belong to a glamorous and fantasy world of elaborate manufacturing that is always embellished.

However, television's magic works differently. Its impact lies in habit. Being present in people's homes, living with them. In their living rooms and their bedrooms. Day and night. For weeks, months, or even years. In television, artists have no other choice than to be natural, and in a sense "real." They are not restricted by a story's concrete fiction. Above all else, they must look close and familiar. Hence the interest in having movie stars also appear on television. For a moment, it brings them closer to people, it makes them more real. It is not difficult to understand the empathy that a familiar face arises in people.

So much so, that if you have a celebrity in front of you, people tend to forget that they do not know that person at all. And without hesitation they treat them with an inappropriate closeness and familiarity. Not only in manners of speech, but even by invading their personal space and behaving, in some cases, on the fringes of harassment. The worst part of this is that it is usually attractive women who receive most of this. All of that may result in very intimidating and humiliating moments.

Although not comparable, comedians also used to suffer particularly irritating situations. It is universally assumed that they are always in a joking mood, ready and waiting to make you laugh, every second of their lives (apart from the additional obligation of having to be funny all the time).

THE FILM AND AUDIOVISUAL INDUSTRY

We already talked about this. The higher you climb in this industry, the more you get away from reality. The type of life that a famous person is forced to carry out is not compatible with any other regular citizen's life. That is the cost of fame. And, at least so far, paying such a high cost means that celebrities are given lots of money. But that is a balance that has changed more than it should, and not for the better. Most television work can give you fame, yes, but not star status and definitely not equivalent remuneration.

If you are in every household in the country for long enough, it can become impossible to walk down the street and lead a normal life. However, if the purchasing power achieved is not enough to raise your standard of living above the majority of people, the result will be a constant friction between the worst of both worlds. Far from being easily solved, this inconsistency is getting worse by the moment. No matter how many new television channels are created, the number of professionals needing a job will always be much greater than the positions that need to be filled; therefore, the supply and demand balance always tends to continue lowering wages and budgets.

At the moment, the biggest destabilizing element is the continuous exposure we talked about before. In this new world of immediate and unnecessary information overload, where every smartphone is a camera and television at the same time, anyone can be famous, at any time, and for any reason. Besides, it is impossible to predict or control, and worst of all is that it is completely free. Can anyone imagine suffering all the inconveniences of fame, without enjoying any of the privileges? It is true that this is an ephemeral type of fame and that some people know very well how to use it to obtain substantial economic benefit, but there are also many irreparable damages caused by the 15 minutes of fame that Warhol talked about.

THE FILM AND AUDIOVISUAL INDUSTRY

CREATIVE INDUSTRIES WORKERS

People who work in show business usually have a bad reputation in the society, which far from causing a deterrent effect, sometimes even works as an engaging effect (it is doubly tempting for certain people). Professionally speaking, this image is not much better, due to the reputation of instability and uncertainty that we already mentioned and totally justified.

Whether they are artists or technicians, like any other person in the world, workers of this sector must strive to do their job well, whatever it is. They must also face tough competition, abusive working conditions, favoritism, nepotism, and many other realities that have little to do with the attractive content of the industry, but rather with the fact that it is a job like any other. The film and audiovisual industry may look nice from the outside and everyone may want to work in it, but when seeing it from within, it may not be what you expect. A common mistake is assuming that these professions are restricted to people with certain personality types only, when there is no generic class of pattern. You can find people with a lot of attitude, self-confidence, and leadership skills, but also people who are tremendously insecure, unstable, obsessive, influenced, and submissive. This is true for any profession in the field, both for famous and profitable positions, and the more modest categories. And contrary to what it may seem, these personality traits have nothing to do with the possible success or failure that someone may have in life. The combinations are incredibly varied and do not imply that a person will have a better or worse chance of succeeding, nor being smarter or dumber, nor even performing their activity with a higher or lower quality. And yes, this also includes producers and executives. Anyone who gets behind the scenes of any company knows that you can find bosses, managers, or directors everywhere who are very good at doing their jobs, as well as others who are as dumb as a stump.

Every job and every case is different but, in the vast majority of modern professions, the interaction with other human beings is one of the main factors affecting both performance and outcome. Hence why many people reach great heights with only amazing abilities in people skills or with simple luck. This also explains why others end up lagging behind, despite their talents, because of a sad combination of bad luck and personal weaknesses, a priori not relevant to the exercise of their profession.

All the productions that we know would not have been possible without the immense number of workers, artists, and technicians that work in this industry. There are hundreds of people working behind the scenes in movies, television, music, video games, and on any other entertainment show or event. They are specialized in various tasks, some more common than others, from an accountant in a production company who prepares payroll, to a digital artist exclusively dedicated to bringing an animated character's long hair to life (perhaps for a whole year). Musicians, actors, animators, cinematographers, and let us not forget the technical profiles, they are all equally important. Only those who belong on the electrical team touch the wiring on set and carpenters are the most important crew members when you must have the set decorations ready for the first day of shooting. Every single job is necessary, commendable, and worthy of recognition.

THE FILM AND AUDIOVISUAL INDUSTRY

There are not many people who stay at the movie theater to see them, but the end credits of a film are there to showcase them. It is a detailed list to recognize all the people who worked on that production, serving also as official proof of the job. There are currently several online platforms where this and other information are properly credited, so that everyone can check out professional careers (in this industry there is nothing more official than that: The closing credits). Let us take a look at all the different jobs that the entertainment industry offers.

There are permanent jobs like working for a company and being paid an annual salary, and there are temporary, discontinuous opportunities that you yourself must look for (basically per project). The simplest and also the most prestigious jobs belong in the second category. They have the greatest uncertainty by default. You can only work on demand and you must wait for someone to hire you (unless you want to pursue something specifically).

Starting with permanent contracts, these are only available within production or service companies, apart from big majors. In film, television, and advertising companies, there are always a few mandatory positions that are needed in order to maintain an active office (mostly administrative and executive jobs, but a few creative positions are likely too). Contrastingly, in animation and video game production, due to the nature of their activity and the current market needs, they can afford a much bigger permanent staff. They can work on their own productions or provide services to other companies, but there are more possibilities that stay afloat. Other permanent jobs are internal workers at television networks and, much less accessible, executive positions like producers and distributors. However, temporary contracts are the most widespread in this sector.

Each production takes form from the specific script that defines it, so nothing can start until it is analyzed and broken down into thousands of tasks, to be performed by hundreds of professionals.

THE FILM AND AUDIOVISUAL INDUSTRY

Since developing, analyzing, and breaking down a script may take more than two years (and of course, the movie may never get to be filmed, even if it has already been broken down and the shooting has been planned), hiring professionals usually does not happen until the last moment. (Time equals money, so just in case, it is better to avoid unnecessary expenses.)

Evidently, this type of industry will always be able to find available professionals, so it is the workers who have to adjust their agenda in order to be eligible for a particular production. These are professional decisions based on personal schedules and according to availability and calendars. Your best resume will always be the mark that your work made on previous productions. So, doing a good job and leaving a good impression on your fellow co-workers will definitely help keep your schedule busy at all times, triggering one job after another. (As a result, that indubitably means that it is going to be harder for beginners, although it always helps to be willing to work for free.) Discouragingly, at the end of each production, all the temporary contracts expire and everyone will have to wait before receiving the next job offer or start searching on their own again.

In special cases, some professionals can be temporarily hired because they excel in their area. This means that their presence singularly contributed to the production's prestige.

Another exception would be hiring a few workers who could be permanently contracted. However, it is more advantageous to hire for only a few months. For example, a production may want to avoid Christmas, summer, or the few months between one production and the next one, because everyone knows in advance that there will be an insufficient budget or workload to maintain such positions as permanent (they would just be losing money).

It goes without saying that with this type of hiring, companies have different tax advantages and disadvantages.

Therefore, the employer will always look for ways to hire employees using the most appropriate formula. According to each country's regulations, the employer will decide whether to opt for a permanent or temporary contract, with a fixed payroll or choose to expressly avoid it, by making use of an external service. When we talk about smaller companies or industries, there are cases in which no contract is signed, leaving workers legally unprotected, even without any force to claim payment for their services (so they will be paid if they are lucky). This is a common practice in less developed industries and difficult for authorities to control, due to the fleeting temporality of the service (and the little relevance it has compared to other illicit activities, in any country). In decent-sized industries, the absence of contracts is rare to see (it is unlikely that a company will have fifty animators working without a contract), so it is more common to have contracts, even if they are mostly unfair or unfavorable for the artist. (Having a signed legal contract does not mean that workers do not suffer from other labor abuses.)

Everyone sees the positives of prestigious and visible positions. Positions like actors, directors, screenwriters, and perhaps even composers. (Although, the reality is, that facing unemployment spells between projects is hard for them.) Apart from the possibility of negotiating your own salaries (depending on your current status or demand), you are offered to sign contracts with longer or shorter durations. For example, TV series, in theory, guarantee more work hours than films do. Besides, if everything goes well, there is the logical advantage of being offered a renewal every year. There are similar kinds of advantages in movies, with sequels, prequels, or spin-offs, where you could be offered a certain continuity. This is not annually though, since movies cannot be produced as quickly as TV episodes. Also note that signing a contract legally attaches you to the project. But nothing says that such subsequent projects are going to be done.

Of course, this is the most desired working status, but also the most competitive and the hardest to reach. The negative side can also be devastating. As in every cycle, you could be working non-stop for years, and suddenly not receive any offers (or at least, with the minimum quality you may require).

THE FILM AND AUDIOVISUAL INDUSTRY

As everyone knows, directors and actors are affected the most by this type of workflow. We have already seen the huge number of factors that affect work opportunities, including luck and coincidences. Now, we also know that we must add the possible negative points that you could accumulate against yourself, due to your behavior and performance (or even worse, because of other people's behavior). It is a constant fear, which you should be careful not to develop into an anxious neurosis. Any false step could destroy your professional career, yes, but it could be that you are just unlucky for a while, for no particular reason.

It is not that easy to get on board with a specific project that wants to count on you, which also interests you, and on top of that, is actually going to be produced. It gets even worse when the competition amongst professionals is extreme. In this industry, months are the minimum time units and professional careers are measured in years (and not too many), so if you are lucky, you will have time to make a few dozen movies in your lifetime. And this is as valid for beginners as it is for the A-list stars.

By the way, for those who are not aware of the division in the so-called "hot list," let us give you a brief explanation: The success and earnings from your previous work, defines your position in a general, conceptual ranking. This is then divided into the following classes: A (this contains the most demanded and expensive actors and directors), B (this contains a more standard celebrity level), C (those that you may remember, but are easy to forget) or D (those that are hardly considered "famous," but are still positioned above the anonymous mass).

There are also a lot of subjective factors that define your personality and, therefore, will define your professional career too. The opinions and prejudices that decision makers have of you, without you even knowing, can turn against you. But there is nothing that you can do about that. Additionally, do not forget that by that same subjectivity, someone can also love you for the same reasons than others dislike you. That is why the best recommendation is always to just be yourself. Imagine someone loving you just as you are. You never know!

Also, you must be careful with this: If there are some rumors circulating about you, they may not have the power to destroy you, but try to avoid anything that could hurt you or your professionalism. Your personal actions should always make others speak well of you. The more you work and the more people you deal with, the more people will have something to say about you. This can be a good or bad thing and, more importantly, true or false. There is no way of controlling what is said about you, nor what certain people hear about you. There could be things that might eventually affect your career, that is true, but facts always outweigh gossip. And a combative person on shoots, in negotiations, or in the office usually end up gaining a bad reputation, just like people who treat others well end up generating positive feedback.

We have already said the norm is usually that everyone says good things about everyone else, even if it is only to keep up appearances. Which brings us to our next point. Whenever you hear gossip about someone else, there are two clear options: Either it is truth that is being spread, or it is a lie that someone is intentionally using to hurt someone else. So that is why being polite, kind, and affectionate with everyone is the most natural and intelligent way to cover your back. There are less chances of making undesired enemies. Also, pay attention to the opposite. Having an enemy is as dangerous as getting the reputation of being gossipy and speaking negatively of others in order to damage them (especially if those things are not true or even if they are). There are deceptive people in all professions, but personal disagreements aside, there is no virtual difference between harmless palace intrigue and high school gossip.

As previously stated, it does not mean that gossiping about a co-worker is grounds for termination or is a valid reason to stop receiving job offers. But it is true that a continued bad reputation that is justified and proved, can affect the opinion of some relevant people. They will end up choosing another person instead of you.

However, on the other hand, we also know that some A-list stars can be the most unpleasant and quarrelsome people in the universe, and they are not going to lose the job (unless they make a really, really big mess). The same applies to any other industry worker. Imagine that you are an unknown artist and you are animating small penguins for a kids movie, in an animation studio office. Now, suppose that you get a reputation for being rude, impolite, unpleasant, and/or disgusting. You might have problems keeping your job, or finding a better one in another studio, because of the references that your co-workers would give about you within the animation community. Now you see why maintaining a positive attitude is so important.

To be fair, even in the most normal conditions, there are many factors that contribute to workers going through a rough patch and having difficulty landing their next job. There might be bad timing between the completion date of what they are currently working on and the dates of new opportunities. This may mean that they would have to reject them. (And obviously, new talent always takes advantage of opportunities.) You could also be unlucky with your choices, and the project you decided to do ends up getting canceled suddenly (or being a nightmare, or never end up paying). In the case of women, you can be affected by long maternity leaves (the labor market re-entry is always difficult). Also, for example, on a more personal level, you could make the decision to devote more time to your family, instead of working so intensely in this industry.

The specific case of actors' appearances deserves a special mention. It is something that would be seriously discriminatory in other professions, but makes sense in this context, as we have seen in the previous chapter. Some changes in appearance can be controlled, such as weight or changing things using cosmetic surgery, or uncontrollable, like the consequences of an accident or illness. But, age is the key factor that determines how long an actor is unemployed.

THE FILM AND AUDIOVISUAL INDUSTRY

It is impossible to avoid time passing and there are inevitable transition periods in everyone's career that is laden with insecurity: Will the public accept this actor as a teenager, as much as they liked him or her as a child? Could this adult keep the same level of fame, now that the teen-star condition is no longer applicable? When is an attractive woman no longer credible as a femme fatale? And when must they begin doing mature female roles? What about that middle age, where you are too old to be the stereotypical, average mother, but also too young to play a grandmother?

Only time will tell if a lack of activity is the end of your career or just a temporary unemployment spell. You can be optimistic or pessimistic, but the uncertainty will always be there. For the best paid professionals, thanks to the money saved during booming periods, they can enjoy a certain stability and live leisurely for several years, if not their entire life. Even without the pressure of having to work as a necessity again.

For those professionals who are not in such a privileged position, their situation is quite different. They should be concerned about managing their wages during stable times and perhaps investing it wisely at the right time. When one starts to earn a significant amount of money (not necessarily a small fortune, but after accumulating several decent paychecks), the smartest move might be looking for other sources of additional income, like financial investments, real estate acquisitions, starting a business, and retirement plans. Basically, it is about finding peace of mind for the future, apart from still having the possibility of getting another job, even outside the audiovisual industry. In fact, opting for a normal life, instead of striving to be a celebrity, can be a very relaxing solution with no public repercussions. The lack of pressure makes it easy to make a simple and personal decision. Even after being relatively famous, some former celebrities prefer normal lives. They want to keep a low profile, only being locally recognized from time to time, or finding places where nobody knows them at all.

THE FILM AND AUDIOVISUAL INDUSTRY

THE FILM CREW

Most people do not know, for obvious reasons, how film shoots actually work. Based on very few details deducted from promotional materials like "behind the scenes" information and DVD/Blu-ray bonus options, people's conceptions of it are quite limited. There is not much you can take away from a group of people standing around a complex and expensive camera, talking and pointing. Or from a partially unfinished set surrounded by lots of lights, and some guys far off in the background, usually with their arms crossed. Basically, it is just a loophole that nobody understands very well, including many beginners and amateurs with little experience. Because amateurs are accustomed to their lack of means, they naively think that the only thing you need to do is put a few people in front of the camera and press the record button. The huge amount of technical and artistic aspects, mechanical equipment, wiring, lighting, food, transport, and office material that is needed for shooting is often unnoticed. Not to mention, all the things that must always be behind the camera, since it cannot be seen on screen.

In Chapter 7: "The Director's Job," we saw a quick breakdown of a film-shoot workflow. We also mentioned that the film's budget and complexity define the size of its crew, as well as how comfortable or precarious working conditions are going to be. We are reminding you, because the specific function of each chain's link is equally important. Maybe technicians changing simple light bulbs do not have to have artistic knowledge of lighting, but it will probably be more helpful to the director of photography if they have it. This whole machine must work perfectly and for that to happen, each one has to properly comply with their responsibilities, deadlines, and quality benchmarks.

If the plan is to shoot some scenes outdoors, at a specific time, with certain light conditions, then everything related to the camera, sound, and lighting will have to be ready. This implies that all the materials must be prepared and tested before, which in turn means the crew must go to the location as soon as possible.

This surely forces everyone involved to wake up at a particular time in the early morning. The same goes for every scene, every day, multiplied by the number of weeks needed to shoot a specific script, according to the director's vision (who has decided the number of shots to be filmed, and the complexity of them).

Since most of the jobs during the shoots are temporary, and last as long as the shooting period does, some of these hires just start shortly after the project is green lit. For example, once the shoot dates are fixed, there is no time to lose. Costumes and decorations must be designed and created as soon as possible to avoid any delays (although during filming, a small team is hired for maintenance and emergencies).

Always on the lookout for the next job, all these professionals survive the same way they started, by word of mouth and pre-established relationships. It is true that there are not many opportunities for newcomers in this closed system. In this arena, more than direct competition, there is a sort of natural selection among the few people who are actually interested in such positions, those who are better qualified, and those who are willing to start from the bottom. Whether by academic training, achievements as an amateur, contacts from friends and family, or just pleading for the first chance, these chances usually show up as an assistant position, and probably an unpaid one. (But that is better than nothing, right?)

After that, once you are inside, depending on the availability, interest, and insistence you demonstrate, new opportunities will keep coming up. The more experience and knowledge you accumulate, the more they will come. At the same time, as your network of contacts continues to increase, it can bring new opportunities in the future. We already stated it, but the more people know you and the better their opinion of you is, the more likely team leaders will remember you and want you to be on their team in the next production (until someday when you may be leading your own team, if that is what you are looking for). Apart from talent and work capacity, the most valuable qualities in these jobs are attitude and commitment.

THE FILM AND AUDIOVISUAL INDUSTRY

These are usually jobs that, in one way or another, you actually love doing. And there might be a point where you do not see yourself doing anything else. Some people feel that the uncertainty that we often mention is actually seen as a life choice that is more free, adventurous, or bohemian. Something that matches with certain kinds of personalities. People who do not want to "restrict" their lives to regular office working hours, like many other people in the world. They may frown upon boring and predictable day-to-day routines that other people see as blessings.

Of course, in this sector, everyone works hard under the orders of a team leader and department director, with all of them being under the subjectivity and tyranny of a director. However, as long as there is proper commitment, your utmost attention must be focused on attitude. Unfortunately, this usually means being willing to put your job above anything else, including family, sleeping hours, and maybe even your own money.

A film shoot is a microcosm. A delicate and diverse ecosystem where all its elements are forced to coexist for months, come rain or shine. Since coexistence is mandatory, you should always try to make the environment as pleasant as possible, both personally and professionally. So many hours a day, every day, is not always easy to handle. There are too many people working at the same time, each with their own objectives and demands that often intersect with each other, and not happening without friction. And, as if this were not enough, add budget restrictions and constantly working against time. (We could also add that it does not help that the working hours allowed by law are always exceeded.)

An interesting note about professionalism and seriousness, has to do with "bloopers." They seem very funny however, because shooting movies requires repeating everything many times, even if nothing has gone wrong, imagine repeating the entire procedures involved in preparing one shot, all because someone said the wrong word, forgot a line, laughed, stumbled, or made any other kind of mistake—it is anything but funny.

Sometimes things are completely unavoidable and some of them are actually quite funny when they happen. What we are saying is that shots can be repeated for a number of technical reasons, because of any team member. But with particular regard to bloopers, it is important to stress that no one should fool around just for fun. In fact, the appropriate and polite thing to do, when bloopers happen, is to apologize.

Every production has a strict, estimated schedule that should be achieved, which means that either everyone stays working late until the daily plan is finished, or the pending parts of the plan are removed and/or rescheduled. That could mean extra expenses, last-minute readjustments, or changes in the director's vision. All of this has an undesired snowball effect, let us say. Because the painful truth is that every day costs money. Literally every time the sun rises and sets. Every unplanned, extra day can be a major setback.

Finally, last but not least, we have accountants, secretaries, lawyers, and other professional profiles that are completely away from the cinematographic content but are also essential in any film shoot.

The best way to observe this peculiar ecosystem and reduce it to an understandable and measurable scale, is to look at amateur and semi-professional shoots. Capable and versatile beginners will immediately get a glimpse of what filmmaking is all about, while they find out many of the real keys of this profession. For a start, since there is no budget or hiring, your crew's motivations (friends, family, and other aspiring professionals) are very different from those of a professional team, so you run the risk of having a misperception of what professional shoots feel like. Some people's commitment and dedication may come from friendship or the desire to have fun and do something different; while those with more professional aspirations could respond listlessly or with apathy. They might believe that the rest of the crew are not in the same league (so the whole thing could feel like a waste of time).

The precarious conditions at these levels definitely does not help (or maybe it does, depending on how you look at it). And facing adversity can be considered character-forming for beginners.

We all have (and continue to develop throughout our lives) some personality traits that affect everything we do. Traits like respect, patience, politeness, and the ability to concentrate. And although it is not impossible to change radically, what usually happens is people evolve more or less in the same direction. There are always people that are easy to work with and people that are difficult to work with. And in general, there are a great number of people in the middle that simply do their job (which is the minimum you could expect from a professional team, if you have one). So many things can go wrong in a working day that there is no time to waste on pointless discussions. As long as there is respect and cordiality, everything should be bearable regardless of the circumstances.

Everything that we have described in these pages proves people may have a lot of reasons for going through a rough time or feeling tense and stressed. With so many personalities together, for so long, in different personal and professional circumstances, it is easy to lose your manners, causing some conflicts.

That is why everyone must make an effort not to infect others or poison the environment. Although you could expect the opposite, the higher someone is in the production hierarchy, the less tolerance they have for problems and frustrations.

It is very likely that a director has been accumulating frustrations from the beginning of a production (if not throughout their entire career), and it does not help when a problem arises in the midst of a shoot, caused by a wrong decision made during planning. It does not matter whether it is the producer's fault (for a random example) or the director's fault (an even greater frustration if you add guilt and shame now), the only thing that matters is what you decide to focus on, the problem or the solution.

THE FILM AND AUDIOVISUAL INDUSTRY

Everyone knows that the director is in charge. So opposition is not a possibility, everything is about fulfilling orders. And, although this is something that no one likes to recognize, sometimes you have to endure impertinence or disrespect from a director. It is true that good directors tend to be quite strict and demanding, but they also know how to measure their words and their politeness and character (or they should). It is a different issue if, as a consequence of their unilateral power, they do not consider it to be an obligation. It depends more on their personality. There are directors who resort to a rigid, dictatorial attitude, because they know the amount of time that can be lost in democratic discussions, different viewpoints, and explanations against what they want to do. So, it is always more efficient to opt for the fast-track: "We will do it this way because I say so."

There are indeed many decisions that could delay the planned schedule. And too many unpredictable elements, so they must avoid bad decisions. The director and production manager live in fear that every minute this may happen.

Moreover, working directly with actors deserves a special mention (again). It is no secret that actors are difficult to work with and it is not that this belief has been perpetuated without justifiable reasons. Actors work with emotions. They control their feelings and body. This means that, even if they are supposed to have a high degree of control over it, they have also automated certain action-reaction codes in such a way, that they cannot avoid some inappropriate tones and gestures in real life. Certainly, this is no excuse to justify their lack of politeness or patience, but rather the opposite. It is precisely their control over these resources that allow them to take advantage of certain situations, dignifying their reactions with great vehemence and emphasis. Or, in other words: Making use of a good "performance." They are able to win or get out of any discussion, with such solvency that it is very difficult to reply with anything less than common sense. Actors, like all people with excessive egos, often see themselves with the moral victory in situations, or with enough skill to make it seem so.

THE FILM AND AUDIOVISUAL INDUSTRY

In the previous chapter, we reviewed their personal pressures of fame together with the harsh demands of their profession. Very few people understand the concentration required to pretend that you are another person, in a credible way or what it takes to live something that is not real, surrounded by so many artificial elements that destroy the context (like spotlights, cables, and dozens of people staring at you). All while connecting and disconnecting your mind for seconds at a time and without following the logical chronological order. Do not forget the need to remember your lines, together with natural and imposed body actions, and how exhausted your body gets because of repetition. Imagine how interruptions, jokes, or the inappropriate attitudes of others can affect you, while you are just trying to do your job.

Filming sets and theater stages are an actor's workplace. (How can we forget the typical phone that rings during Hamlet's soliloquy.) It is difficult to remain calm and stay cool, with the same attitude you have with fans, the press, or on television. In some of these moments you are also working, of course, playing the empathetic celebrity character, but there is less pressure. The film has already finished and all you have to do is sell it. And to be honest, the film's success or failure will not depend on what you say in an interview. Promotion actually serves to enhance the star system more than the movie (showing the trailer and saying the release date are more than enough).

It seems that we have moved away from the subject, but not really. Actors are the best reference for talking about the atmosphere on set. Everything revolves around them. The camera is pointing and chasing them around. It is unavoidable, they are the focus of attention. When they move, there are always handfuls of people behind the camera who must move with them, so that everything on the screen remains as perfect and as wonderful as it should. The atmosphere will always depend mostly on the attitudes of the actors and the director. They are the most influential figures, and the gauge for the spirit of the troop. When they are nice to each other, everyone works well together. It does not matter how different each personality is.

THE FILM AND AUDIOVISUAL INDUSTRY

Whether they are calm and quiet people, as well as pranksters or chatty ones. Some may be nicer or more annoying, but everything depends on the level of connection and understanding they have with each other. That is why some teams, either artistic or technical, try to work together as much as they can.

Once such a close professional and personal collaboration is finished, the most important thing is the overall impression you get from the experience. It may have been nothing special (the least you can expect, this is not a bad thing), negative (due to a lack of understanding or some specific frictions), or positive (because of mutual understanding, admiration, and/or special connection). The most diverse relationships are forged throughout the shooting days, reaching the zenith at the famous wrap party (to celebrate the end of the main photography, where lead actors and most of the crew are no longer required).

These events release accumulated tensions, in any possible sense. Without being allowed to share any information about it (no need to explain why), little by little mixed feelings emerge. As alcohol intake increases (and anything else you can imagine) all the friendships, frictions, rumors, and affairs that have taken place or have been gestating during the shooting, are released on this special night. One last night without future consequences. An unusual explosion of sincerity that nobody will seem to remember a few months later at promotional events, festivals, and other public appearances. There is a bit of everything, apart from the usual falsehoods of the business (everyone should love the film they did together, no matter how terrible it may be), you will find elusive looks, tense greetings, effusive pretend love, chitchatting, and gossip. All this will be demonstrated with the utmost professionalism, as much as there will be, of course, some authentic signs of affection too. Despite the cliché, not everyone loses their mind at these parties or in their private lives in general. There are those who never attend these parties. (Some may show up just because it is strictly necessary to show themselves and leave before the Dionysian craziness begins.)

THE FILM AND AUDIOVISUAL INDUSTRY

After filming a movie, the fact is, every participant would have left an imprint on each other. For better or worse and on a personal or professional level. This greatly affects, as we said before, the possibility and/or desire to work together in the future. Unfortunately, the decision to repeat artistic teams (actors, art directors, directors of photography, etc.) is not very easy to achieve. Do not forget producers can also intervene in those decisions. So, although directors have the right to propose the team they want to work with (including the main cast), they are usually not in a position to present that as a requirement. Perhaps the most privileged directors could negotiate with more weight, but they also have to be careful with the cards they have, and the hands they play.

As for the technical teams, every audiovisual worker knows the level of professionalism and quality required to fulfill their tasks; however, the hiring responsibility belongs to the whim and hierarchy of each department chief. They will always check amongst their favorite circle of regular collaborators first. They will call certain people, depending on the different responses, availabilities, and interests.

THE BENEFITS OF BEING A SALARIED EMPLOYEE

Whether we like it or not, reality is like a harassing shadow that is always behind us, pushing us all toward the same black hole. Our daily lives costs money. That is why most people get into this industry with high aspirations (all these things about chasing your dreams and the like), sooner or later there is a point where those dreams are left aside, against the possibility of obtaining a safe, stable job (although you feel less passionate about it). Probably even in a different industry, as it is not uncommon nowadays for people to work on something that has no relation to their academic studies. The truth is, at present, it is not impossible to get a permanent job in the audiovisual industry. For instance, more and more people are needed by big production companies, for technical and creative work within animation, video games, and visual effects. Live action films are worlds apart (we have already covered enough of that), but these relatively new branches of the sector have put themselves in an enviable position, within the corporate world's highest standards. Even the smallest production companies can provide, to a greater or lesser extent, stable, permanent jobs at their offices, with good salaries, benefits, and legal guarantees. Whether they are totally independent, big subsidiary companies, or just average third-party service vendors, these companies can offer a certain degree of stability (much greater than the other options seen so far).

Typically, they depend on the health of the industry, in their respective countries; and particularly on the number of projects in development for the upcoming years. But according to each company's capacity and your professional quality, you may have a lot of possibilities in finding a permanent job or, at least, gaining temporary experience little by little. This way, your resume will start to look attractive enough to other companies and in order to opt for a better job each time.

Although the global economy recovery is palpable in general terms, there are still people who are often forced to change jobs, cities, and/or country of residence. The only positive side is that not having a job at all is even worse and, actually, traveling around the world is something that many young people find interesting and attractive. Besides, in such an international sector, you can expect that any decent company works by default in the English language. So, this is the most common thing for young artists who are looking to get experience and find their place.

Sadly, in some less fortunate countries, it is worrying that even senior workers are forced to look for another job now and again (even immigrating to other countries), after each project ends or is canceled. Many small companies cannot afford to maintain a stable workforce until they get funds for the next project (which may take several months or years). The luckiest companies can at least survive with the main founders and company partners or, at most, the veterans and essential positions.

Seniority and quality are essential for companies. Nothing is better than trying to keep the so-called "core" stable, once they have proven to work well. There are levels of coordination, understanding, efficiency, and quality in both the technical and artistic aspects which are not easy to find. There are also cases in which companies have been created specifically to produce one only film and decided to cease their activity once the production was finished. At least, in these cases, there were no surprises and the workers were already aware that they would be working on that project only.

Audiovisual production is expensive therefore, outsourcing services are always an option, and are usually well paid. Working at one of these companies, providing external services, tend to be good jobs with decent salaries. Although, the work-life balance is not always the most desired. The situation is far from the old days when Disney had its animators sleeping on the floor, working weekends, without being paid for being the great artists that they were, or even publicly recognized. (There was a struggle for the control of the company. Its highest executives were competing to take all the glory from their films in the 90s, totally forgetting about the workers who made them possible.)

In every company, there may be inevitable workload peaks from time to time. But, while some companies support working overtime, most decent, modern corporations do their best to reconcile the personal and professional lives of their employees. This is one of the reasons why the practice of outsourcing has become more and more frequent. In any sector, the most repetitive and least-qualified work has been commissioned to external factories in Asia or Eastern Europe, where the value of money is lower. Expenses are reduced and responsibility is derived to others. This is especially convenient since labor laws and workers' rights are more "flexible" in these countries.

Thanks to the progressive modernization of our world, the artistic and technical quality has ceased to be a barrier. External remote work is possible, at any production phase, for every type of necessity.

THE FILM AND AUDIOVISUAL INDUSTRY

Outsourcing is very useful to reduce costs, solve unexpected workload peaks, make last-minute changes without affecting other phases, or simply maintain a manageable internal team size for important tasks, without having to hire an unsustainable number of permanent or temporary workers in your company.

From a political perspective, outsourcing is not a very popular option, because it does not generate as many jobs in a country or company. Not as if everything were solved in-house. But certainly, efficiency and economic profitability are great benefits. So the firm, and the project itself, are actually helping to improve their local and national industry, at a higher level.

It is better to contribute this way, with a solid company of thirty people as a permanent workforce, than being a company of one hundred and fifty employees that will have to go out of business three months later.

As a consequence, many countries are supporting the creation of such companies (animation, VFX, and video games), and their expansion to new offices in other countries. This causes, among other things, the flow of new job offers to be more or less constant. Perhaps not so many offers as to cover the immense demand, but again, the challenge of social competitiveness is here, using the law of supply and demand to overcome and grow as a professional. In this sense, outsourcing initiatives can be considered complementary to everything that was said before. The best national talent gets a fair reward at their proportional value. At the same time, productivity and efficiency with high profitability but less demand, are outsourced to other countries. (Which in turn, usually poses a professional and corporate challenge for their standards of quality, and are proportionally paid above average, within their own industry.) Usually, these companies offering external services are highly profitable, so they offer good jobs that have permanent contracts, social benefits, flexible hours, a modern and positive culture, and fair salaries (usually, to compensate punctual peaks of stress, in most cases).

THE FILM AND AUDIOVISUAL INDUSTRY

We must recognize the impressive revolution of CGI 3D (Not meaning the one with the stereoscopic glasses, but any digital image rendered with 3D software.) and its decisive contribution to the actual development of the industry. The computer-generation of these images require a large number of artists, technicians, and animators, with a high degree of specialization. So, this is not only reinforcing the growth and competences where these companies operate, but also opening new frontiers in artistic and technical matters. They are enriching the sector with new professional challenges, and therefore, new necessities for educational training. At this moment, it is enjoying more than moderate stability and still has a huge margin of growth.

This specialization is also striking evidence of how fabricated the business has become. This is not good or bad by itself, but it teaches us that even the most artistic things end up being anecdotal in a mass manufacturing chain. Many things have changed and the digital format is finally the industry standard, after all the false controversy about transitioning from film projection to digital screening. Perhaps you remember those foolish arguments. The emotional warmth, the beauty in grain and imperfection, and the nostalgic "magic" of film. For those that are too young to remember, it was an unnecessary and false polemic, invented as a simple excuse to justify (and make a few headlines about) the transition being so slow. The controversial issues found in this unavoidable technical transition could basically be summarized into these three aspects: The first one is the investment that every movie theater in the world would have to make into digital projectors. (Some governments even granted public aid for this digital transition, until producers and distributors agreed to pay a private economic compensation to theaters, in order to amortize the investment.) The second are the changes that a new digital copying system would imply for distributors, considering the obvious savings compared to the old process for printing copies, in several cans of celluloid per film (which derived in the compensation fee that was just mentioned).

And finally, the inevitable bankruptcy that the AGFA, Fuji, and Kodak empire had to face. Because of the unstoppable advances in digital photography, film sales continued to decline and never recovered.

Even in visual terms, all films seem to be over-manufactured. Everything looks so industrialized that it seems as if some tricks or mannerisms "must" be used as an automatic formula. Audiovisual creation is becoming a library of resources to be applied in a mechanical way. Even at the level of art and photography, which can be considered more free and creative, there are certain apprehended standards that are now manifestly consolidated. They deliberately end up being imposed on any possible alternative. A fistful of aesthetical, subjective, and stylistic tricks that have become, in some way, a sort of quality standard. This hinders the room from maneuvering those with a different vision (not necessarily innovative, but just different) to the predefined pattern of the whole industry. A pattern made of elements that, in reality, are nothing more than extractions of previous achievements from other colleagues. Details, ideas, or solutions that now are "trendy" innovations, which must be included in your film for it to be fashionable.

Within this model of global industrialization, digital work has a lot of routines that are impossible to avoid. All tasks are a lot more mechanical than you would expect, and not so different from those in other, less creative sectors. In the most extreme cases, there are positions where you do not even need any artistic talent.

For example, creating rigs (the virtual skeletons of 3D characters), programming software tools (so that other artists and technicians can work better), designing and generating levels for video games (which may go from pure coding to map planning), or the so-called rotoscope (the task consisting of tracing the silhouettes of actors or elements in motion, frame by frame over footage, to separate them from the background). This work requires more patience and attention to detail than technical or artistic skill, that is why it is usually outsourced to countries with a cheaper labor force.

There are similar tasks like those, which can be considered "technical art." In some ways, they have a certain artistic impact to the final result but not by themselves. For example, the typical 3D models representing everyday elements like furniture, food, clothing, vehicles, buildings, etc. In the virtual environment of any film or series, you cannot (or should not) notice that the table, car, or building are digital. 3D artists must emulate the shape, volume, and texture as close to reality as possible. Hence why it is so important to use accurate documentation as references. Like the engineering plans of a real object or the construction drawings of a real building. As well as real pictures, textures, and lighting samples. Pure imitation can be a laborious process, but no special artistic talent, interpretation, or creativity is required. Unless we are talking about 3D animation for kids, where you need a greater degree of creativity to do the job. All the elements must look as nice and as cute as the characters and environments that were created for that world. Furthermore, as secondary objects, they should not draw too much attention, in comparison to the main elements, so these tasks can also be delegated to less qualified professionals, like in-house juniors or they can be outsourced abroad. Under some strict guidelines and the eye of a competent supervisor, everything should be fine (and logically, providing better quality means less supervision is needed).

In regard to more creative roles, like lighting and photography, you can apply more individual uses of artistic criterion. Although you are always subject to supervision within your team (and of course, at the orders of the director), each artist must make good personal use of the color theories and have advanced knowledge of visual composition. It is inevitable to work under another person's supervision, but the artists in charge of colors and lighting usually very much enjoy working with pens (digitally or traditionally). As in any other job, your daily routine can end up feeling repetitive, as if it were "directed" by others. But these artists tend to have a more personal satisfaction than other positions, especially when the movie starts to look more finished.

THE FILM AND AUDIOVISUAL INDUSTRY

However, there are not many positions available for lighting and photography. (In comparison to the number of modelers or animators needed.) There are not many people within the same company, who are true experts in photography, with an outstanding talent for light and color.

Besides, digital 3D art is constantly offering new tools and solutions to emulate, with impressive accuracy, light's realistic behavior. This reduces the need for over-qualified professionals, and makes these tasks simpler. The only indispensable role that is usually needed is a good digital director of photography, and perhaps one supervisor or lead artist, with a good sense of lighting and color. Something similar happened to realism in painting: The amount of work, precision, and skills needed to capture a real image on a canvas, became merely admirable with the advent of photography. Realistic imitation was no longer a technical requirement and that kind of virtuosity ceased to be amortizable.

Fortunately for them, painters found other ways of recreating, causing painters' abilities to mutate towards a more creative, emotional, and conceptual exploration. There were catastrophic voices announcing the end of the painter profession.

And although it is true that it changed forever, no one could imagine how rich, diversified, and multidisciplinary the profession would become nowadays, for both photographers and painters (well, digital painters, at least).

In less distant times, coinciding with the change of the century, artistic visual representation by using computers also had great challenges to face. But they were all resolved with loads of effort and talent by a young company called Pixar. The company was created by a few former workers of "Industrial Light & Magic" (the visual effects company owned by George Lucas) and sponsored by Steve Jobs (who cunningly decided to invest in all the research and development needed during that time, allowing 3D animation to be where it is now).

THE FILM AND AUDIOVISUAL INDUSTRY

To his day, exactly like what happened with traditional painting, the secrets of photographic hyperrealism are now within everyone's reach (It is technically feasible with any computer, and it is only a matter of time and money.), so the few advances that remain to be done, always go in the same direction: toward efficiency. (That is to say, reducing speed and costs, while still getting the best possible result.)

From a business point of view, the creation of this type of sustainable employment has a broad economic and political interest. In theory, it is an ideal breeding ground for job creation. Unlike most modern factories, where few people are needed to manufacture a massive number of products, this industry needs many people to obtain a few minutes of entertainment. And the artistic specificity of each product makes its total automation impossible, so the human factor remains necessary. Because of all this, the only decisive factor for this industry's survival remains, for the moment, in the return of investment.

THE FUTURE OF ENTERTAINMENT

If we must talk about the industry's future with regard to the next generation, we have to talk about research. What the radical expansion of virtual reality and holography will mean for entertainment can hardly be compared to anything seen before. During the 20th century, the video game industry began experimenting with virtual reality helmets and gloves (as a legacy from NASA and military usage in the U.S. Air Force). Unlike a pair of glasses, an accessory atop our whole head managed to cover our entire field of vision and hearing. The audiovisual experience was completely immersive, at least in theory. Unfortunately, in practice, the computers at that time were not able to process 3D graphics in the quantity, quality, and speed necessary to obtain a decent result. The limitations on the number of polygons, textures, resolutions, speed calculations and interactive responses, made such a promising idea but a failed attempt.

But there was also something positive, it was very clear that it would only be a matter of time until they got there. Any smartphone today has several times more power than those old computers, so it is not difficult to imagine the realism that virtual technology is going to reach in a few more years.

Overnight, another invention appeared as the first advance of what is about to come. A way to connect your own mobile device to a binocular mask with a strap, allowing a stereoscopic effect on your 3D app, in real time. (This is basically like having one part of those primitive virtual reality helmets, except with the use of your smartphone).

At the same time, once all the devices in the world had their own camera, it was possible to take the next natural step, which is called "augmented reality." It is a process by which virtual images are added to your device screen, in real time, during the microseconds that pass from the moment the images are captured by your phone, to the moment they are displayed on the screen. So, you can see things on your device that are obviously not there in the real world.

It is just a workaround, rough-and-ready solution, as a foretaste of what we can expect from holography. Holograms will someday be such a common element in our lives, just like television or cell phones are today. Although, at the moment, it is still in the early stages of improvement and research, since the results required for global use do not make sense yet.

Unlike the poor concept of augmented reality, holograms do actually appear before you, in a particular real place, where it is projected from several angles at once. This provides a real three-dimensionality to the holographic object that, despite being visually present in reality, has no physical mass. It is only light that has been emitted by several projectors, which converge at certain points in space. In theory, this means that it cannot be touched. Not in a strict sense, at least. But you have to combine other technologies such as motion detection, haptic gloves, or electrode pads.

THE FILM AND AUDIOVISUAL INDUSTRY

You can simulate a hologram that is reacting to your contact, even without being a real, physical object. And why not? If it is what you want, you can complete the experience by programming all these devices to provide you with a real feeling that you are touching the hologram (with all the complex derivations that this implies).

Therefore, there are two different ways of approaching the same immersive concept: Either you lie to your body, making it believe that it is in another world, or you add virtual elements to the real world, where your body is so it can obtain the interactive experience. In fact, we might wonder: What is, after all, audiovisual narration as we know it so far? It is just a simulated reality, which we see displayed on a screen. Let us remove the screen and add interaction. When we do this, we will get virtual reality, which will be the undisputed winner in the future of entertainment. Even above holography or cybernetics. While the first one will tend to focus on information and advertising, the second one will clearly be dedicated to the mechanization of the human tasks that we want to stop doing (what comes to be the fourth industrial revolution).

The only doubt is when to begin enhancing this new form of entertainment. It is still being discussed whether it will be more convenient to release this to the market while experimenting with the medium itself, or whether it will be more profitable to wait for the realism of the experience to reach much higher levels. The dilemma is not trivial because, if it is a satisfying experience, virtual reality could be an irresistible temptation.

The psychological implications of this immersive world are far from simple. If society is not properly ready for this, said temptation could become a serious necessity and a dangerous vice (an addiction completely comparable to the hardest drugs). If it ends up being much better than any other option for leisure, and totally affordable for home consumption, it could propose the immediate death of any other form of entertainment. Maybe any other form of life. Is the industry ready for that? Or even worse, are human beings?

THE FILM AND AUDIOVISUAL INDUSTRY

It is one of everyone's greatest concerns regarding this new medium, even if the inevitable is known to happen. We have already mentioned several examples. For technological changes transition are required to be done little by little, in different scales and done safely for everyone in the industry. It is not convenient to invade the market just to get it over with. It is advisable to generate expectation (as it is being done) and create the impulsive desire to have these devices in the future, of course. But in the meantime, the current, existing options must be slowed down as much as possible, even if it is certain that they will soon become obsolete. (It also would not make sense to abandon them before they reached their full potential.) If you think about it, in regard to humankind, everything ends up collapsing sooner or later. But, at the same time, nothing collapses without drawing a proper reaction plan ahead of time.

Without a doubt, the future of show business will be inevitably linked to these concepts of "alternative" reality. Much has been discussed in recent years (and much more to come) about the extent of this evolution. Its physical, social, and ethical limits: Will the immersive experience kill the traditional concept of the screen? Will ultimate interactivity end with passive types of entertainment? Will virtual reality lead us to a life of alienation, with no possible return? We have faced similar crossroads before and, as much as the most alarmist voices say, progress has always addressed living better and more comfortably.

Because of the first Industrial Revolution in the 19th century, a lot of people lost their jobs, we all know that, right? But we also know how much the standard of living improved for the modern world, and how much we owe to that revolution, as much as to the next ones. Out of it came science, health, urbanization, and social and labor conditions.

No other time in history had so many professional artists in the world, nor of such varied condition and origin. Except for those few privileged enough to live under the protection of kings and nobles so many centuries ago. Artists have never lived and worked under such a stable, recognized, and well-paid status.

THE FILM AND AUDIOVISUAL INDUSTRY

We can say a lot of horrible things about capitalist economies and the industrialization of work, but we cannot deny that humankind has never lived better than they do now, nor have they ever enjoyed such an offer of leisure and entertainment. The best example of this is the extreme narcissism we live with every day of our lives. The excessive importance that we have given to fictional entertainment like film, television, music, or video games. Momentary escapes focused on the pleasure of the senses at the most basic level. And nothing is more primitive than the pleasure of the senses. So, as long as this remains the same, and it is likely to continue to be so, the entertainment industry will not stop growing and generating wealth.

Enjoy it.

Printed in Great Britain
by Amazon